To Abraham.
You were the
first few in
the world but the last
not
I hope
from the author.
8.11.80.

*From
Leningrad
to
Jerusalem*

Norwegian Sea

Pechora

Murmansk

Boden

Dvina

Sin

Perm

Kirov

Sortavala

Oslo

Helsinki

Leningrad

Kazan

Stockholm

Tallin

Vladimir

Gorky

Chi

Baltic Sea

North Sea

Copenhagen

Riga

Kalinin

Saransk

Kaluga

Moscow

Berlin

Vilna

Minsk

Warsaw

Dniepr

Don

Volga

Amsterdam

Bonn

Kiev

Bern

Vienna

Dniestr

Budapest

Kishinev

Odessa

Belgrade

Bucharest

Danube

Black Sea

Sofia

Rome

Ankara

Tigris

Athens

Euphrates

Ba

Tunis

Mediterranean Sea

Beirut

Damascus

Amman

Tripoli

Jerusalem

Cairo

- - - -	Operation Wedding No. 1
•—•—•—	Operation Wedding No. 2, 3
++++++	To Kishenev Trial, Return
——	The Gulag Way
▬▬▬	From Gulag To Jerusalem

km   0   200

© carta. JERUS

From Leningrad to Jerusalem

The Gulag Way

HILLEL BUTMAN

————————————————

Translated from the Russian
by Stefani Hoffman
Edited by Carol Talpers

BENMIR BOOKS
BERKELEY · CALIFORNIA

Book Design by Wolfgang Lederer
Technical Consultant: Tom Relihan
Printed in the United States
by Braun-Brumfield, Inc.

ISBN 0-917883-04-7

Contents

Foreword

For an individual to be thrust onto the stage of history is more often than not a combination of one's place, time, and circumstance. Hillel Butman seized that moment of his life and thereby helped to shape the destiny of his people.

The place was the Soviet Union. The time was the late 1960s and early 1970s. The circumstance was a young man, seemingly alone in his passion for his people. Discovering that he was one of many who felt the same concerns, he resolved to attempt the unthinkable for himself and countless others whose names and faces he did not know.

As a Jew, consumed by a love for and identification with his people and his land, Hillel Butman sought to begin the process of opening the barred doors of the Soviet Union so that his people might begin the long march to freedom in their own land of Israel. A Jew in a world where it was dangerous to be a Jew; a Zionist in a land where to proclaim one's love of Israel could bring down the wrath of the state; an individual committed to educating each and every Jew in the Soviet Union where such a program was forbidden. All of this and more drove Hillel Butman to meet his fate.

The story of his monumental effort is told here in his own words. A magnificent testimony to human courage, it also reminds us of those days when the struggle to free Soviet Jews was just beginning. Butman's eloquent exposition of his dramatic story compels us to consider once again the roots of the movement which began the great modern Exodus of the Jews from the Soviet Union.

Too often we have forgotten that the revolution of Soviet Jewry began with the rebirth and continuing struggle of the state of Israel. Butman describes the roots of the movement by reminding us that the objectives were precise and clear:

". . . to foster the struggle for free emigration to Israel of all Soviet Jews who desired this, and to awaken the Jewish consciousness of Soviet Jews, particularly the young people, by disseminating information about Jewish culture."

When Butman articulated these two principles in Leningrad in November of 1966 he laid the framework in formal terms for all that was to follow in the movement to free Soviet Jews.

Did Butman realize that his pioneering effort would have such an earth-shaking impact? Did he know that he was articulating the hidden desires of hundreds of thousands of his fellow Jews? With the outbreak of the Six Day War on June 5, 1967, the tide of passion could not be contained and within a few years the mighty commissars were faced with a flood that could not, would not, be stopped.

As I take pen to paper to write this brief foreword I cannot help but reflect on how far we have come, and how much further we have to go in the struggle to free Soviet Jewry. How well I remember my own experiences traveling in the Soviet Union as a student in 1969. The hopes and dreams of those whom I met remain with me to this day.

On December 24, 1970, I was in Jerusalem. It was Christmas Eve and the city was preparing for that observance when the word arrived that the sentences in the first Leningrad trial had been handed down. As if driven by some unseen force, I went with countless others to the Western Wall where a mass of free Jews gathered to raise their voices in protest against sentences of prison and death. We came to that sacred place to join in solidarity with our fellow Jews— miles away in distance but close in our hearts that night. We were joined in protest by an anguished humanity: only one week later, the death sentences were commuted. As we rejoiced in that moment of relief we knew that the struggle had just begun. Who would have imagined that a decade later they would be free and living in the land of Israel? It was Butman and his friends who commanded our attention and whose names were emblazoned on our minds and hearts. Even as we struggled for them, new names, new cases, and new trials all emerged to form a banner for a struggle to free our people in the Soviet Union. As those whose names we know passed to freedom, the ranks swelled with those struggling to be free. As more escaped to freedom, there were more who wished to follow.

Why have we in the West been so gripped by this struggle for freedom by a people so long repressed? The drama of their striving could not help but move us into action. Yet there was another motivation behind our response. It was the conscious knowledge that but for an accident of history—if our parents, grandparents, or great grandparents had not walked to freedom—those for whom world Jewry raised their voices might have been us.

Hillel Butman could have been any one of us had history dealt a different hand. In him we felt the passion for freedom, the commitment to being a proud Jew, and an undying devotion and love for the land of Israel. Butman and his friends became the symbol of our struggle to insure the survival of our people in the Soviet Union. Hillel Butman was the right person, in the right place, at the right time. Butman is a hero of our time and his story is the essential link in understanding the inner dynamics of that time. His story reminds us of the struggle which continues today to be Jews, in our own land.

I have no doubt that even as the novel *Exodus* by Leon Uris has had an impact on Soviet Jews, so Butman's story will move the current generation of Soviet Jews who are seeking their roots.

I have never met Hillel Butman face to face, and yet I know him. He is my brother and I will always remember that to him we owe so much. In embracing this book, we embrace him, free today in Israel, and we pledge to continue our struggle for the day when the trip from Leningrad to Jerusalem will be direct.

John F. Rothmann
Past President
Bay Area Council for Soviet Jews
March, 1990

Acknowledgments

The material in this book was originally published in two volumes in Russian by the Library-Aliya Publishers in Israel, under the titles *From Leningrad to Jerusalem—With A Long Stopover* (1981) and *A Time To Be Silent and A Time to Speak* (1984). The English translation by Stefani Hoffman of these two volumes was made possible in part by a grant from the Jewish Memorial Fund, New York. These translations have been adapted and edited by Carol Talpers for the non-Russian reader.

The support of the Jewish Memorial Fund and the early interest in the manuscript by Ruth Frank, then Executive Director of the Jewish Book Council, are gratefully acknowledged. The dedication to the task of translating the work by Ms. Hoffman, the editing of the translations by Ms. Talpers, the generous and informed foreword by John F. Rothmann, and technical assistance by Tom Relihan are much appreciated.

Hillel Butman
Jerusalem
March, 1990

Introduction

On a raw afternoon early in November of 1966, I met with five friends in a park near Leningrad. There we formed a Zionist group. Our goals were to foster the struggle for freedom to emigrate to Israel for all Soviet Jews who so desired, and to awaken the Jewish consciousness of Soviet Jews by disseminating information about Jewish culture. That brief meeting determined much of what has occurred in my life since then.

During the next three and a half years our numbers grew and similar groups came into existence in other cities in the Soviet Union. We obtained, copied, and distributed Jewish literature, both poetry and prose. We taught Hebrew and Jewish history. We nurtured the dream of leaving Russia and living fuller, freer lives in the country we thought of as our homeland. But our activities were considered "anti-Soviet" and so were forbidden. Only a few Jews were permitted to leave for Israel during these years. The dream of *aliyah* continued to be just a dream.

Some of us devised a plan—Operation Wedding—to hijack a plane, fly to Sweden, and then hold a press conference that would draw international attention to the thousands of Soviet Jews who wanted to emigrate to Israel. But when we sought advice from Israel, we were told to abandon the plan.

As the sun rose on June 15, 1970, KGB agents at the Smolny Airport outside Leningrad arrested a small group of Jews about to board a plane bound for Sortavala, near the Finnish border. The men and women taken into custody had planned to board a commercial plane, hijack it, fly to Sweden, and from there go to Israel.

Later that same day, when I arrived at the dacha where I was vacationing in Siversky, I found that three KGB agents had searched our rooms and were waiting for me. As I put my four-year-old daughter to bed before they took me off to be interrogated, I was only vaguely aware that it might be a long time before I saw her again.

I was not a party to the hijacking that had been aborted that morning. But I was a Zionist, and I had been one of the originators of the earlier plan for a different hijacking which never came to fruition. My abandonment of that plan did not save me from almost nine years in Soviet prisons.

The KGB used the attempted hijacking as a pretext to smash Zionist groups thoughout the Soviet Union. In addition to those arrested at the airport, about two dozen others were arrested and tried for anti-Soviet agitation and propaganda; some were charged with treason. The defendants were sentenced to prison terms varying from one to ten years, and after serving their prison terms were allowed to leave the USSR. All except one (Viktor Shtilbans), who elected to remain in Leningrad, emigrated. As of summer 1989, sixty live in Israel, four live in the USA, two live in Austria, one in France, one in West Germany, and one in South Africa.

The fact that I am a Jew determined my life as a Soviet citizen—from my experiences of personal and of institutional anti-Semitism to the years I spent as a prisoner in the gulag.

Writing this book has been difficult for me, but it would have been even more difficult for me not to write. I have tried to write an unbiased account, realizing at the same time that this can only be my own subjective view of what occurred. Differences may linger about specific incidents, behavior, and attitudes. But the significance of the larger story cannot be denied. The events described here played a major role in opening the gates for the emigration of Soviet Jewry.

PART 1

Operation Wedding

CHAPTER ONE

June 15, 1970—Morning

Monday, June 15, 1970, began as an ordinary summer day. The alarm clock was silent that morning: I didn't have to rush off to work. I could sleep as long as I wanted. In two days, my three-week vacation with my family would be over. Then I would have to say farewell to the shady dacha in green Siversky and return to work. Back to feeling someone's elbow in my ribs on the bus and getting buttons ripped off in the metro, back to the factory, to the monotonously drumming engine of the test stand in the laboratory.

On the 16th I would return to Leningrad. Eva had returned to the city on the 14th, leaving a long list of instructions for me, so that instead of wondering how to run the house, I could think about more interesting subjects.

For example, the soccer score. We had tied with Italy and Sweden. Unfortunately, we had lost to Uruguay. But after all, there are only three million of us and we hadn't been playing soccer for long. "Hooray for our boys!" I thought to myself and imagined how the ball quivered between the Swedish goal posts.

"Our boys." There was a time when I would have said, "Hooray for the Israelis!" But in June 1970 I said "Our boys!" And every cell inside of me sang "Ours, ours!" In Leningrad there were Jews walking around who didn't even suspect that far away in Mexico, Israel was among the sixteen best teams competing in the world soccer championship. Israel had already made it to the quarter finals—among the top eight—while Russia had lost again. Most Soviet Jews didn't run out in the morning to look for *Soviet Sport*. For me, however, it had become a sacred ritual.

While we were on vacation, I took my daughter Lilya and my sister's daughter Annie to the library each morning so that Mama could clean the house. Both girls pored over picture books, waiting impatiently for me to finish looking at the newspapers. Then we would leave the library for the twenty-minute walk to the dacha. The girls were at the "tell me why" age and each day we played a new game as we walked. That Monday we called out the names of trees.

"Birch," cried Annie.

"Oak," corrected Lilya. She was a year older; soon she would be four.

"Maple," I declared. "Look at its leaves." Jumping up, I broke off a leaf.

I glanced from their flashing little feet and shorts to their identical white sun hats. Although dressed exactly alike, they looked completely different. Ann—a blue-eyed blonde—looked Scandinavian, while swarthy Lilya looked Semitic.

I turned my eyes to Lilya. We were good friends, and when Eva was at work, we were never bored together. It was hard to believe that my little friend hadn't even existed four years earlier.

My little friend Lilya. When did our friendship begin? The friendship of two people, one who was already thirty-seven and the other not yet four. No, it never began—it always existed. When she was only a baby she began to establish a special relationship with me.

One day after I got home from work, I lay down on the sofa and dropped off to sleep. In the middle of a dream I sensed that I was somehow having trouble breathing. Opening my eyes, I discovered a slipper lying on my face. Lilya, panting hard, was dragging a huge, dirty winter boot from the hall, to put next to the slipper. She did this with the best of intentions. Let's get friendly. You see how much I care about you!

By June 1970, at the age of three and a half, Lilya was a grown-up person. She loved to help, especially with the ironing. While I would iron, Lilya handed me the linen. The trick was not to give me what was closest—after all, Daddy could take that himself. Instead, she dove into the heap, pulled out a handkerchief, and brought it to me. A shirt fell onto the floor and a sheet slid off the pile. But that was just part of the cost of production.

The work sped along and the mountain of ironed linen kept growing. We had to finish our surprise for Eva quickly, because she would soon return from work.

"Daddy, I'm your helper."

"Right, right, darling, you're a real helper."

After all the laundry had been ironed, the tired but happy pressers sat at the table and waited. Lilya looked at me coyly and suddenly leapt at me—I barely managed to jump up and catch her in the air.

"I love you very much, Daddy," she whispered as she kissed me on the cheek.

The three of us turned down the street and walked toward the dacha where we rented rooms. The girls started a new game—a race—and ran toward the fence in front of the house.

As I reached them, I glanced at the porch. My mother's face—rather, her eyes—startled me. Eyes full of anxiety and horror, trying to tell me something. But her mouth was silent. Then I noticed three figures on the porch: a heavy-set man in a double-breasted leather jacket, and two affable-looking younger men in identical light gray suits. Three KGB agents.

I had encountered such "affable" types before, in the Big House (the notorious KGB investigation prison in Leningrad) on the Liteyny ten years earlier, in 1960, when three of us were picked up for listening to Voice of Israel broadcasts, studying Hebrew and reading the *Israel Herald*. Then the KGB had interrogated Solomon Dreizner, Natan Tsiryulnikov and me for three days in a row; we had refused to answer. Solomon and I were not prosecuted. Natan served a year in prison for circulating the *Israel Herald*. Solomon got off easy—he wasn't even thrown out of his institute. But I was sacked by the Bureau of Criminal Investigation, where I had been working as an investigator, and switched to repairing refrigerators. That's how things were then. What would happen now?

The girls tugged at the gate. Up on the porch the three men rose in greeting.

"Hello, Hilya Izraylevich. We've been waiting for you a long time."

They apparently had been searching the dacha for two hours. How long can you search a room that is ten square meters and doesn't even have a bookcase? Or a kitchen in which there is nothing but a refrigerator, a table and shelves for dishes? For a long time. Looking clever, you can knock on the thin wooden partitions between the rooms, pour milk from the bottle into a pot and back again, sift flour with a fork and then slowly sprinkle it until the sleeve of your light gray suit turns white. You can do a lot.

I went inside with the three men. According to Soviet law, two civilians had to be present as "official witnesses" during a search. The witnesses were waiting in the house—I recognized one, but not the other.

"Listen," said one of the official witnesses, "I was searched in 1938, but it wasn't like this."

This man was renting a room on the second floor of the dacha and until that moment we had said little but "Hello" or "Good evening" to each other. He was obviously tired from sitting on the uncomfortable couch for more than two hours. The small room was full of people and there was no other place for him to sit.

I was not worried about the results of the search. The house was "kosher." The day before I had loaned the only "unkosher" book to a new acquaintance. It was a short book, and if he was a fast reader he might have walked in at any moment to return it. That would conform to the universal law that if anything can go wrong, it will. In Russia it is sometimes called the law of the sandwich: the bread always falls with the buttered side down.

The KGB agents might have found *My Glorious Brothers* by Howard Fast. The Leningrad Organization's publication committee had just gotten hold of it, it hadn't been copied yet and hardly anyone had read it. But after the last meeting of our Committee Lev Korenblit gave it to me to read because I was going on vacation. At the dacha, whenever I had sat down to read, Lilya had run in to ask whether I had finished so that we could go play house. Finally, I hid from her in my mother-in-law's room on the second floor and must have left the book there.

The light gray suits came and went, but leather jacket stayed in the room. He kept shaking out our bed linens. The pants I had worn at the last Committee meeting were hanging on the headboard. In the back pocket was my telephone book. Only I knew that the last two digits in each of the telephone numbers were transposed. But that's a very primitive code and could easily have been broken. I had been using a more complicated code but had gotten tired of having to decode a number each time I made a call.

In that little phone book was a folded piece of paper, a list of the people from Leningrad who were to go to the Zionist summer camp on the banks of the Dniestr in Moldavia. The men from the Kishinev branch of the Organization had set up this tent camp for the first time. The group from Leningrad was to send Hebrew and history teachers as well as students. According to the preliminary estimate, there would be about one hundred people attending from all over the country. That camp was to be a trial balloon. We planned to have more teachers, students and courses the following year.

How could I snatch my notebook? I could do it if the two gray suits left and leather jacket turned around. How would the official search witnesses react? The one who was arrested in 1938 could hardly bear any love toward these men. He would be quiet. But what about the other one? I didn't know him. Perhaps he was one of those witnesses who were on permanent duty with the KGB and were taken along, the way a dog is taken to the scene of a crime.

The gray suits went out of the room. Leather jacket moved between me and the pants, and discovered his first "trophy."

"Look," he triumphantly told the witnesses, "the schedule of a foreign radio station!" He waved a slip of paper that he had found behind the cornice of the front door. Just a few days earlier I had learned that a Swedish radio station had begun to broadcast in Russian—I wrote down the wave band and stuck it behind the cornice.

"Foreign radio station . . . broadcasting schedule . . ." The witnesses, who had almost fallen asleep, came back to life. "Maybe this jerk isn't so innocent after all. . . ."

No matter how long you anticipate an arrest, when it happens it is unexpected. And it never follows the scenario you imagined. I had thought a lot about the possibility of an arrest, even before I met Mark Dymshitz. I had even worked out a plan. "They," of course, would come to our Leningrad apartment in Kupchino and knock on the door. From behind the door, I would ask, "Who is it?" Undoubtedly I would hear a suspicious male voice answer, after a second of hesitation, "Open up. We're from the housing office." Or something like that.

"Wait a second," I would answer, and then I would run to the balcony, which faces the other side of the building. "They" would have forgotten to post someone there, and I would quickly scramble down and run for a bus. I would borrow money from Aunt Sonya and hurry to Moscow. There I would go to the apartment of Lyusya Muchnik or some other Muscovite friend. I would hold a press conference, and then I would turn myself in to the Lubyanka.

This plan presented one technical difficulty: I would have to climb down very quickly from our fourth-floor balcony to the street, while "they" were cooling their heels at the front door of my apartment. I carried out a series of trial runs. The ceilings in the new buildings we lived in were about eight feet high. When I climbed down from the balcony, the scariest moment was when I was hanging by my hands between the fourth and third floors. My toes barely touch the railing of the balcony below me. Standing on tiptoe, I pulled away one hand and leaned against the smooth wall of the building—feeling as if I was about to lose my balance. Then I removed my other hand and leaned my body slightly forward, hoping to land inside the balcony and not out. Between the third and second floors I was more confident, and between the second and the first floors I could breathe evenly and deeply.

Naturally, I practiced during the day, when the other apartment dwellers were at work. Nevertheless, I was soon in demand. A neighbor from the fifth floor appeared first. Hemming and hawing a bit, he said that his door had blown shut with the key on the inside. I climbed up from my balcony and unlocked his door.

Then Galya Gelman came over from the neighboring building.

"Listen, my husband lost the keys again," she said. "I heard that you can . . ."

I climbed down to her balcony from the one above it. A week later a strange woman appeared and said sheepishly:

"You don't know me. I live in building number five. My oldest daughter left the house and took the keys with her, and I can't get in. I don't know what to do—you're my only hope."

I realized that if I didn't say no to her, I would set a precedent that would leave me no peace, and that would also guarantee the attention of the local police. I refused.

The girls were playing in the next room, which my sister was renting. On the floor they had built a long curved train out of their toys. The "cars" of the train stretched all the way across the room toward the porch. The adults had forgotten the girls—no one even came in to put them in bed for a nap. Lilya didn't come into our room. She knew that "comrades" had come to visit, and she left me alone.

Finally the search was concluded and a record was made of it—when it took place, who was present, what was found. Then I undressed Lilya and put her to bed while Mama took care of Annie. Lilya dove under the blanket and lay, as usual, on her side with her face to the wall. I could see how she was forcing her lids to stay closed—she was thinking that the sooner she fell asleep, the sooner she could get up and play house with Daddy and Annie.

I looked back at Lilya from the doorway. When you get up from your nap, darling, I won't be here, I thought. Would I be there when she would wake up tomorrow morning? Or the day after tomorrow? As I passed Aunt Sonya's room, I opened the door slightly. She was a sick woman and the visit of the KGB agents had only made her feel worse.

"Good-bye, Aunt Sonya. Best regards to your Solomon," I called out before I was led away.

Aunt Sonya had no Solomon. After they took me away, I knew she would stay with the girls while Mama ran to the train and went to Leningrad to warn Solomon Dreizner, and then he would warn the others. Or so I thought at that moment.

It was four o'clock in the afternoon. I didn't know that I was one of the last to be picked up. If I had been in town instead of at the dacha, I would already have been with Solomon and the others.

We went down the steps from the porch and walked over to a black KGB Volga waiting by the gate. It hadn't been there when I came back with the girls. Mama overtook us by the car and thrust a quilted jacket into my hands. Where did she find it, here at the dacha, and why was she giving it to me? Ten years earlier, when they took me away the first time, she hadn't given me a quilted jacket.

A dog ran by. Two women stood at the corner chattering. Leather jacket sat in the front of the car, next to the driver. A gray suit sat on each side of me. The Volga turned onto the road and headed toward the local police station.

We spent an hour in the courtyard of the police station while leather jacket kept trying to reach some number in Leningrad. The line was busy. He tried another number—again the line was busy. He came back to the car, nervously smoked a cigarette, then went back to the telephone. Finally he managed to get through, received the OK he needed, and we set off on the Luga-Leningrad highway.

Leather jacket turned around from time to time to check the back of the car. Reassured that I was still there and that the gray suits were not dozing, he went back to looking out the window. Everyone was silent.

Yes, this arrest was different from 1960. This time they had searched the way it is done in the movies. They had even taken some blank pieces of paper from a pad—perhaps they thought something had been written on the paper invisibly. Probably they would iron the paper or dip it into some chemical to check for an invisible message.

They had hidden the car intentionally, to avoid frightening the people at the dacha. And it had taken leather jacket an hour to get through on the phone, even though a call clearly had been agreed upon in advance. Something was going on, I thought. Was I being detained as a suspect for interrogation or was I being arrested as a defendant? Had they taken just me, or the others too? It seemed unlikely that they were going to crush our Organization; we hadn't had any warning signals. It's true, we were always on the razor's edge, but we tried to keep our balance.

CHAPTER TWO

Pushkin Park

On July 16, 1966, Geula Gil, the Israeli singer, was performing in Leningrad after a tour in Riga. At each of her concerts she was greeted with tremendous enthusiasm—but this inevitably led to battles with police. At her performances in Riga several Jews had been arrested and several had been wounded in clashes with police, but more than one Zionist was born there.

For her Leningrad concert only the lucky Jews were able to get seats in the summer auditorium of the Recreation Park. Jews who were less fortunate crowded the aisles, and Jews who had no luck at all waited outside for the intermission, hoping to sneak in for the second part of the concert.

A mime was performing on the stage. He portrayed a soldier carrying a white flag. A strong wind blowing in his face filled out the white flag like a sail and drove the soldier back, but just for one step. With a tremendous effort of will and muscle, the soldier straightened out the flag. Pushing against the winds, he stepped forward and, planting the other foot behind and turning his body slightly, he awaited the next gust. Only his tightly compressed lips and the narrowed slits of his eyes showed what a price he was paying for this small step forward.

Another step forward . . . and another. How did Soviet censorship let this act slip through? I looked at the spectators: everyone understood perfectly. No, this was not an abstract representation of man struggling with difficulties. That was not simply a white flag above him. The blue and

13

white flag of our homeland was fluttering above the soldier! He represented the people of Israel in their difficult march forward! He was a soldier of the Israeli army, and he fought against heavy odds, one against ten, because the Jews of the Soviet Union could not rush to his aid and support the flag with our strong hands.

The second part of the concert began and we went back inside the hall. I carried a bouquet of flowers. So did my friend Solomon Dreizner. So did many others—all for Geula Gil and her guitarists, and the mime Arkin. But someone had prudently foreseen all the possibilities and prevented any possible contact between the Jews in the hall and the Jews on stage. There would be no demonstration of unity: that's why a car for the performer had been brought directly to the inaccessible back entrance and why the side staircase leading from the hall to the stage had been removed. That's why the ushers weren't allowing anyone close enough to the stage to throw flowers. The Leningrad KGB had learned some lessons from the events in Riga.

In principle it was possible to reach the stage from the hall by climbing either of the two tall columns on each side. But the columns were guarded by ushers and you couldn't get around them. The only thing you could do was distract them.

The plan worked perfectly. Brandishing his bouquet, Solomon rushed toward the left side of the stage. Immediately a figure stepped away from the column: "Young man, that is forbidden."

For an instant, the column was unguarded and I began to climb. The audience understood my intentions: there was complete silence and then a hushed whisper. And finally, when I reached the stage and Geula held the flowers in one hand and offered me the other, and we lifted our joined hands above the stage, applause thundered forth. The

Yemenite Jewess from Israel and the Soviet Jew interlocked in a symbolic handshake.

"*Le-shana ha-baa b-Yerushalayim* (Next year in Jerusalem)," I whispered into her ear because, standing side by side, we could hardly hear each other over the deafening applause.

The journey to Jerusalem began three months later when the Leningrad Organization was created on November 5, 1966, in a park in Pushkin. Offices and factories closed early because of the holiday commemorating the October Revolution. After work a group of us met at the railway station and took the train to Pushkin, site of the former suburban imperial residence, less than an hour from Leningrad.

David Chernoglaz lived in Pushkin. He had graduated from the agricultural institute there and knew the town well. He met us near the grounds of the Tsarskoye Selo Lyceum and led us into the deserted park with its bare trees. There we sat on damp benches near the lone wooden table, facing the Lyceum where 150 years earlier the liberal ideals of the Russian intellectuals were first articulated as they planned the insurrection against the tsar.

It was a gray, dank day. Whipped by a piercing wind, we pressed close to each other. On one side of the table, representing one group, I sat with Solomon Dreizner and Rudik Brud—they had graduated from the architectural institute together. On the other side were Aron Shpilberg, David Chernoglaz, and Vladik Mogilever. Aron was an engineer, David an agronomist and Vladik a graduate student in mathematics. I was the only undergraduate in the group. At the time of that meeting, I was working by day as a refrigerator repairman while studying at night, taking correspondence courses at the Leningrad engineering college. Two people were missing: Ben Tovbin and Grisha Vertlib, my friend from law school.

There in the park we adopted a program that united the two groups. I suggested that our program should be based on that of the first Zionist Congress, held in Basel in 1897, but adapted to the Soviet reality of 1966. Our program was to have two goals: (1) to foster the struggle for free emigration to Israel of all Soviet Jews who desired this, and (2) to awaken the Jewish consciousness of Soviet Jews, particularly the young people, by disseminating information about Jewish culture. The six of us present in Pushkin Park that day voted unanimously for that program. We agreed to collect membership dues but not to write a constitution yet. The cold November wind discouraged lengthy speeches or discussions. We separated, agreeing to meet again, next time at my aunt's home.

The young men who gathered in Pushkin Park that day represented the generation of the 1930s. Our parents had not been Zionists. When we began to think about how we wanted to live our lives, our parents couldn't guide us— political and economic circumstances in the Soviet Union had been different when they were young.

Our parents' attitudes toward the Soviet system had been formed in the time of great purges, when everyone was in jeopardy and many were in prison. During those years shopkeepers and revolutionaries alike were at risk, and so was anyone who failed to follow the numerous zigzags of the party line.

When the "thaw" began in the mid-1950s, our parents realized that it might not last—they knew that the political climate could freeze over again at any time. They wanted their children to be outstanding pupils in school, to win scholarships at the university, to become indispensable specialists at work, to find and marry girls from "good Jewish families," to live peaceful lives. Our parents were not Zionists. So the young people of my generation came to Zionism without role models.

I don't mean that our parents had lost their Jewish identity. I heard Jewish songs from my father and from others of his generation—songs sung in Russian or in Yiddish. The heroes of my parents' generation were Jews who successfully evaded the traps set by non-Jews and by the GPU (now the KGB). The Jews of that generation looked backward, not toward the future. They longed for the good old days. Our parents couldn't answer our most basic questions—Where are we heading? What future awaits us? Where do we belong?

Who, then, were our teachers? How did we find the answers that led us to seek our heritage, that led us to Zionism? We were taught by our years as Soviet citizens, by the experiences of our lives. We were born in the 1930s, when churches were being blown up, when individuals and entire social groups were shot and killed. The great experiment was in full swing. The separate identities of all the groups within the USSR had to be submerged—national and religious cultures, customs and traditions were being subjected to russification. It was the time of industrialization, collectivization and passportization—requiring everyone to register with the local police.

When we were born, our parents had not yet been embarrassed by their Jewishness. They registered us on our birth certificates with the names of our deceased grandparents. In 1948 when we went to get our passports we had a good laugh. That's when we learned that Grisha Butman was Hilya Izraylevich Butman, that Syoma Dreizner was Solomon Girshevich Dreizner, and Misha Shmuylovich was Meir-Yankel Isakovich Shmuylovich.

During the Israeli War of Independence, we worried about the Jews in Israel. The newspapers reported on the military aspects of what was happening—that six hundred thousand Jews were winning a war against Arab kings and imperialist Britain which stood behind the Arab millions. We believed that it was necessary to fight against forced assimilation. The Soviet regime had closed Jewish kindergartens and schools, shut down the Jewish press and theaters, and physically annihilated the bearers of Zionist ideas. One result was a generation of Jewish youth without ideological, cultural or religious roots.

That day in Pushkin Park, I expressed some reservations about the creation of a formal organization. And I was not alone in having such reservations. Groups in other cities in the USSR—people who shared those feelings—chose not to form such organizations.

Was an organization necessary? At the time, the disadvantages seemed much more obvious to me than the advantages. A program, bylaws and membership dues—the usual features of an organization—could provide a formal basis for prosecution.

Later, many dissidents in the Soviet Union have decided against the creation of legal organizations because this has proved to be the surest, most direct route to a labor camp. But, looking back, I feel that we were completely justified in forming an organization, even though we knew from experience that people who form such organizations put themselves in jeopardy. If effectiveness is the goal, then an organization is like an orchestra that can play a richly textured score beyond the reach of a soloist.

Experience also has shown that if the KGB has its eye on two people who are acquainted, it will accuse them of organizational activity against the state, whether or not they accepted a joint program, worked out statutes or paid dues. When I was in the camps, I often met such "members of organizations"—people who had not met face to face until their trials. So it mattered little whether we acknowledged, by creating an organization, that we were actually participating in Zionist activities. If the KGB decided to accuse us, they would not need an organization to justify their action.

The pale of settlement laws during the tsarist rule restricted the area in which Jews were permitted to live but allowed community organizations, cultural and religious studies and the observance of tradition. Under the Soviet state Jews could not openly study their language, observe their religion or freely pursue their cultural heritage. The heritage that had been passed on through the centuries was in danger of being erased in the Soviet Union.

A nation can be destroyed by genocide, or it can be destroyed by forcing its people to assimilate. Stalin—self styled "Leader of the People"—was about to embark on the former path when he died in 1953. Those who followed him rejected genocide and, instead, energetically pursued policies of forced assimilation. Hybridized by those policies, Jews became raw material for the rootless nation, the homogenized "United Soviet People" that Brezhnev and his brave-new-world creators wanted to breed in a huge cage surrounded by an iron curtain.

Anything that obstructed or contradicted the government policies and party line became a target of the KGB. Even when the BBC and Voice of America could be heard in the USSR, the Voice of Israel could not break through the deafening noise of the jamming apparatus. Jewish tourists who packed for a visit to the USSR and wrapped their slippers in pages from illustrated Israeli journals found those same slippers rewrapped in brown Soviet paper when they claimed their baggage from customs.

The Soviet government devised an almost impregnable barrier against information, ideas and influence from outside the country. Under such conditions, the ideological annihilation of Soviet Jewry could be prevented only by activities such as ours within the Soviet Union. Each Jew, better informed about Jewish culture and tradition, could potentially join the stream of Jews that would flow from the USSR to Israel when Jews finally were allowed to emigrate.

When would that be? In 1966, emigration of Jews from the USSR to Israel was only a dream. Even the most optimistic did not imagine that only four years later large numbers of Jews would be granted visas and allowed to go to Israel.

The local organization that we started on November 5, 1966, was active for almost four years. During the first two years we were very cautious about choosing meeting places. We assumed that the authorities would bug our apartments. So in the summer we met in parks. When the Leningrad cold forced us indoors, we borrowed keys from relatives or chance acquaintances and tried to make our meetings look like gatherings of old friends who were escaping their wives for a few hours, getting together for a few drinks and some camaraderie. Once we even got the keys of a propaganda center. During that meeting, photographs of the founders of Marxism looked down from the walls at the clandestine Zionist crew. Karl Marx seemed the saddest. His face seemed to say, "My God! What will I see next?"

But someone who hasn't been burned will not be wary of fire. By 1969, when our organization was gaining momentum, we had become over-confident. Just when we had the most to hide from the KGB, we began to meet in our own apartments. At first we covered the telephones with pillows. Then we stopped doing even that.

Most of our activity up until 1969 was educational work. A few weeks after our founding meeting in Pushkin Park, we decided that the two groups would operate independently but would coordinate their work. The liaison member of our group was Solomon Dreizner. Theirs was David Chernoglaz. Later, as other similar groups were formed, liaison members from all groups formed the Organization's Committee.

CHAPTER THREE

Equality for Jews—Soviet Style

In the summer of 1950, I believed that all university applicants were treated equally in the Soviet Union, regardless of age, sex, nationality or religion. And I believed that anyone who thought otherwise retained vestiges of capitalist prejudice.

My consciousness was free of such vestiges. Because I knew German better than anyone else in my school, I collected my documents and took them to the Institute of Foreign Languages. Bogdanov, the only other graduate from my school who was applying there, had a mediocre record—a lone B in German, C's in everything else. My transcript was more impressive—all A's in the humanities.

While I was sitting in the vestibule of the institute filling out the application, two women students—both obviously Jewish—approached me.

"Young man, they won't take you. They don't take Jews," one of them said quietly.

Since they appeared to be students, they seemed to be telling me that, although Jewish women were accepted, Jewish men were not. Well, I would see for myself. I submitted my documents to the selection committee.

Strangely, Bogdanov with his mediocre record was waved through by the committee. He passed his exams and eventually became an army translator. But I. . .well, the girls were right.

So, the selection committee of the Foreign Languages Institute contained anti-Semites. That's not the end of the world, I told myself. Fortunately the whole process, from application to decision, took hours, not months. I decided to apply to the Journalism School at the Leningrad University that same day.

I went over to the University with my documents and got in line. The secretary of the entrance committee, an elderly, gray-haired woman with a tired but benevolent expression, was sitting behind the counter. When there were three people ahead of me but none behind me, I heard her say, apparently to no one in particular, "I advise you not to apply."

At first I didn't realize that her comment was directed at me. When she accepted the documents of the person in front of me, she said the same thing again, but louder. And this time she looked straight at me, almost angry at my slow-wittedness.

"You won't pass," she added sharply.

I hadn't believed the girls at the Institute, but they had been right. Now the official secretary of the entrance committee was clearly telling me what would happen. I took my documents and left.

For years in school I had dreamed of being either a translator or a journalist. I was one of the few who knew what they wanted before graduation. Now, in one day, my plans had been dashed. The officials hadn't even looked at my passport or glanced at my transcript. All they saw was my nose. What the hell was going on?

I understood, of course, that many Jews were "enemies" and "cosmopolites," but I was not one of them. The history I cherished was that of Alexander Nevsky, Dmitry Donskoy, Peter the Great, the Decembrists and populists who preceded the revolution and the heroes of the first Soviet state: these were my heroes. Had I lived at the time of the October Revolution in 1918, then I, too, would have fought against the Whites, the Greens, and all other enemies of the Soviet regime. It was unjust—all Jews were being punished for the "guilt" of a few who were considered to be anti-Soviet.

I was seventeen—an age of dreams and optimism. I applied and was admitted to Law School. Grisha Vertlib, and other Jews as well, entered with me. So, even if there were anti-Semites at the Foreign Languages Institute and the School of Journalism, there weren't any at the Law School. As the saying goes, the blindest man is the one who doesn't want to see.

How could I allow myself to realize that I was living in a country of organized state anti-Semitism, where the policy I had found at the Institute of Languages and the School of Journalism was the rule, and the policy of the Law School was the exception? How could that be true in a country where socialism had overthrown the tsar and destroyed the power of landlords and capitalists? After all, the pale of Jewish settlement had been abolished and Leningrad was full of Jews. The tsarist five-percent quota for Jews entering institutions of higher learning had been abolished; almost all of our parents and uncles and aunts had graduated from colleges and universities. All privileges, titles, and ranks had been eliminated—everyone was equal. The Criminal Code even included a statute against inciting national hatred.

When I was denied admission to the Institute of Languages and to the School of Journalism, I had to acknowledge the existence of some institutionalized anti-Semitism. I had already gotten used to anti-Semitic incidents on buses, in stadiums and on the streets. I began to sense a strong anti-Semitic atmosphere around me. If this state was unjust, then where was there justice? In America, where, as I was told, bellies are swollen from both hunger and overeating? If I acknowledged that the Soviet state was unjust with regard to nationality, then I would have to admit that it was unjust in other respects as well. How could I live in an unjust society without opposing it? As I began to be aware of injustices in Soviet society, I began also to accustom myself to the life of a second class citizen. The process of parting with my illusions progressed slowly and painfully, as life continued to teach me and I continued to learn.

In January of 1953, some outstanding Jewish doctors in Moscow were accused of poisoning Soviet leaders. The so-called Doctors' Plot was staged by Stalin just before his death, and was accompanied by an "anti-cosmopolitan" campaign in the media which implied that all the criminals were Jews. But then in March 1953, after Stalin's death, an amnesty was declared by the Soviet government and people began talking about a "thaw."

The summer of 1953 was a strange and mysterious season. Stalin died. He was mourned loudly and quickly forgotten. Beria, then head of the KGB, halted the case against the Jewish doctors. He released them and reinstated all their rights. For the first time, enemies of the people were rehabilitated while they were still alive! And then, suddenly, Beria was assassinated.

That summer I decided to apply for admission to an air force jet fighter training school in the Ukrainian city of Kremenchug. At the time, Komosomol, the Communist Party Youth Organization, was recruiting jet aviators, but the response was poor. I was eager to prove that Jews could fight. So I quit law school, applied to the air force, received an assignment from the district military headquarters and left Leningrad for Kremenchug.

We lived in tents in the courtyard of the school. Only those recruits who passed medical and qualifying exams would be admitted. Recalling the outcomes of my applications to the Institute of Languages and to journalism school, I was apprehensive. But the doctors—"murderers in white gowns"—had been cleared, a thaw seemed imminent and the aroma of the blossoming Ukrainian gardens roused my youthful enthusiasm.

Two of us among the three hundred original candidates were Jews. After the medical exam, I was the only Jew left. Those of us who passed awaited the decisions of the credentials committee.

My tent housed about thirty men, almost all from Belorussia. After taps they had long conversations, most often about their healthy instincts and the women who could satisfy them. But one blue-eyed fellow with curly blond hair, who presumably could have talked about many amorous adventures, always steered the talk in a different direction.

He told of how the Jews in his native Bobruisk had become impudent, and he said it was impossible to get rid of them. He and his friends had finally procured weapons and gone to the Jewish neighborhoods to set things right. But then, he said, the Jews got together and retaliated. And then the whole cycle began again. From his words I concluded that the Jews in Bobruisk had organized a self-defense league that boldly repelled attacks and let no incident go unanswered. I felt a wave of pride. I also felt a love for those unknown Jews, with whom I had much more in common than with the men who were lying near me in the tent, listening with great interest to those stories about Bobruisk.

Several times I tried to get this fellow to shut up. One day he and I were standing in the school courtyard guarding a training plane. Just the two of us and no one else.

"Look, Yuzef," I said to him, "every evening you talk about how you beat up Jews. I'm a Jew. We're the same age. Let's put it to the test. Prove you're not a liar."

Verbally Yuzef agreed, but in deed he kept procrastinating; he never put his manhood to the test. It was my little victory.

Meanwhile, the credentials committee was making its decisions. The day before the official announcements, a black-haired fellow in an air force school uniform came up and spoke to me in an Armenian accent.

"Listen, you're waiting for nothing. You won't get accepted."

"Why?"

"You're a Jew, aren't you?"

"Yes."

"I came here after a special school. We were all taken into air force schools without any tests or entrance committees. Everyone who arrived with me was enrolled, but the officials kept postponing my enrollment. You know why? My sister married a Jew. They kept asking me why she married a Jew. 'What's the matter, why couldn't she find an Armenian?' "

His words stirred up ominous presentiments, but I didn't have to agonize for long. A few days later it was my platoon's turn to appear before the committee. One after another the fellows went in and one after another they came out smiling, enrolled.

A tent-mate with whom I'd gotten on well came out. He didn't want to enter the school and had done everything he could think of to avoid enrollment. The medical commission had found something the matter with him, he had failed two examinations and he drank all the time. From the expression on his face, I could see that even he had been enrolled.

Then it was my turn to go in.

"Surname? First name? Patronymic? Date and place of birth? Nationality? Short autobiography!"

I answered apprehensively. Among the officers I noticed an elderly man in civilian clothes. He had an intelligent, strong-willed face, short hair that was graying in the back. He leafed through a folder and occasionally glanced at me. Finally he asked, "Do you have any relatives abroad?"

I really didn't know if I had relatives abroad. Once, when I had been listening to a conversation between my mother and her brother, they seemed to be saying that their father's step-brother had emigrated to America at the turn of the century. He had come back to Russia as a tourist before the war, and even wanted to remain in Russia, but had not been permitted to do so. He was kind of a relative, but he wasn't Mama's real uncle. No, I comforted myself, he's not the kind of relative that one has to report.

"No," I answered, faltering slightly. I didn't like to lie; and I wasn't good at it.

"Do you understand why I'm asking you in particular about this?" I heard the gray-haired civilian ask. "The Jewish people are dispersed throughout the world. Many have relatives in various countries. Intelligence agencies of imperialist powers utilize this, and we must take this into consideration. Go, you are enrolled."

I flew out into the bright Ukrainian day. The fellows slapped me on the back, and even the Armenian from the special school smiled, although he looked confused.

So, after all, there was no official anti-Semitism in the Soviet Union. There were anti-Semites—in personnel departments and on entrance committees. But where people did their jobs honestly and honestly followed the party line, there was no anti-Semitism. Hadn't I been accepted into law school? And now I was enrolled in the air force school. And look how frank and honest the chairman of the commission had been with me. And I understood his point of view. I was even a little embarrassed that I hadn't been completely honest. After all, it could be said that I had relatives abroad.

To celebrate, we went to the Dniepr to swim. None of us had passes, but there were so many holes in the wooden fence around the school that all thirty of us were able to crawl out simultaneously.

That evening everyone had a haircut and changed into military uniform. Everyone but me. I was told that I was being dismissed from the school because of my unauthorized departure from school grounds. They offered to transfer me to the aviation school where specialists were trained to service the jets on the ground. I indignantly rejected the offer. If you're born to fly, you do not crawl on your hands and knees.

The next day I set out for home with a loaf of bread and four rubles, eighty kopeks for the four-day journey to Leningrad by way of Moscow. My military pass made it easier for me to get onto the trains, which were crowded with people returning from summer vacations. When I finally arrived in Moscow, the loaf of bread was only a memory; so I spent my last ninety kopeks for a dozen undernourished crabs—a bargain that stuck in my throat. I had never before eaten crabs—nor have I since.

Then I didn't even have five kopeks for the Moscow subway. While I was standing near the turnstile feeling the hunger pangs in my stomach, I noticed a large family going through. The father, who held all the tickets, was behind the rest of them. I sneaked into the middle of the group. What's one son more or less? While the ticket taker was still counting the tickets, I was gliding down the escalator.

A few days after I got home to Leningrad, I took my documents to the military registration headquarters and asked the military commissar for the application I had submitted—having it would save me the trouble of filling out another, if that became necessary. He handed the application to me without turning around. In the answer to the fifth question, which calls for one's nationality, the word "Jew" was underlined with a thick stroke of blue ink. I was a so-called "invalid of the fifth question." In all official Soviet questionnaires, the fifth question—after identification of surname, first name, patronymic, date and place of birth—

deals with "nationality." Jews are expected to identify themselves as such, and automatically become ineligible for a variety of benefits. Thus they are euphemistically called "invalids of the fifth question."

With some difficulty, I managed to be readmitted to law school for the final year.

I finished law school in 1954, at an interesting time. During Stalin's rule, the country had come to the brink of disaster. Even though bread prices were regularly reduced—slightly but with great fanfare—there were still bread lines all over, even in Moscow and Leningrad. Industry, deprived of any economic stimulation, produced only a perpetual deficit. What the government described as "temporary difficulties" were really permanent conditions. Most men who weren't in prison were serving in the army. Satirists of the post-Stalinist period said that people had stopped wearing shoes and had put on boots instead—because the country was ankle-deep in crap.

The collective leadership gradually began to loosen the reins, for fear that the harness would break. The slaveholding system, centralized and regimented, was undergoing transformation. Trains brought rehabilitated prisoners from the labor camps of Kolyma, Siberia, and the Urals. Trains full of demobilized soldiers needed for the moribund factories and kolkhozes—collective farms—set out from the western borders. Political satirists were no longer arrested. The extremes of the political repression were abandoned but the old principles were retained, including the "wise Stalinist nationality policy"—a euphemism for anti-Semitism.

Soon after we graduated from law school, we were given work assignments. No one wanted to leave Leningrad, especially those of us who were natives. Graduates did their best to avoid assignments in the provinces that might result in the loss of their permits to live in Leningrad. Many of the young women graduates became pregnant to avoid being sent out of the city.

I was assigned as a criminal investigator in the prosecutor's office of the Karelo-Finnish Soviet Republic. Grisha Vertlib was assigned to the Kirovsk region, and all the other Jewish graduates were sent to similarly uninhabited expanses of the Soviet north and east. The non-Jews, who had come from these same expanses to study in Leningrad, almost without exception were assigned to work in Leningrad—even though they lacked housing.

I hadn't yet totally abandoned my Komosomol enthusiasm and managed to conjure up exciting images of myself as a district investigator in desolate Kareliya. There is nothing in most of Kareliya but forests, lakes and sawmills with drunk or semi-drunk woodcutters—my future clients. I equipped myself with a double-barreled shotgun and enough ammunition to destroy all the wildlife in Kareliya and I set out for the Karelo-Finnish Republic. I arrived to find that my position had already been filled and they didn't need me. A few days later I returned home.

In 1953, after Stalin's death, the situation of the Jews gradually changed for the better—I wouldn't say it was good, but it was better than it had been during the last few years of the Stalin regime.

Those who had not lost their jobs during the great purge sighed with relief. Those who had lost their jobs learned that it was almost impossible to find new jobs. Snub-nosed heads of personnel departments became experts in the art of refusal. They told women that resolute men were needed; men were told that diligent women were required; the young were informed that they needed experience; older applicants were told that they were too old. And even if your passport listed your nationality as Russian but you looked Jewish, you knew in advance that you would not be qualified.

Many of us, although desperate for work and willing to take any kind of job, remained unemployed for months and years. I will never forget those times. I envied people in workers' soiled uniforms. But I couldn't be hired as a laborer: "What, the government wasted money on your education for nothing?" I was embarrassed to look my mother in the eye. The bread stuck in my throat. I began to avoid people and noticed with some amazement that I was surrounded by similar "invalids of the fifth question"—our common rejection united us.

Then I got a job as a proofreader in a printing house. I worked there for a year and despised the work. I had never thought it possible to read a book and see only letters, commas and exclamation marks.

During that year I began studying at night school, in the physics and mathematics department of a teachers college. After all, I had to give some thought to the future, to somehow change the present. I worked as an instructor of tour guides, but that wasn't a promising career for me, either.

Suddenly I got lucky. I helped catch one of two muggers who had beaten up a Czech student and stolen his camera. The head of the Leningrad Police Department, Commissar Solovyev, appeared on the scene. When he learned that I had graduated from law school, he invited me to work for the "organs," the generic term used in Russia to describe police and security forces. Even though Commissar Solovyev had personally offered me a job, the personnel department was opposed and kept me dangling for a long time. Finally I figured out that I was supposed to invite the major in charge of my case out to dinner at a restaurant.

When a bottle of cognac had been emptied, the major told me, "Don't worry, everything will be all right."

And so, in the summer of 1957, I began to work in the Leningrad Criminal Investigation Department. I had a fire-proof locker and a pistol.

CHAPTER FOUR

Jewish Awakening

At the Twentieth Party Congress in February 1956, Khruschev made his famous speech denouncing Stalin's rule of terror. After that, everyone's eyes were opened. Those who had previously discerned a Communist paradise on the horizon realized that communism, like the horizon, was an imaginary condition that grew more distant the closer one got to it.

Soviet society became ideologically disillusioned, and an almost all-pervasive cynicism replaced the discarded ideology. Not everyone was cynical. Some—and I was among them—could not live without faith. I retained my faith in socialism as the system of the future in which personal labor would be the only criterion for prosperity and for society's attitude toward the individual. It was clear to me, however, that socialism in the Soviet Union had at some point in time taken a wrong turn.

I rejected capitalist society in principle, as a society in which the pursuit of profit at any price demoralizes people. The October Revolution had been right. The class struggle was right. Dictatorship of the proletariat was necessary. The bourgeoisie had to be weeded out. Lenin had been 100 percent right. Stalin had perverted Lenin's cause.

It was with this perspective that I later came to Zionism. And it was not until much later that I learned to make independent decisions about what I saw and read, instead of trying to fit all ideas into a rigid framework and throwing out those that did not fit. Once I had stopped thinking dogmatically, I understood that the facts at my disposal could lead to conclusions very different from those being pushed by the official line.

The more that Soviet society excluded me, the more strongly I was drawn to my own people. When World War II began, I was eight years old; and when it ended I was twelve. I knew that the Germans murdered Jews. At the wedding of a relative, I met a boy who had been wounded in a mass shooting and had fallen into a ditch. Later he regained consciousness and crawled out from under the heap of bodies. Until I heard his story, the Holocaust had touched me only obliquely. Since then it has pierced me through and through.

Millions of Jews were murdered because they were Jews. Huge gas ovens smoked in Poland, but no one tried to bomb the crematoria. Two million Soviet Jews in the Nazi-occupied territory were doomed. They could not believe that they were about to be murdered, or they hoped that they personally could somehow survive under the Nazis. Many Soviet Jews remembered the arrival of Kaiser Wilhelm's Germans and their liberal occupation of the Ukraine during World War I. These Jews found it difficult to see the situation during World War II as really different, and that is why many of them decided not to leave their homes when they could. Any Jews who might have resisted the Nazis had been left leaderless by the Soviet regime's systematic elimination of Zionists before the Germans arrived. Local centers of resistance arose only in places where the militant Zionist youth had not been destroyed during the early years of the Soviet regime.

During World War II, darkness and death descended on European Jewry. Six million perished. But this tragedy went unnoted in the Soviet Union. There was no monument to the Jews who were murdered at Babi Yar or at thousands of other ditches and ravines. In Kiev in 1976, a monument was dedicated "to the victims of the German Fascist invaders at

Babi Yar." There were inscriptions in Russian and Ukrainian, but there was no mention of the Jews. When journalists wrote about the millions of Soviet citizens killed by the Nazis, they told about the "Russians, Ukrainians, Belorussians, Lithuanians and others." The Jews were among the "others."

Soviet authorities converted synagogues into warehouses. They repressed Jewish culture, language and traditions. They shot members of the Jewish Anti-Fascist Committee. Stalin, like Hitler, was solving the "Jewish problem."

In my mind I connected the two events—the Nazi Holocaust of European Jewry and the Russian persecution of Soviet Jews in Stalinist times. These were only the most recent of such events—and there could be more in the future. I developed an insatiable interest in Jewish history and read everything I could get my hands on. The more I read, the more I wanted to know. Growing awareness of and pride in my Jewishness led me toward Zionism. Anti-Semitism in Russia was creating Zionism, not eliminating it.

The Israelis' 1956 campaign in the Sinai set my head spinning. During Israel's War of Independence, I had been a schoolboy. Then I had identified with an army that, in fighting against the Arabs and their British imperialist protectors, was defending Soviet interests as well as its own. But in 1956, after my inner crisis, I was rooting for an army that, in defending our Jewish cause, was also opposing the expansion of the Soviet empire in the Middle East.

It seemed that the links of Jewish history did not lead only to the past. New links were being forged in our time in the Middle East: for the first time in two thousand years, the Jews were the blacksmiths of their future. I felt the excitement of a proselyte. I spent all my free time at the public library, where one could still read the London Times. I couldn't read English, but I spent hours staring at the photographs of bearded Israeli soldiers in the Sinai desert.

The year 1956 was one of political turmoil. Soviet tanks stood at the crossroads of Budapest, and soldiers from Uzbekistan marched along the banks of the Danube to quell the Hungarian revolt. Poland was in turmoil and Gomulka made his way from jail to the chair of first secretary of the Communist party. The Hungarian revolt stirred the conscience of many Soviet people, who felt the need to bring about changes in Russia. Many Jews belonged to these groups and again, as they had in 1917, they burned with the desire to sweep out the dirt and bring order into the home where they were viewed as undesirable lodgers. It was at that time in my life that I had to choose between Zionism and the Soviet democratic dissident movement. My meeting with Leah Lurie helped me find my way.

The awakened Jew in me sought kindred spirits, but I searched in vain. At the public library I met no young Jews, only retired old men who spoke Yiddish to each other. They politely slipped away from my attempts to start conversations about Israel. But then, in the fall of 1958, I finally found what I was seeking.

Each year on Simchat Torah, Jews gathered in the courtyard of the Leningrad synagogue. This holiday was the only time during the year when young men and women could assemble, to see and be seen, to meet and begin acquaintanceships and friendships. Many young isolated Jews saw this gathering as an opportunity to meet other Jews and perhaps find a spouse. These young people were not Zionists. But they were Jews. They crowded into the synagogue, listened to the cantors and breathed in the Jewish atmosphere.

I don't know when this annual gathering began to be a tradition. But each year the size of the group increased. Eventually the authorities got worried. They began sending police guards. Lermontov Boulevard was closed off, and empty Black Marias, the Soviet version of paddy-wagons, stood by the synagogue gates awaiting their prey. The police loudspeaker thundered in the courtyard:

"Citizen Jews, have a conscience. You are disturbing the sleep of sick children. Have mercy on them. . . . Disperse." A wing of the synagogue had been confiscated and turned into a children's hospital. Now it provided an excuse to arrest those gathered outside the synagogue and fill the Black Marias.

Agents mingled with the crowd in the yard and wrote down the names of the students. Afterwards the KGB made the students' lives miserable, ousting them from the Communist Party youth organization because "religion is incompatible with membership in the Komosomol," and expelling them from their institutes "for immoral conduct."

But the more energetically the police "participated" in the celebration of Simchat Torah, and the more scuffles there were between the young Jews and the plainclothesmen in the synagogue courtyard, the more the scene attracted Jewish youths who were defiant with awakening national pride. By the late 1960s, Simchat Torah had become a powerful festival and a demonstration of Jewish spirit.

But way back in 1958 on Simchat Torah, the synagogue yard was half empty. A cluster of young people crowded near the small synagogue. As I approached, I noticed a woman of about fifty with a small boy. She was standing in the center of a cluster of young people, and I realized that she was talking about Israel. She alluded to letters from an uncle there.

I was fascinated. Israel was suddenly transformed from a mythical country on another continent to a land where real people—including this woman's uncle—lived and wrote letters. I decided I had to get to know her. But when

I moved around the circle to get closer to her, she looked at me suspiciously. Finally, interrupting her story, she said good-bye, took the boy by the hand, and slipped out of the courtyard. She was almost running. Looking back, she saw me following her and walked even faster. I managed to overtake her a few blocks from the synagogue.

I could understand her fear—the Stalinist period was still too fresh in all our memories, and she, apparently, had been terrorized. But I felt that I had no alternative. "I don't know your name, but I have long dreamed of meeting someone like you. You can't imagine how important it is to me . . ."

"Young man, leave me alone, or else I'll call the police."

"But for me to meet you . . ."

"Stop pursuing me. . . . Sasha, what does he want from me? What did I do to him?" She passed her fingers over her lips and adjusted her glasses over her nose—simultaneously indicating that I should be silent and that she was curious about me. I burst out laughing, and the ice of distrust began to crack.

It was not easy for me to persuade Rosa Epshtein that I really was not a threat. But when we parted, I took with me her address and telephone number. And I knew the address wasn't a fake—I had accompanied her home and saw her unlock the door.

Two weeks later Rosa introduced me to the world of Leah Lurie, to her home and her family. Soon I brought Solomon Dreizner along with me into this world. Solomon and I were childhood friends. His father fell in defense of Leningrad in the early days of the war. In order to help his mother and three sisters he went to work at fifteen, and attended an evening high schoool. After graduation he entered an aeronautical school and from there entered military service as an officer. He was sent to an eastern Siberian district, where the life of the military in this barren frontier zone consisted mostly of drunken brawls. For Solomon, as a Jew, chances of transfer or advancement were nil. Eventually he was discharged and returned to Leningrad, where he entered an engineering school. After graduation, he got a job in a design office. He was one of my closest friends and we shared an intense interest in Israel. We entered the home of Leah Lurie as emotional Zionists. We departed from it as informed people who knew what we wanted and where our homeland was.

Leah Lurie was born in Riga in 1912. Her father, Sender, was a physician, and her mother Eugenie, a renowned beauty. Eugenie created the environment and set the tone in the Lurie household during those early years of this century. French and German were spoken in the home. The Luries, and especially Eugenie, had an active social life that included parties, receptions and horseback riding. She was elegant and strong willed.

When Eugenie became pregnant, she did not want to sacrifice her beauty. And so she wore a tight corset during the months she was carrying her child. The infant, Leah, was born with deformed limbs. As little Leah began to grow, her parents discovered that she could not walk on her own or move her hands normally. Even so, Leah was energetic, playful, curious. Her cheerful optimism would have been admirable even in someone who had not been disabled from birth. She was interested in music, and the Leningrad radio archives contain recordings she made of children's songs.

The Holocaust and postwar anti-Semitism disturbed Leah deeply and made her a Zionist. Because of their Zionist activities, she and her father were arrested on the same day in 1949. Sender Lurie was taken away in a Black Maria, and Leah was carried off on a stretcher.

Leah's father loved his daughter deeply. He believed that, for her, arrest meant certain death. Even strong men do not often survive interrogation and imprisonment, and Sender Lurie believed there was no hope for his physically disabled daughter. Without Leah he did not want to live. Unaware that Leah had survived incarceration, Sender Lurie died in prison.

But Leah returned. Her face was still beautiful and her thoughtful gray eyes were still shining, though wrinkles had appeared around her eyes, and gray strands streaked her cropped auburn hair.

That is how Leah looked when Solomon and I first saw her, in the late fall of 1958. And that is how she looked when she died in January of 1960, at the age of forty-seven. That year of our friendship with Leah imbued our lives with meaning. We found what we had been seeking—kindred spirits. She made many people welcome in her home, among them those who were ready to leave for Israel at a moment's notice.

Leah was one of the few who, having survived all the horrors of the "Beria Preserve," found the strength after her return to continue her life's work. During the time between her release from prison in 1954 and her death in 1960, Leah supported herself and her aged mother by giving lessons in French and German. She also taught Hebrew, which she learned from the radio, but she did not charge for Hebrew lessons. She began a translation of *The Uprising in the Warsaw Ghetto* from Yiddish to Russian. Only Eugenie saw Leah as she turned the pages with her tongue and tried to write with her deformed fingers.

Leah dreamed of teaching the children of Yemenite Jews, people she loved dearly for their industriousness and devotion to the land. She gave Solomon and me the gift of eight lessons in Hebrew.

During our time with Leah, Solomon and I learned and

our Jewish awareness grew. The call letters of the "Voice of Israel" became the signals calling us to a new life. The songs of Yaffa Yarkoni and Shoshana Damari rang in our hearts. Each new kibbutz in the Jerusalem Corridor was our victory. Endless conversations about Israel made it seem nearer and more real. I began to dream about living in Israel, and that dream came to engross me completely.

Leah Lurie died under the surgeon's scalpel. Some thought she was murdered, but I do not think so. After her death, searches, arrests and interrogations of her friends began. She was buried in the Preobrazhensky cemetery next to the synagogue in Leningrad. An epitaph in Hebrew was engraved on her tombstone: "Leah Lurie of Blessed Memory, 1912-1960. A faithful daughter of her people." "Unknown hooligans" broke the tombstone, and it was replaced with one inscribed in Russian. The phrase "a faithful daughter of her people" had been dropped.

If it is true that there are immortal people, Leah Lurie is one of them. Her gray eyes still smile at those who had the good fortune to know her. When we think of her we are reminded of Hillel the Elder, the sage of the first century, and of his words that we learned from Leah—"If you are not for yourself, then who is for you? But if you are only for yourself, then what are you?" Six years after Leah Lurie's death, our illegal Zionist organization was founded in Pushkin Park. Two of the founders—Solomon Dreizner and I— were disciples of Leah Lurie, whom we all called Lilya.

That same year, 1966, my daughter was born. My wife and I named her Lilya in memory of my beloved mentor.

CHAPTER FIVE

Happier Times

When they came for me in 1960, I was working as a police investigator. They had already picked up Solomon Dreizner. As soon as they took him away, his mother got on a bus and came to me. I was ill in bed at home, but I got up quickly and cleared out. Later I found out that I had done the right thing. Since "they" didn't know that I was ill, they had gone to the Kirovsk Regional Police Department, where I was employed. There everyone became alarmed. Immediately, my locker—which contained my Makarov pistol, the personal weapon of a Soviet police officer—was sealed. Hours later they went to my home.

All day long I wandered through the streets of Leningrad, waiting for some news about Solomon. He was released about midnight and called his mother with the good news. After I learned of his release we met, taking every precaution to avoid observation by the KGB. Solomon told me about his interrogation, that he had to report to the KGB again tomorrow; we agreed on a story. We decided that even if they pressed hard, we would refuse to answer any questions. The one who refused first would stick a match, head up, into the flowerpot in the corridor near the interrogation room. When they came for me early the next morning, I was psychologically prepared.

At that first interrogation in 1960, Colonel Rogov, chief of the Investigation Department of the Leningrad KGB, flashed a big smile as he entered the room where I was sitting. He wore that smile as confidently and easily as he carried the six-foot body of an athlete and darling of fortune. He shook my hand firmly, in a friendly manner.

"Well, hello. How the devil did you get into this business. Never mind, it's not so terrible. Everyone makes mistakes."

And again he smiled cheerfully, as if to show that the situation was not really serious. His manner seemed to suggest that we would work out this misunderstanding together, and then I would return to my job and he would continue to protect the state against its enemies.

Seeing my dejected look, he added, "Butman, you're a lieutenant and I am a colonel, but we are both officers. We both work for organizations that defend the state, and we both have to do our duty now."

Adrenalin starts flowing into the bloodstream at a time of stress when there is no way out or, worse yet, when there are two ways out but both are fraught with danger. Perhaps I should tell Rogov everything I knew; after all, we didn't do anything so terrible. So we got together, we listened to Israeli broadcasts, we discussed Israeli problems and looked through copies of the *Israel Herald* that Natan Tsiryulnikov brought from the Israeli embassy when he traveled to Moscow for his work. The paper contained only objective information about Israel and steered away from any mention of the Soviet Union. And what can be so wrong with Hebrew lessons?

What if I stand firm and don't answer any questions? I'll be sacked from my job, and finished professionally. Try starting life all over at the age of twenty-seven!

Well, it's just as well that I have no choice. Solomon and I agreed on everything last night. We considered all the possibilities and made our decision. And Solomon will act accordingly—that's for sure.

On the third day a match appeared in the flowerpot— head up.

From my experience with the police in 1960, I knew that silence was the only strategy that made sense for us. If a case concerned activity over a period of time, and not just one or two incidents, even if only two people were involved, they could not foresee and agree on everything in advance. More than two people and more than two incidents produced a situation with more unknowns than anyone could anticipate. So if one person talked, the second was bound, eventually, to contradict the first person at some time during the interrogation.

Ever since childhood I have found the idea of lying to be repugnant. But it is quite another thing to be silent, even though silence can be a form of lying. Silence cannot be contradicted, even unwittingly.

Vladik Mogilever was the only one of the Committee who objected to the decision to be silent. During an earlier investigation (of the case of the dissident Ronkin-Khakhaev group), he had been interrogated as a witness several times. Vladik had come to the conclusion that the investigators from the Leningrad KGB were naive and that it was possible to fool them. He contended that you could guess from the investigators' questions what they knew and what they did not know, what interested them and what did not. But Vladik was out-voted. If interrogated, we would be silent.

This decision created some questions: Was silence to be maintained from the very beginning? It was suggested that we give the basic facts about ourselves, but not answer any questions about the substance of the case.

But the KGB could start an informal interrogation without first covering the basic personal data found in the passport of the individual being interrogated. If that happened, we were to try to determine where informal questions ended and substantive ones began.

We decided to try a rehearsal, an imaginary investigation. Grisha Vertlib believed that none of us should answer any questions. So, in our rehearsal, we interrogated Grisha.

"Hello, Grigory Solomonovich," we began. "How are you?"

"Hello," he answered, and then fell silent. After all, "How are you?" is a question.

"How is Galya?" he was asked. "How are things going at her job?"

"I refuse to give testimony. I do not consider myself guilty in any way, and I don't know of anyone who committed any crimes."

"Grigory Solomonovich, you are an intelligent man, but you are not behaving rationally. Do you know your sister Galya? Yes or No?"

"I refuse to give testimony. I do not consider . . ."

We decided to be silent from the very beginning.

In 1960, after I lost my job at the police department, I got a job in a refrigerator repair shop. The handcuffs and revolver of an officer were replaced with a pliers and a wrench. At the age of twenty-eight I was starting again. But it was a time in my life when opportunities were found as well as lost!

My friend Boris Markhasev, a physician, invited Solomon Dreizner and me to celebrate May Day of 1961 with his young nieces at their home on Vasilyevsky Island. We were to contribute our share of food and drinks. On the evening of April 30th we set out with some friends, heading for the address Boris had given us.

Our hosts had invited other friends, too—Ira, Fira, Slava and Ella—and they arrived soon after we did. Ella, I noticed right away, was very attractive and naturally modest. I didn't manage to sit next to her at dinner, but after the party I accompanied her home.

Before long we were talking about Jewish topics. I mentioned a translation I had of *The Uprising in the Warsaw Ghetto* and she asked if she could borrow it. I told Ella that I was not really Grisha, but Hilya Izraylevich Butman, and that I was a Zionist, not a Komosomol member. For some reason, I added that my future wife would have to go with me to Israel. And she, for some reason, asked:

"But what will be the patronymic of your children? You have such a strange name."

Before we parted, I asked Ella if she was free the following Monday. She said she was busy. After a moment's hesitation I asked about Tuesday. She was busy. Very hesitantly I asked about Wednesday. She was also busy on Wednesday. I said good-bye and left.

At twenty-one, without a diploma, Ella was working as an engineer at a military factory. At twenty-eight, and with a diploma, I was working as an apprentice mechanic in a repair shop. Perhaps she just was not interested in seeing me again. I had no way of knowing that she really was busy Monday, Tuesday and Wednesday.

Several weeks later I came upon the three notebooks containing the translation of *The Uprising in the Warsaw Ghetto*. I had Ella's telephone number at work and called her, and we made a date to meet that evening at the lighthouse near the Palace Bridge on Vasilyevsky Island.

I arrived at the bridge a little early. The minutes passed, and time dragged by—no Ella. It was a holiday—the anniversary of the founding of Leningrad. Hundreds of people were celebrating all around me. But I became more and more morose. Finally I climbed up on the pedestal of one of the decorative posts on the bridge to see if I could find Ella in the crowd, but in vain. Later, I learned that she had come, and had even arrived on time. But she had gone not to the Palace Bridge, but to the bridge of Lieutenant Schmidt.

On April 30, 1962, just a year after our first meeting,

Ella Bekman became Ella Butman. And later, when I changed the name on my passport, she did the same, and we became Hillel and Eva.

I had not had a lot of luck in my life until then. Eva has been my good luck. But our life together has been hard for her. And the hardships started right away. After our wedding, we went back to our separate homes—the room we had rented was still being fixed up.

After a few days we were able to move in. We learned that it's not easy to live in a communal apartment with eight other families. But our biggest headache was night school at the technical institute. The bright dream of emigrating to Israel was supplemented by a dull dream of getting enough sleep. During those years—and especially after Lileshka was born—I fell asleep on buses, at lectures, while working. I had trouble thinking, no less studying. Eva did the work for two, and somehow she dragged me from course to course.

Although I had been forced by circumstances to enter the technical institute, I remained a humanist. I could not master descriptive geometry. Just joining two points with a straight line had always seemed difficult—drawing the intersections of complex geometric figures in space seemed impossible. Eva, who dealt with the construction of nonstandard equipment at the factory, grew hoarse trying to explain to me which edges should be visible in the sketch and which ones should not. And I had to face the exam.

The instructor, Marianovsky, was Jewish, and he sympathized with us. During the exam he turned away intentionally, so as not to see Eva sketching and explaining a drawing to me. This was our second attempt. The first time I hadn't been able to explain to him what was so beautifully drawn on my paper. I had had to leave. And Eva had left, too, saying that she was not prepared. Another failure would be disastrous.

Marianovsky absent-mindedly listened to my answer, looking first at me and then at Eva. Finally he interrupted me in the middle of a word:

"All right, young man, wait outside the room. Leave your exam book here."

I waited a long time. Finally Eva appeared, with two exam books in her hand. I looked at mine—it was a C. Eva also got a C.

"He waited until I was the only one left," she said. "Then he examined me, and I answered my question, and did it well. Then he said to me, 'Unfortunately your husband doesn't know descriptive geometry and never will. If I simply give him a passing grade, that would be dishonest. How about my adding his grade and yours, and then taking the average?' "

Eva beamed with joy.

In the summer of 1969 Eva and I took our final exams, defending our diploma projects. Thanks to her efforts, we had been able to complete a six-year course in eight years, although on the average people finished it in eleven years. Eva finished the institute twice—once for herself and once for me. And she also managed to give birth to our Lileshka.

"What will be the patronymic of your children? You have such a strange name," Ella Bekman had asked at our first meeting. On our daughter's birth certificate we wrote "Hilevna," daughter of Hillel.

Eva had been a member of the Komosomol committee in her factory, and she did not become a Zionist right away. Just as I had not. Nor had our peers. After all, we were the generation after the generation referred to by Elie Wiesel as the "Jews of Silence," those whose "tongues had been removed" by the Yezhov-Beria terror.

When the judge at the Second Leningrad Zionist Trial asked Eva, "How are you related to the accused Butman?" she replied:

"I am the wife of Butman, Hilya Izraylevich, and I'm proud of it!"

CHAPTER SIX

Underground—Books and Ulpans

During the first few months of its life, much of our Organization's time, money and attention went to the dissemination of literature. Decisions had to be made about what to distribute and how to go about it. How could we provide effective counterpropaganda to oppose the avalanche of slander about Israel, Zionism and Jewish history?

The Leningrad Organization consisted of small groups; each group had a librarian who was responsible for circulating literature. The librarians handed out the material to group members, who in turn passed it on to others. We operated like a real library. In our efforts to obtain materials to reproduce and circulate, we focused on three topics: the ideological foundations of Zionism, Israel's domestic and foreign affairs, and the problems of *aliyah*. Some of the literature was taken from out-of-print Russian texts that we found in local collections, some was brought into the country illegally in single copies. Some of the texts were in foreign languages and had to be translated into Russian. All of these had to be reproduced in multiple copies, mostly by typing and retyping.

As one of our early projects, we condensed a translation of Leon Uris' *Exodus* and typed a shortened version. Many hours were spent discussing which parts of the book were to be omitted. Then Vladik Mogilever, who at the time was responsible for collection and distribution of books of interest to Jews, made an arrangement with a retired woman who spent at least six months typing twenty-one copies of the abridged version of *Exodus*. This project cost us half a year's budget and left the cash-box empty.

How many people could read twenty-one copies of a book in one year? Probably about two hundred—and there were about two hundred thousand Jews in Leningrad alone. Among these were tens of thousands of young people who were still capable of adopting new ideas and fighting for them. When would they get a chance to read Uris' *Exodus* or Bialik's poetry or Jabotinsky's *Feuilletons*? Would they ever experience the feelings aroused by Bialik's "City of Slaughter"? At the rate we were going, the Jewish youth of Russia would be old men and women by the time our literature could reach them.

From the first months of the Organization's existence, we had discussed the idea of disseminating leaflets during mass gatherings. Twice a year—on May 1st and again on November 7th—all of Leningrad goes out into the streets and an endless stream of demonstrations flows across Palace Square. At the factories they give the day off to anyone who agrees to carry a red banner for several hundred meters during a demonstration.

Leningrad is not Rio de Janeiro or New Orleans, with noisy, colorful carnivals. But people need relaxation. It's pleasant to get away from the daily aggravations, to put on a new jacket and a white shirt, walk around the festively decorated city, enjoy the music and buy pretty balloons for your children and beer and smoked fish for yourself.

The people in these holiday crowds have long been indifferent to the slogans and appeals that reach them over the loudspeakers, although sometimes a strictly local appeal—such as "Hurray for the glorious collective of the technical school of public nutrition!"—might rate a response from some passing enthusiasts. But even just a hundred leaflets addressed to the Jews of Leningrad, falling into the Palace Square during a demonstration, would arouse interest. Jewish youth would learn that an organization of Zionists existed in Leningrad. And that knowledge could kindle the flame in those who were still capable of burning emotion.

But how could we do this? It was possible to just pull out a bundle of leaflets and throw them around. That would be suicide. It would also mean the death of the Organization.

With tens of thousands of people on the square, how great was the chance that a KGB agent would turn up nearby? Very great. During one holiday, Kolya Bondar, a university teacher from Ivano-Frankovsk, arrived in Kiev and joined a demonstration on the Kreschatik. In his hands he carried a picture identical in size and shape to those carried by dozens of the people around him. The slogan on his picture, like theirs, began with the words "Hurray for," but those were followed by the words "an independent Ukraine." Kolya managed to go several dozen meters before he was arrested. Later I met him in a labor camp in the Urals.

In February 1917, the Zionists of Russia warmly welcomed the revolution that brought the promise of freedom, equality of opportunity, ideological pluralism and parliamentary rule based on division of power. As the years passed, it became evident that much of this promise would not be fulfilled.

The attitude of the KGB toward Zionists was based on the idea that the government must "keep and not let go" any Jew who seeks to emigrate from the USSR to Israel. This was an extension of the idea that anyone who does not support the government and the philosophy of the USSR is someone who opposes that government and its philosophy. If the KGB could look at Zionism with a more open view, it would be evident that Zionism serves positive functions, not only for the Jews but for the Soviet Union as well. Zionism deflects the tendency of many Jewish young people to interfere in internal Russian affairs and this discourages attempts to change the existing order. Zionism gives these young people a different goal—to emigrate from Russia to Israel, to build a home in their homeland, based on their own traditions, to defend that land from its enemies, and to secure the future of their children, grandchildren and great-grandchildren.

Our Organization fought the existing Soviet regime on very specific issues: we sought the right to emigrate, and to awaken Jewish consciousness. It was not our goal to change the existing order in the USSR. Nevertheless, our activities "rocked the boat," and the government could not tolerate the existence of our Organization.

Ulpans—informal groups for studying Jewish history and the Hebrew language—became the means of Jewish education. In an ulpan, young people were organized into groups with common interests. Their national consciousness was aroused and enhanced as they learned the language and heritage of the Jewish people. The ulpans also gave us an opportunity to decide which of the students could best handle the responsibilities of participation in Zionist activities.

The first ulpan in Leningrad was organized in early fall of 1967 by David Chernoglaz and Vladik Mogilever, who taught history and Hebrew there. Through an acquaintance, they had been able to rent a huge house on the shores of the Finnish Gulf in the Leningrad suburb of Repino. During the summer this house was the dacha of some party boss; the rest of the time it was the site of the ulpan.

In the classrooms of the Repino ulpan it was possible to

accommodate two dozen students. Among them were the first members of the Organization and their acquaintances—most of them students or recent graduates of technical institutes. The teaching level at that first ulpan was high, and the exam given at the end of each course was tough.

The ulpan students prepared hot meals in the sparkling clean kitchen stocked with flour, cereal and sugar. This spacious building had only one defect—it was devilishly cold on frosty days. Those on duty heated the classrooms from Saturday night to Sunday, but even near the stove our breath was visible as vapor.

Solomon Dreizner and I organized the second ulpan a month after the first one. Solomon took care of business matters and I taught Hebrew. Our ulpan, in a rented wing of a private dwelling, was also in a Leningrad suburb, but several train stops closer to Leningrad than the Repino ulpan. All we had was a room of about fifteen to twenty square meters, and a small entryway. When everyone was assembled, we had to sit very close together. This warmed us, in every sense of the word. The students on duty took turns arriving earlier than the rest in order to warm up our modest quarters.

Every student who could brought a meal, and some brought extra food for those who had less. During the long recess, the men played soccer in the snowy street while the women set the table. Then the men came in and their playful spirit continued through the meal, with jokes, witticisms and teasing. I do not remember a gayer time than those Sundays.

At this ulpan, study was less important than the sharing of the Jewish spirit and values. The academic level was much lower than at Repino, but almost all the students who finished our ulpan, although they did not become fluent in Hebrew, did join the Organization.

The Riga group sent us color slides of Israel. First we

showed them at the ulpan. Then they made the rounds of private apartments and attracted new students to the ulpans. During their studies at the ulpans, people progressed from passive sympathy for Israel to active desire to emigrate.

Aron Voloshin, Sasha Halperin, Kharik Kizhner, Shimon Levit and Lazar Trakhtenberg—all from Kishinev—had joined the Organization when, with Tolya Goldfeld, they finished the Polytechnic Institute in Leningrad. After they returned to Kishinev, they created an autonomous unit affiliated with our Leningrad group and they maintained close ties with us through Tolya.

But before they departed for Kishinev, they studied Hebrew. Vladik Mogilever organized intensive Hebrew classes for them so that they could teach Hebrew in Kishinev ulpans. Their teachers were Avram Elinson (a member of the Union of Soviet Writers and a future member of the Israeli Writers' Union) and Vladik Mogilever. For ten days, ten hours each day, the five men studied Hebrew. Advanced materials were used for the course: a chapter from Genesis, excerpts from *Eugene Onegin* in Avram Shlonsky's translation, and also his translation of Simonov's poem "Wait for Me," Krylov's fables in the brilliant translation of Khanania Raikhman and the latter's verse, aphorisms and epigrams. And many exercises.

During breaks, students and teachers ate quickly and then sang popular Israeli songs. The course ended and the exams were completed. During the final evening everyone talked about meeting at home in Israel. Their dreams would, eventually, be realized. But the Kishinev group's road to Israel would pass through the Mordvinian labor camps.

At the end of the course, Avram Elinson gave each of his students a book in Hebrew from his personal library. He picked books that were also available in Russian, so that his students could continue their studies after they got back to Kishinev.

In the winter of 1969 1970, preparations began for a summer camp that students and workers would attend during their vacations. Every effort was made to avoid arousing the notice of the KGB. The tent camp was to house about a hundred people the first year, perhaps more in subsequent years, in several shifts. A site was chosen on the banks of the Dniestr, not far from Kishinev. Passwords were agreed upon in all the cities in which we and the Kishinev group had connections. We managed to procure such basics as food, tents and textbooks.

The first shift was to start in the middle of June, and the first teachers flew from Leningrad to Kishinev a few days early. Lev Yagman, a member of the Committee, was to teach during the first shift. He took a vacation and flew to Kishinev with his wife Musia and their two little children during the first week in June. Courses hadn't started yet, so the family spent a few days in Odessa. They rented a room, settled in and put the children to sleep. Lev took a wash basin and went out to the courtyard to wash his feet before going to bed.

But he was able to wash only one foot. He was arrested before he could put the other foot into the basin.

In Leningrad during the late 1960s we all had ordinary working days, holidays, days of good spirits and days of depression. With both joy and sorrow people went to the apartment of Sasha, Dr. Alexander Blank, their adviser and comforter. Sasha lived alone, and his apartment was a Jewish club, a Jewish dining room, a Jewish hotel.

"Soviet power—*in drerd an ort* (Yiddish for "it should be buried"). Here is what you must do . . . ," he would say to a guest as he gave advice and poured something strong into a shotglass.

Although he lived by himself, Sasha was never alone. People flocked to his apartment night and day. I remember one evening in particular. Eva and I had guests from out of town, and we gave them our apartment. Eva stayed with a friend. Sasha lived nearby—across a vacant lot—and I went over to his place.

I arrived late, after midnight, but the apartment was still full of people and conversations. Sasha was bustling between the kitchen and the living room, offering food and drink to his guests, talking with several people at once, and studying new words in Hebrew while he washed the dishes. The radio was blaring, the television was on, and the front door kept banging as people came and went.

Sasha worked in two clinics and had to go to both his jobs the next day. Some evenings he worked, without charge, as a physician on duty at the symphony, so that he could be in the world of music. I had to be at the factory early the next morning. How could either of us sleep in the midst of all the activity? Sasha shrugged his shoulders. "Well, what can you do?"

Not until about 2 am did the guests begin to disperse and the phone stop ringing. Sasha set up our beds; we lay down and fell asleep instantly. A knock at the door woke me, and for a moment I couldn't imagine where I was, or why. Sasha was already at the door, yawning but inviting Vladik Mogilever to come in. Vladik was on his way to the airport. He had two hours before his flight was to leave, and he had stopped by to discuss something.

I turned the light on and looked at the clock. It was 3 am—we had slept about an hour. Vladik left at about 5 am. The phone began to ring about an hour later. In the morning I was exhausted. But not Sasha. For him it had been an ordinary night, no worse and no better than any other.

Sasha's lifestyle was enough to destroy a strong young bull, and he was not that. In World War II, during a disorganized winter attack in the North Caucasus, he had lost part of his leg along with his Komosomol illusions. At eighteen he became an invalid for life, but he never lost his independence of mind.

In 1969 Sasha decided to apply for an exit visa. But first he had to extricate himself from the Communist Party. When he had joined in 1942, in a snowy trench at the front, all he had to do was write a few words on a piece of paper. But to leave the Party in 1969 was far more complicated. At a party meeting, Sasha "honestly acknowledged" that he felt himself unworthy of being a member of the great party of Lenin. He said that he was increasingly under the influence of a religious opiate—and that he had even begun to perform circumcisions.

The dissatisfaction of the others at the meeting was clear: the party had no place for a man who performed circumcisions and planned to go to Israel. They voted unanimously to expel him. Some people even insisted on submitting the case of Sasha's betrayal of the motherland to the court. But the deed was done, and Sasha believed that he had a chance for a visa.

Shortly before Sasha left the Communist Party, he discovered the existence of a "sister" in Israel. She inundated him with letters, and he sent telegrams to her. They had to be reunited; clearly they could not live apart any longer. But at the OVIR (visa office), the officials laughed:

"Listen, Blank, you were only two years old when your . . . what is she? . . . sister left the USSR. Here you still have plenty of brothers and sisters with whom you grew up. What kind of strange love is it that you have for that Israeli sister?"

"You can't order the heart. It knows who it loves and who it doesn't," Sasha answered.

That same year he received a visa. The festivities began in Leningrad. It was hard to find a Jew who didn't know Sasha. He was the first member of our Organization to leave. Now we were sure that Israel would find out about us. Maybe we would even get some help.

Solomon Dreizner and Vladik Mogilever accompanied Sasha Blank from Leningrad to Moscow when Sasha left for Israel. After they returned to Leningrad, they reported to our Committee that almost all the Zionists in Russia had gathered in Moscow to say farewell to Sasha. They also told us of the formation of the All-Union Coordinating Committee (AUCC) in Moscow. From that time on, the work of the Zionist groups in Moscow, Leningrad, Riga, Kiev and Tbilsi would be coordinated by the AUCC.

The creation of the AUCC was a major step for the movement. The resulting coordination of the activities of the Zionist groups fueled all of us with new energy. We were encouraged by the knowledge that somewhere in distant Tbilsi or Kishinev someone else was taking a risk for the same ideals. Coordination also had practical results, in that members of the AUCC began to exchange ideas.

When the AUCC was created, intense disagreements arose over the organizational structure of the Zionist movement. The groups from Leningrad and Kiev insisted on an organizational structure with corresponding disciplinary demands. The other groups considered this unsuitable.

The AUCC operated without a home base. At each session, the group from one of the five cities was given the responsibility for organizing the next meeting. The second AUCC meeting was held in Riga in November of 1969. When AUCC met in Kiev in February 1970, the Zionist groups of Minsk, Vilna and Kishinev became full members of the AUCC.

By December of 1969, Vladik Mogilever couldn't fulfill all his publications commitments. And so the Leningrad group formed the Publication Committee. Lev Korenblit took on the editorial responsibilities, and Viktor Boguslavsky did the production work. Not long after the formation of the AUCC, publication of the journal *Iton* (the Hebrew word for newspaper) began. Then we had even more work to do, reproducing and distributing it. At the time all we knew about *Iton* was that it came from Riga; only two issues were published. The third issue remained in a half-finished state. Later, in the camps, I met some of the people who had been involved with *Iton*—in Riga—Misha Shepshelovich, Tolya Altman and Iosif Mendelevich. Boris Mafzer was also part of that group, but I didn't meet him while I was in prison.

Gradually the Leningrad group acquired some money. Membership dues alone brought in more than a hundred rubles a month. And occasionally someone would make a gift of money. For example, Lev Korenblit and his colleague from work, Monus Sominsky, both doctors of science, each gave the organization 110 rubles before they even joined. Publication projects consumed the largest share of the money. During the life of the Organization we purchased several typewriters, and for those we had to buy paper and carbons. Members traveled to Riga to help with *Iton*, and to other places to obtain or distribute materials we published.

David Chernoglaz served as our treasurer until May 1970, when he was—briefly—succeeded by Lev Yagman. During the month or so that Lev was treasurer, one member of our group, Lassal Kaminsky, brought a significant sum of cash from Moscow. They money was left by a professor from Novosibirsk who had received an exit visa. He donated the money for the use of the All-Union Committee. But within weeks, before we had time to use it, we had all been arrested.

From Moscow we received several hundred copies of the textbook *Elef Milim* (Hebrew for one thousand words). These had been reproduced on a copying machine in a city in Siberia. We thought, how wonderful it would be to possess such a machine! And then, unexpectedly, we had a chance to turn this fantasy into reality.

Several such copying machines were located in an institution in Kishinev. The person in charge of the machines went on vacation and entrusted the keys of the building to David Rabinovich. David was a friend of Organization members Aron Voloshin and Sasha Halperin. The three of them decided to take advantage of the situation.

They removed the copying components from one of the machines and told us what they had done. At the next Committee session it was decided that the components should be sent to Leningrad, where we could assemble a machine that could make use of this valuable object. We gave this project the code name "Launch." Solomon Dreizner was in charge.

The parts were delivered to Leningrad, along with the technical descriptions of how to assemble them. The missing parts were manufactured, and then four Organization members—Natan Tsiryulnikov, Hillel Shur, Boris Starobinets and Boris Loitershtein—began to assemble the pieces. They worked in Hillel Shur's apartment.

But while the copier was being assembled in Leningrad, an angry investigation evidently was beginning in Kishinev. In the USSR every copying machine is registered. As soon as the loss of the components was discovered by the institution, panic ensued. Since David Rabinovich was responsible for guarding the machine, he had to pay for the missing components. And it seems likely that the officials also checked his connections and began an investigation.

The Committee in Leningrad collected 200 rubles for Rabinovich, and sent the money via Sasha Halperin when he came to Leningrad for a visit. The work in Hillel Shur's apartment was almost completed, and the copier was ready to be "launched." For their technical efforts on this project, the group in Leningrad—Dreizner, Shur, Tsiryulnikov, Starobinets and Loitershtein—were, later, given "credit" by the special commission of technical experts appointed to investigate. During the trial in May 1971 the Kishinev group was accused by the KGB of stealing the parts of the copying machine. The Leningrad group was accused of "unpremeditated harboring of stolen goods."

At the end of 1969, the Riga group proposed what came to be called the Pushkin project—they intended to collect information and publish a book of facts about state anti-Semitism in the USSR. This project gradually died, although not for lack of facts. Only theoretically could one meet a Jew in the USSR who had not experienced anti-Semitism. A few rare Jews could be found who said that they had not noticed anti-Semitism, but that did not mean that they had not run into it. The concepts of "run into" and "notice" are as different as the concepts of "listen" and "hear."

No, Project Pushkin died for ethical reasons. We didn't feel that we had the right to reveal incidents of discrimination without the permission of the people affected. To do so would almost certainly have jeopardized, and even ruined, their future "peaceful lives." Besides, for practical reasons, many people would consequently refuse to confirm these facts.

CHAPTER SEVEN

The Letter and the Suitcase

One day at the beginning of 1967 while I was out for a stroll near the Russian Museum, I had an idea that struck me as unusual and promising. I presented it, first to Solomon, Grisha, and Rudik, and then to a meeting of the eight original members of the Organization.

I suggested that we compose a well-reasoned and strongly worded letter. In it we would discuss two problems—the forced assimilation of the Jewish minority in the USSR by the intentional annihilation of Jewish culture, and Soviet violation of the 1948 United Nations Human Rights Declaration, under which all Soviet Jews had the right to depart for Israel. Such a letter would arouse international public opinion in support of *aliyah.*

We would send this letter to the Kremlin and circulate it in the USSR. And we would not do this anonymously. Each of us would sign the letter, and each would affix his real address and place of work. We would also send this letter to the address for which it was really intended—abroad. I believed that this bold, open approach would attract worldwide attention—such a letter would be the voice of Soviet young people with Komosomol cards in their pockets. The letter would address the two problems that our Organization intended to solve. And this approach—being open and providing our names and addresses and workplaces—would protect us from retaliation from the Soviet government and might even result in our being expelled from the USSR.

The group decided that I should write a draft of the

letter I had in mind. Grisha Vertlib, who was enthusiastic about the idea, wrote a second version.

My draft filled an entire composition notebook; once I started, I couldn't stop. But I was cautious and wrote only about the Jewish aspects of life in the Soviet Union. My letter concluded with a demand that the UN Declaration of Human Rights be observed and that all Soviet Jews who so desired be permitted to leave for Israel.

I read this draft to the group, and they edited it only a little. Grisha Vertlib inserted into my letter several ideas from his draft. And then our letter was ready to start making its way toward its many destinations.

This was several years before the famous letter of the eighteen Georgian Jews that was transmitted by the Israeli government to the United Nations and which broke the silence that surrounded Soviet Jewry. Our letter was prepared long before the writing of open letters became commonplace, and long before Yasha Kazakov, who acted in a similar manner, succeeded in getting exiled from Moscow, not to the Far East but to the Middle East.

But our letter was never sent. Our Organization was not a military unit with a single head. It was a democracy with all the attendant advantages and disadvantages. Some people in the Organization were just as doubtful as others were certain that the letter was a good idea. Some members suggested that we use this letter as a kind of trump card—and that we should publish it with our signatures, and thus risk arrest, only when we actually faced arrest for the activities of the Organization. The letter would thus be transformed from an instrument of attack on the assimilation policy of the Soviet Union and an instrument to help us achieve *aliyah*, into an instrument of personal defense.

Solomon, Grisha, Rudik and I were unwilling to use the letter that way. We wanted to use it according to our original plan. Who was wrong and who was right? We decided to find the answer in Israel. This was easy enough to decide, but it was difficult to make contact with someone in Israel. Finally we did manage to talk with Mr. Efrat, a member of an Israeli delegation accompanying Labor Minister Yigal Allon on a visit to the USSR. But then Efrat disappeared, and we waited for a response which never came.

A few months later, in the spring of 1967, we gathered with our then customary caution in the Komosomol Park near the Narvsky Gates. After we had finished with the agenda, Aron Shpilberg announced that a whole suitcase of books would be sent to us from Riga, if we could figure out a way to receive it safely.

The group entrusted me with the job of devising a plan. I assumed that our contact would travel from Riga with a "tail" as well as with a suitcase full of Zionist literature. The Riga KGB would undoubtedly get in touch with the Leningrad KGB, who would await the train from Riga with as much anticipation as we would.

I tried to imagine how I would act if I were a KGB agent. It seemed to me that I would be less interested in the suitcase and its contents than in the people who received it. Logic suggested that the KGB would follow the suitcase until it reached its destination—and then they would take in the people to whom it was delivered. We had to find a way to shake the KGB tail along the route.

Here my knowledge of Leningrad was helpful. I knew of an unusual street layout in one of the old districts of the city. There, an intricate arrangement of passages and court-yards makes it possible for a resident—and anyone else familiar with the area—to go quickly from Khalturin Street to the parallel road, Moika Quay. But a stranger to the area, walking down either of those streets, would see only a solid wall of buildings. He would be unaware that any of the building entrances led to passages that connected to the parallel street. He would not know which entrances were left unlocked and which passages connected the two streets. And so this stranger would have to go down either of these streets for a distance of perhaps two bus stops before finding a cross street that would get him from one street to another. In contrast, anyone familiar with the area and with the entrances, courtyards and passages, could—even while carrying a heavy suitcase—run the length of the passage from Khalturin Street to Moika Quay in a minute and a half.

I devised a plan that took advantage of the peculiar features of this area. One member of the Leningrad group would meet the contact from Riga at the railroad station. They would pretend not to know each other, would discover that they were going to the same part of the city and would share a cab as if economizing. In the taxi they would be silent. When the cab would stop at the first address, No. 8 Khalturin Street, another member of the Organization would come out of the building and collect the contact and the suitcase. The two of them would race, with the suitcase, through the connecting passages to Moika Quay. The member who had met the contact at the railway station would tell the taxi driver to proceed to another address.

When the two men with the suitcase reach Moika Quay, another taxi would be waiting with another member of our Organization. Our man with the suitcase would get into that taxi and away it would go. The contact from Riga would take off along one of the bridges across the Moika.

But what if our contact was picked up right after he got off the train in Leningrad? He could tell the KGB that a stranger at the Riga station had asked him to drop off the suitcase in Leningrad, and had paid him well. He could say that he had never before seen the man who met him. And if the KGB asked, he could give them a plausible description of the "man who gave him the suitcase" and a plausible (but inaccurate) address for its destination.

But what if the KGB men eventually drove up to No. 8 Khalturin right behind us? For this I had planned something special. The elegant old building on Khalturin Street had been a private home but now was an apartment house. At the front entrance were two glass doors. In the lobby behind the glass doors was an elevator. And behind the elevator, not readily visible from the lobby, was a door into a narrow passageway that led to a courtyard from which one could enter another passageway to Moika Quay. If the two men carrying the suitcase could manage to get from the street into the lobby and the passageway, they could bar the door behind them and gain the minutes needed for escape. And while the KGB tried to break down the barricaded door, they would lose time they could have used to jump in the car and drive around to Moika Quay.

Solomon and I shaped a heavy piece of wood, drove over to the Khalturin Street house and measured the piece to make sure it would be exactly the right length to bar the door. At almost the last moment Grisha Vertlib, David Chernoglaz and Ben Tovbin changed the plan so much that it was nearly unrecognizable. They replaced the Riga contact man traveling to Leningrad with a Leningrad man going to Riga and coming back with the suitcase, and they rejected the idea of having a taxi waiting at the Moika Quay exit of the passageway from Khalturin.

But the idea of using a wood strut to barricade the door was retained. All eight of us, Grisha Vertlib, Aron Shpilberg, Solomon Dreizner, David Chernoglaz, Ben Tovbin, Rudik Brud, Vladik Mogilever and I, were to take part in receiving the suitcase.

I suggested Pinhas Shekhtman as the contact to go to Riga. Pinhas was a young laborer proud of his Jewishness. In the late 1960s he had made a daring but unsuccessful attempt to escape from the USSR by crossing the Finnish border. And Pinhas had another important attribute—he did not know the other members of the organization. Pinhas immediately accepted the proposal, and he did his job well.

On the chosen day, Pinhas flew from Leningrad to Riga. At the Riga airport, using prearranged signals and passwords, he met a man with a suitcase who introduced himself as Ruva. Ruva accompanied Pinhas to the Riga railroad station, and they stood on the platform near the train for a few minutes. Just a moment before the train was to leave, a third man arrived with another suitcase, which contained the literature.

Pinhas took that suitcase and got on the train just as it began to roll out of the station toward Leningrad. The third man left the railroad station. Ruva took his empty suitcase, which he had brought along to confuse the KGB, and went home. Before Pinhas left for Riga, I introduced him to Grisha Vertlib. When Pinhas' train from Riga arrived at the Leningrad station the next morning, Grisha was there waiting.

I got up very early that morning. Without even stopping to eat breakfast, I took the piece of wood and left the house. When I arrived at the meeting place on Khalturin Street, Aron Shpilberg was already there. The others soon arrived and then dispersed to their posts.

I was the receiver. With the stick in one hand, I stood behind the glass doors at No. 8 Khalturin. Solomon stood near the doorway across the street. The rest spread out within sight of each other, up to the first cross street, along it, and along the Moika Quay. If the KGB got there first, the look-outs would warn me when I emerged from the last connecting courtyard onto Moika Quay.

Apartment dwellers from No. 8 went out shopping, returned, went out again on business and returned again. Each time they went through the entrance, they looked at me suspiciously—who is this strange character hanging around for more than two hours, and with a stick! They'll call the police, I thought.

Finally Solomon looked at me, signaling that I should get ready. Then he turned away indifferently, removed his hat, and wiped his brow with a handkerchief. That was the signal I had been waiting for. Now the suitcase would appear.

I saw Grisha Vertlib first. He was walking along the other side of the street, looking at the numbers of the buildings. Finally he saw No. 8 and began to cross the street. Then Pinhas appeared, wearing his dark imitation leather jacket with a knitted collar. He had the suitcase and was dragging it laboriously along the sidewalk. His face revealed anxiety, exhaustion, pain.

In the final plan, Grisha was not to go up to Pinhas at the railroad station. Instead, he went to the streetcar stop. Pinhas, with the suitcase, followed at a distance. They got on a tram, then switched from one car to another. Grisha kept checking to see if anyone was following them.

Pinhas had been up all night on the train. He was exhausted and hungry, and he was having difficulty lugging the huge suitcase as he followed Grisha's zigzags. Grisha, nearsighted and worried about whether they were being followed, was not aware of Pinhas' struggle.

As Pinhas approached the front entrance of No. 8, I could see from his face that he was close to the breaking point. I jumped out of the entry and onto the sidewalk and took the suitcase from him. We ran into the entrance of No. 8, then from the lobby through the doorway of one passage, and immediately barricaded the door with the wooden strut. Together we dragged the suitcase through the courtyards and passages to the exit on Moika Quay. And then, as planned, Pinhas disappeared, leaving me with the suitcase.

Only then, as I started to drag it myself, did I fully understand the expression on Pinhas' face. I learned then what any political prisoner knows—that a suitcase filled with books seems to weigh far more than a suitcase filled with platinum. Every five or six steps I had to stop and switch the suitcase to the other hand. Why had I let the others cancel the taxi that was to have been waiting at the Moika exit? I felt so weak that the KGB could have knocked me down like a scarecrow.

For the next half hour I dragged that suitcase through the streets of Leningrad to my destination—the apartment of a friend. I had arranged with her to leave a suitcase there. When I arrived she did not question me about the contents. Perhaps, since I was a refrigerator repairman, she thought it contained spare parts. I hoisted the suitcase up and shoved it onto a shelf in her apartment. And then I went home.

The next time we got literature from Riga, Silva Zalmanson brought it in a suitcase directly to Solomon Dreizner's apartment. Perhaps that was risky, but it was a lot simpler.

A month after the traumatic arrival of the suitcase, it was still locked and nailed shut. Solomon Dreizner, Rudik Brud, Grisha Vertlib and I wanted to put off opening it. Aron Shpilberg, David Chernoglaz and Ben Tovbin wanted to open it so that the literature it contained could be disseminated immediately. Vladik Mogilever, as he often did, tried to work out a compromise.

Why were the four of us so resistant to opening the suitcase? At issue was the use of the letter we had written months earlier but hadn't yet sent, pending advice from Israel. If we opened the suitcase, began to distribute its contents, and brought the KGB down upon ourselves, we would then have time only to use the letter as a "shield" but not enough time to make the best use of its potential for arousing international public opinion in support of *aliyah*. And we strongly believed that the letter would be far more effective in advancing the goals of the Organization than would the entire contents of the suitcase.

Then suddenly Israel was embattled in what came to be called the Six Day War. We could not wait any longer. The suitcase was broken open. Inside were hundreds of books— Uris' *Exodus*, Jabotinsky's *Feuilletons*, Bialik's poems and other material.

Now we might need the letter as a possible defensive instrument. We still wanted an answer from Israel and we had to somehow transmit the letter there. In the spring of 1969, a group of Zionists from Riga unexpectedly received permission to emigrate. One of the people in this group was a former prisoner of Zion, Iosif Khorol. Years earlier I had been to Khorol's apartment, where I had seen a huge portrait of Zeev Jabotinsky on the wall. As a Zionist activist he was less likely to refuse us.

Khorol did agree to take with him a copy of our letter— unsigned. We devised a code system by which we could, after Khorol reached Israel safely, communicate to him the names to be added to the letters. After he received the names and added them to the text, he would be able to publish the letter to protect us if we were arrested.

A month after Khorol left, another acquaintance of ours—a man named Iosif Yankelevich, a Herutnik who had suffered through many years in labor camps—also was allowed to emigrate from Riga to Israel. I planned to accompany Yankelevich and his family, including his thirteen-year-old daughter Sima, to the Moscow airport. I decided to ask him to take the list of signatures to Khorol.

Grisha Vertlib encoded the list and gave it to me on a double sheet of notebook paper. Just the sight of all those numbers made me uncomfortable. In movies about vigilance, Soviet KGB always caught people with just such codes.

I traveled from Leningrad to Moscow with this incriminating piece of paper in my pocket. How would I explain this sheet of numbers if I was picked up by the KGB during the journey? I tried, without success, to think of a satisfactory explanation. When I showed the paper to Iosif at the airport, the color drained out of his face.

"If it's very important, I'll take it," he said, "but you understand . . ."

I understood. He had survived sixteen years in camps and in exile in the Urals and Siberia, dreaming only of Israel. Now, in another two hours he could be in the Schonau Castle near Vienna, safely on his way to Israel. Or he could be in the KGB office in the Lubyanka Prison. This scrap of paper could ruin everything. I snatched the paper from him and went quickly to the nearest lavatory, where I flushed it down the toilet. Then I returned to him calmly, empty-handed.

Before I left Leningrad, I had memorized all the information that was on that sheet—the seventeen names in alphabetical order, the professions (those were the easiest, since most of the people were engineers), the birthdates and address. Now I had to give Iosif as much of this information as I could in a few brief moments.

Fortunately he had with him a lot of photographs taken during the farewells in Riga. I couldn't find a photo with seventeen men, but there was one with eleven men and another with six. On the back of each of those I wrote something like: "Remember us fondly, Iosif" and then listed the names in alphabetical order.

Iosif was too shaken to do anything but put the photos back in his bag. The tension, customs formalities, and a stream of requests and instructions from those saying farewell had all but incapacitated him. He indicated to me that I should tell Sima, his daughter, anything that needed to be memorized.

Sima was only thirteen then, but she was bright and

alert. Born while her parents were in exile near the North Pole, she learned early to understand things that other children are not even aware of.

One day, while riding on a Riga tram with Iosif and his family, I began to tell jokes in Yiddish. Sima, for whom Yiddish was a native language, almost fell off the tram with laughter—my Yiddish was so bad. When I turned to Sima that day in the Moscow airport, we had already made a connection that created trust.

"Simochka, listen and remember. In Vienna, tell Papa, the second is a doctor, the fifth a lawyer, the thirteenth an electrician, the fifteenth agronomist. All the others are engineers. Will you remember?"

Sima moved her lips, repeating silently to herself what I had said to her. Then she replied, "Yes."

The last sips of wine had been drunk. All of us stood up and we shared final kisses, embraces. The Yankeleviches went out to the staircases that went up to the departure gate. The rest of us were not permitted there—we stood below, at the border between "the living and the dead."

At the last moment Sima ran back from the stairs and whispered in my ear,

"The second is a doctor, the fifth is a lawyer, the thirteenth is an electrician, the fifteenth an agronomist."

"Good girl! Have a safe journey!"

The plane took off, rose toward the clouds, and headed west to Vienna. In another forty-eight hours they would be in Israel, they would be home. What did the next two days, months, years hold for those who stood watching as the plane disappeared?

Later I explained to Rina Maslenkovskaya, then a student in our ulpan and later a teacher of Jewish history in another ulpan, how to signal Israel that we'd been arrested and that the time had come for the letter to be published. It was never published.

CHAPTER EIGHT

Simply Fly Away

In 1968, Eva and I celebrated Israeli Independence Day in Riga in the apartment of painter Iosif Kuzkovsky—a member of the Union of Soviet Artists. When we entered Kuzkovsky's home, we realized immediately that his apartment, like Sasha Blank's in Leningrad, was a "Jewish club" where all Jews were welcome and talk about Jewish subjects and issues was constant. But at Kuzkovsky's apartment, it was his paintings, not the man himself, that did the talking. I don't remember one picture in that apartment that didn't cry out about our terrible past, didn't lament the diaspora, didn't evoke thoughts of Zion. His response to the Six Day War was a pastel entitled *David and Goliath*: little David atop the slain giant, who is portrayed as an Arab, wearing a suit of armor and the helmet of Russian folk heroes. In another canvas, entitled *Stepmother*, Kuzkovsky painted a withered old hag with the nose and eyes of a witch—wearing a Russian peasant's kerchief and stroking a Jewish boy. Her bony hands with long nails try to draw the stepson to her. They boy tries to escape from her embrace but he cannot. A painting entitled *Hora* depicts a joyous dance of young boys and girls, arms interlaced around each other's shoulders. The faces express self-confidence, independence. The entire circle of young dancers rests in the hand of a man. A closer look reveals that the man holding the dancers is Kuzkovsky, whose face radiates the gentleness and happiness of a father holding his children

A painting entitled *33.3* depicts a man bending impatiently over a radio receiver. Only Jews who have lived behind the Iron Curtain can understand why this picture was titled *33.3.* For years, thousands of receivers in the USSR stayed tuned to that wavelength—the owners only turned those sets off and on. As soon as the melody of "Hatikva" was heard through the jamming noise, life in many apartments came to a standstill and the only sound to be heard was the Voice of Israel. In August 1969, Iosif Kuzkovsky was allowed to emigrate to Israel. Five months later he died there of a heart attack.

The Kuzkovskys were among the dozens of families who were allowed to leave the USSR while thousands were refused permission to emigrate and were persecuted for their request for exit visas. This Soviet government policy was a calculated move to counter the rising voices in the West pleading the case for Jewish emigration. After all, they had to let a few Jews out, so that the world could see that some Soviet Jews were permitted to emigrate to Israel. But for the thousands who wanted to leave, this trickle of exit visas held out no hope for emigration.

In the fall of 1969, with five ulpans operating within the framework of our group, we had room for more students. Through friends I sought potential pupils. In response to one of my inquiries I was told about a former army flyer, Mark Dymshitz, who was trying to study Hebrew on his own. I asked that an invitation to attend an ulpan be extended to him.

Mark came to me within a short time. He was then about forty years old, with a youthful face, straight dark hair combed back, and thick black eyebrows. We introduced ourselves and began talking. Mark was polite, seemed reasonably frank—and was enthusiastic. Military discipline seemed to suit him: he exuded reliability.

Our first meeting was brief; each of us was sizing up the

other. Fulfilling my role at that meeting, I dispatched Mark to the ulpan in the apartment of one of our members, Misha Korenblit, who was a dentist. Misha's namesake, Lev Korenblit, was teaching Hebrew there.

Mark lived with his wife and two daughters not far from my wife and me, and he used to drop by to talk about his ulpan studies. Our conversations soon moved from Hebrew to Israel, and it was clear that we thought alike about many things. Mark had held the same illusions I had about the Soviet Union. For many years he had adhered to official party views, and even in the fall of 1969 he still carried the red booklet of a Communist Party member.

During the blockade of Leningrad in World War II, Mark, then fifteen years old, lost his parents. He was evacuated from Leningrad with an entire orphanage, was placed in a special school, and then entered an air force flight school. In 1949 he graduated and married a Russian girl who had been evacuated from Leningrad on the same barge with him.

Mark entered the service with one of the last groups of Jews accepted into the air force. But he finished flight school during a period of violent anti-Semitism, and his years in the air force were bitter ones. In 1960 he was offered a choice: demobilization, or a demeaning appointment. Mark—a natural pilot, a major at the age of thirty-three, a navigation officer in his regiment—chose demobilization.

He returned to Leningrad with his wife and two young daughters. There he tried in vain to find work in civil aviation. Everyone who could have hired him was afraid to let an "invalid of the fifth question" fly—especially in Leningrad, so close to the border. Still, the air beckoned. Mark left for Bukhara, where he got a job piloting twelve-seater AN-2 planes. Eventually he went back to Leningrad and completed night school at an agricultural institute. In the fall of

1969, when we met, Mark was working as an engineer in an institute that planned poultry-breeding complexes.

There is a saying—"If you sow habit, you will reap character; if you sow character, you will reap fate." The strongest feature of Mark Dymshitz' character was will. Once he reached the conclusion that his place was in Israel, Mark was fated to follow through to the end.

Even before he began to study Hebrew at the ulpan, Mark had begun to think about escape to Israel. His earliest plans (first to construct an aerial balloon, then to build an airplane) were fantasies, products of his isolation. He understood even then that seizure of an existing plane made more sense, but he knew he could not do that alone. After he began to study at the ulpan, he was no longer alone.

One day early in December 1969, Mark and I were strolling near my house. By then he had come to trust me. Our conversation circled, not for the first time, around the problems confronted by Jews who sought to emigrate to Israel. Suddenly Mark said,

"You don't need to fantasize, you can simply fly away."

"How?" I wondered.

"Hijack an airplane," Mark said calmly, and it was clear that he had long since thought it out. He really did have a plan: Fly to Erevan, in Armenia. Buy tickets for a small AN-2 airplane and order the pilot to fly to Turkey. If the pilot refused, Mark would fly the plane himself. Everything Mark described was simple, clear, and frightening.

I thought about Eva and our little, helpless Lileshka, and realized how such a scheme threatened them. And so my first impulse was to refuse immediately. But I didn't refuse. Mark's crazy idea went to my head. The more I thought about it, the more it stuck. Perhaps this was the one chance I would have in my lifetime—if I missed it, I would never forgive myself. Also, this could be the tenth plague, the one that would force the "Pharaoh" to capitulate! Perhaps we could use such a daring escape to startle the world and get people to realize finally what needed to be done to help the Jews of Russia emigrate to their homeland.

If we were to follow Mark's plan and succeed, we would solve only our own individual problems—all the rest of the Jews in Russia who wanted to leave would still be stranded. If we were going to take a chance, then we must take a bigger one which would help to solve the emigration problem.

We needed to hijack a large airliner. And all the passengers on it would be in on the plan. We couldn't do that in Erevan, so it would have to be done in Leningrad. It did not make any sense to land in Finland. The Finns have a consular agreement with the USSR about handing over turncoats, and they carry it out scrupulously. They would hand us over to the Soviet authorities.

We needed to fly to Sweden and land there. And we needed to have a press conference there, as soon as we landed, to talk about the situation of the Jews in the USSR. The sight of dozens of men and women and children who had just risked their lives to emigrate to Israel would convey a great deal to foreign journalists about the intensity of the desire of Soviet Jews to emigrate. The impact on world opinion would be enormous and immediate.

Was Mark Dymshitz what he seemed to be—a Jew who yearned to emigrate to Israel, an experienced pilot prepared to take great risks, a strong-willed but reasonable and calculating man? Or was he a KGB agent who didn't know any more about airplanes than I did?

That day I asked Mark several technical questions, then said that I needed to think about this idea. This reply was no more startling to him than if I had given him a definite "no." Only the answer "yes" would have surprised him then.

By December 1969, the Organization was composed of about forty people dedicated to the idea of *aliyah*. The first person I talked to about the hijacking was Solomon Dreizner. My enthusiasm for the idea was transmitted to Solomon: maybe this way we would still achieve our aim— free emigration of Jews to Israel. We agreed that Solomon, a former officer who served in the Far East, would put Mark Dymshitz to the test. I invited Mark to come over on December 20, and Solomon came, too. We had supper and something to drink, and the two of them talked the entire evening. The plan to hijack a plane was not mentioned. But it turned out that Solomon and Mark had served in the same Zabaikal military district and that they had acquaintances in common.

It was late when Mark left. Solomon summed up the evening:

"I don't know who this fellow is. But I am sure that he is a pilot and I am sure that he served in the Zabaikal district."

We began to meet with Mark. Soon we were getting together almost every day. I asked a lot of questions about the technical problems of hijacking a large airliner and flying to Sweden. How, for example, were we to avoid interception while we were in the air over the USSR or Finland? What did Mark think the chances were of a favorable outcome?

Gradually Mark and I sketched out the details of a plan. It would be best, we decided, the seize a TU-124 aircraft (48 to 52 passengers) or a TU-135 aircraft (44 to 64 passengers) on the Leningrad-Murmansk line, along the Soviet-Finnish border. The flight from the predetermined point on the line to the Finnish border would take five to ten minutes—not enough time for the anti-aircraft defense to be activated.

During the flight, we would seize the pilots' cabin and suggest to them that they fly the plane along the route we had planned. If both pilots refused, Mark would sit at the controls and take the plane down low enough so that it would be below the range of anti-aircraft defense radar but high enough for a safe flight.

What would we say if air controllers asked questions over the radio about why the plane had changed course? Muffling our voices by speaking through cheesecloth, we would say that two unidentified people had forced us to change the course of the plane and fly to Helsinki. This reply would lead the authorities to believe that there were only two criminals on board, and that the rest of the passengers were loyal Soviet citizens—and that, we hoped, would deter them from shooting down the plane. And the authorities would be relieved (because of the consular agreement between the USSR and Finland) to learn that the plane was flying toward Helsinki.

We considered the possibility that, if we flew over the Baltic Sea, the plane could be shot down and then disappear into the sea, hidden forever from the rest of the world. So we decided to fly over land, skirting the Gulf of Bothnia along the northern coast. Our goal would be Stockholm and we would, while still in the air, contact a Swedish radio station and set up a press conference to take place when we landed. If the fuel ran low, we would land on a straight section of empty highway or at a military airport.

I was startled when, during one of these planning discussions, Mark took out a small caliber, handmade revolver. The revolver was as small as a toy and fitted easily into the palm of Mark's hand. It could be used, he suggested, as a weapon of intimidation.

I hadn't yet made any commitment other than a willingness to discuss the hijacking idea. I hadn't said "yes" and I hadn't said "no." Mark waited patiently.

I called the members of the Committee together for an extraordinary session on the first Saturday of 1970. We decided to borrow my father's place for this meeting on that frosty January day. It had been ten years since I'd lived with my father. He had never been involved in politics and could hardly have been on the KGB register. Besides, he had just moved, and at his new place the telephone—always a cause of concern—was out in the corridor.

Before the meeting, I spoke on the street with each of the Committee members individually. I told each one what we were meeting to discuss, and made them promise not to discuss the subject with anyone without my consent. All of them were as startled as I had been when Mark first talked to me about his idea. Only Tolya Goldfeld, the representative of the youth group, immediately supported me. It turned out that when Tolya was still a student, he and some of his friends from Kishinev had fantasized about hijacking a plane.

Once inside my father's place, we gathered around the table. Why had I called this meeting of the Committee? According to the bylaws that we had adopted, the Committee's only function was to coordinate the activities of the groups of the Organization. We decided procedural questions by a simple majority. Questions of principle were decided as they are in the Arab League: a unanimous decision of the Committee was binding on the entire Organization, but a nonunanimous decision was binding on only those groups who had voted for it. That meant that if the other members in my group agreed with me, I could act independently of the decision of the Committee. But for a matter this serious I wanted to consult with the entire Committee. I wanted to hear the opinion of each of my friends.

By the time the Committee met, I was completely in favor of Mark's plan. But this was a serious and dangerous proposal, one that could have devastating consequences for all those who participated in the hijacking, as well as for the organization. I could not commit the Organization without speaking first to these men.

In the days since I had called the meeting, my friends had had time to think carefully about Mark's plan. Even so, I again described the plan: the escape to Sweden aboard a hijacked plane, risking the lives of several dozen Soviet Jews. The Western countries, responding to the words of the escaped Jews at the press conference, would exert pressure on the Soviet Union at a time when the USSR was interested in Western credits and technology.

Then I proposed that we vote on this question: "Do we have the right to hijack a plane to achieve our just and legitimate goal?" In other words, was the operation morally and ethically acceptable to us?

The men asked about the chances of success. I answered in Mark's words, because I had asked him the same question: "About 80 to 90 percent, if the KGB doesn't know in advance."

"But what about the other 10 to 20 percent?"

"But what if the KGB does find out?"

I knew what to say—the answers had been ripening inside me during the difficult days and nights.

"For us, a successful escape is of only secondary importance. Those who participate will take this risk, not for themselves personally, or at least not only for themselves. Our primary goal is to implement the first and most important objective—to attain freedom of exit for all Soviet Jews who wish to emigrate. The escape of several dozen Jews is not just a resolution of their personal fates, but a way of drawing attention to the national Jewish problem in Russia. It is also our contribution to Israel's struggle.

"I don't think that the Soviet anti-aircraft defense would shoot down the plane because they wouldn't know that the passengers were Jews. If we succeeded in landing in Sweden, the Swedish authorities might arrest the organizers of the group but permit the other passengers to continue to Israel. We would sit for several years in Swedish prisons, and then we would go Home! What a wonderful dream!

"If we were arrested in the USSR, that would be worse, and not only for the participants. It could also mean the annihilation of our Organization—including the closing of the ulpans. But we created the Organization to achieve certain goals, and this operation could mean the achievement of those goals."

David Chernoglaz began to ask technical questions about what the hijacking group would do once it was on the plane. I realized from his questions that David was inclined to oppose the operation—he just needed a pretext and was using potential technical problems as justification. I also knew that David often disagreed with me. What was important was that he wasn't saying anything about the ethical acceptability of the plan.

Again I stated the question as I had presented it for the vote. Technical problems, I said, could be clarified if we found the operation morally acceptable.

Solomon Dreizner spoke next, and then Vladik Mogilever, and their viewpoints were similar—they agreed that the operation would probably be beneficial and that we shouldn't miss this chance. On the other hand, they said, this plan could be harmful. This was a difficult decision. They said that if the operation were carried out, each of them would do his best to help but would not take part.

They had good reasons—Vladik had a newborn baby and Solomon's wife was pregnant.

That day, the only one who firmly supported me was Tolya Goldfeld—evidence of his character and of his youthful ardor. Tolya was younger than the rest of us, unmarried and not encumbered by family responsibilities.

Tolya and I voted for the operation. Solomon and Vladik abstained. And David didn't vote. In the absence of a unanimous vote I considered the operation acceptable—at least for those who voted in favor.

After we had settled that, we voted—unanimously—to allocate money to investigate whether it was technically possible to hijack a plane. To do this we would take trial flights. As treasurer, David immediately gave me 100 rubles from the Organization's membership dues. And on the way home, Solomon and I decided to add another 25 rubles from each of our groups. The trial flights would be costly.

I felt encouraged that this unusual and dangerous plan had not been voted down by the Committee. Certainly I could understand the cautious questions that had been asked.

The next time I met with Mark, I gave him half of the one hundred and fifty rubles, as a sign of my agreement in principle. We agreed that he would draw up a detailed plan. I would take care of the organizational side of the operation.

In January 1970, for the first time since my graduation from the Institute six months earlier, I was suddenly called to military reserve training exercises. These consisted of several weeks of evening classes, after work. The hall in the Institute of Railroad Transport Engineers was full of overripe lieutenants like myself, men who hadn't been called for a long time.

The classes were tedious. Tired after work, we were drowsy during the lectures and came to life only during the practical exercises: at the end of each class we had shooting practice with small-caliber pistols. When practice started on the first evening, I noticed that the pistols were the same caliber as Mark's revolver—5.56 millimeters. I thought about filching some cartridges as a "nonreturnable loan." The instructor left the box of ammunition unattended several times when he went to check the target after a round of shooting. In the presence of the entire platoon, I stashed away a dozen cartridges—and no one seemed to care.

During January, February and March of 1970, I selected the passengers for our plane. I described the hijacking plan in general terms only to those to whom I was closest, the people I considered the most reliable. I told the others that perhaps there might be a possibility of escaping illegally to Israel—that it would be risky but would be likely to succeed if we were cautious and no one found out about our plans.

That is all I said, for two reasons. First, I was, concerned about security: the less each person knew, the smaller the chance of a leak. Second, I was even more concerned about the psychological stress. If the participants were aware from the beginning of the extent of the danger, they would be under great stress for a long time. Few people can sustain emotional stress for months. The first burst of enthusiasm subsides, and then the instinct for self-preservation begins to provide one justification after another for not taking the risk.

By the beginning of April I had a list of about forty people. Some had agreed to take part in hijacking a plane. Others, without knowing the details, had agreed to take the risk of trying to escape from the USSR. I had not introduced any of these people to each other. I had spoken with each one on the street, and each had sworn to remain silent and wait. I was trying to stay in control of the situation and assure the security of the plan and of these people.

I compiled the list of potential participants in a form comprehensible to me. Then I rolled the sheet up into a tube and hid it in one of the rooms of our apartment. A few days later I took it out and hid it in a different place. But I kept worrying about that piece of paper. One day I walked slowly through the apartment: two rooms, kitchen, bath-room, toilet. No place to hide.

Then I noticed the ventilator grating near the ceiling in the bathroom wall. It covered the opening to the ventilator shaft. Eva had tied a nylon cord from it to the shower cur-tain rod, and from this line she hung laundry. To make sure that the line could take the weight of the clothes, she had wound the cord in and out of almost every hole in the grate. It would take a lot of time and tedious work to undo that cord. I pulled the end of it through the grate and into the bathroom, unwinding enough of the cord from the grate so that I had a piece of cord a few feet long. Then I tied it around the tube, pushed the tube and the cord through the grate, and made sure that the list dropped down into the ventilation shaft. Now the only way to retrieve the tube would be to unwind the cord from the grate. If someone cut the cord, the list would drop down the shaft, beyond reach. And so the list was safe. It may still be there today.

One of the first names I put on that list was that of Misha Korenblit. Misha and I were in the same group in the Or-ganization. He had come to the Organization from our ul-pan. Misha lived in an apartment that belonged to his aunt, Anna Jacobson. Our group used that apartment for meet-ings, and an ulpan operated there.

All this activity was going on in a place owned by a woman who, until 1937, had been an active member of the

Communist Party of the United States. Then she and her husband, who had fought in the Spanish Civil War, had gone to the USSR, the country of their dreams—just in time for the savage purges of the late 1930s. Anna and her husband saw up close what had seemed so tempting from afar. Anna's husband began to have seditious thoughts that he shared with Anna—and probably with someone else. He went on a business trip, by train, and didn't return. Although he had survived years of struggle in the United States against the FBI, and long months of war in Spain against Franco, Mussolini and Hitler, he did not survive in the Soviet "paradise." The authorities told Anna that while her husband was asleep in a lower berth on the train, the gun of the officer in the upper berth was jolted out of his pocket, and as it was falling the gun went off. The bullet, accidentally, went into the head of Anna's husband, the authorities said.

Anna kept her thoughts to herself. She also kept her Party card—it served as a constant reminder of how easy it was to fight for Communism in the United States and how difficult it was to survive Communism in the USSR. Anna loved her nephew Misha. And we all loved this solid, short woman. She realized that her apartment had become a small Jewish republic, that she couldn't keep the refrigerator full, that she didn't even have a place to lie down and rest when she came home after work. She just smiled and tugged on her ever-present pipe.

Misha, honestly dedicated to Zionism, had been immediately enthusiastic about the idea of hijacking a plane. I would have been surprised had I not already known about his hot-tempered nature.

Misha was usually my most active supporter in the Organization. In the early months of 1970, Misha, Mark and I planned the operation. In February, Misha flew to Kishinev with two objectives. First, during the flights to Kishinev and back to Leningrad, he was to observe the flight procedure and make note of everything that could be useful to us. He even planned to try, somehow, to get into the pilot's cabin. And second, we wanted to get in touch with Sasha Halperin and his friends in Kishinev to determine whether they were willing to take part in a risky flight to Israel. If Sasha answered in the affirmative, Misha was to invite him to come to see me in Leningrad.

Equipped with money and addresses, Misha flew off to Kishinev. Not long afterwards, Sasha Halperin arrived in Leningrad. The foursome from Kishinev were willing to take their chances. I knew three of these men from the days when they had studied at the Leningrad Polytechnic Institute—Sasha, Aron Voloshin and Kharik Kizhner. Participation of the fourth member of the Kishinev group involved complications. That man planned to "steal" his small son from his wife, who had no intention of going to Israel. This presented a moral problem. In the end, that man dropped out.

Mark Dymshitz made a test trip to Moscow on a commercial flight. The crew on the plane included a pilot with whom he had flown some time earlier, in Bukhara. So Mark was able to visit the crew compartment and had time to familiarize himself with the layout, the seating arrangements, the equipment and so on. When they got back to Leningrad, Mark and this pilot went out to dinner at a restaurant. During their leisurely evening, Mark put out feelers, trying to find out about the crew's weapons. The pilot told him that weapons were issued, but usually the crew did not carry them. During a flight, they put their pistols in the navigator's case.

Now we were getting some idea of what to expect. On board an airliner we would probably find a cabin crew of five people: pilot, copilot, navigator, radio operator and engineer. Sometimes the fifth was missing. Usually on domestic flights there was no steward, only a stewardess.

It seemed to us that if a crew were faced with a sudden attack by hijackers, they probably would not be able to use their firearms—we would be able to prevent them from getting into the navigator's case that held the pistols. But, we now knew, we would be able to attack suddenly only if both doors—from the passenger cabin into the connecting corridor, and from there into the crew's cabin—were open. A delay of even a few seconds would give the crew enough time to get their pistols out of the navigator's case.

We had to find out more about those two doors. Are they both kept unlocked during flight? If they are kept locked, are they locked with a key or with bolts so that the crew can open the doors only when they want to, when they know that one of them is about to enter? Did anyone guard the connecting passage? We had to be able to enter the crew's cabin during the flight quickly enough so that the crew would be taken by surprise.

During the winter, Aeroflot sold tickets to students at half price. I managed to get a student ticket—we had to economize—and flew to Riga on February 19th. I had two goals: to enter the crew's cabin, and to find people in Riga for the operation. My flight was on a Friday afternoon. I would stay in Riga until Sunday evening and be back at work on Monday morning.

Just before take-off, I bought a bottle of wine and put it in my carry-on bag. When I boarded the plane, I put that bag and my jacket and coat in the space for carry-on luggage, and then went on into the passenger cabin. You could pick any seat you wanted, and so I sat in the first row, right in front of the entrance to the corridor leading to the crew compartment. Perhaps from there, I thought, I would be able to see something without entering the corridor.

February is a slow month for Aeroflot, and barely two-thirds of the sixty-four seats were occupied. The pilot announced that we were flying at a height of about seven kilometers. Visibility was good—only a few clouds floated below us. I was able to see clearly how the pilot changed course near Tallin, turning to fly along the coast to Riga. If at that point in the flight he was to follow the original course without turning, he would be over the Swedish island of Gotland in the Baltic Sea in about half an hour. I had to tell Misha and Mark about that.

I went to the baggage rack and got the bottle of wine and my jacket. We were getting close to Riga and I still hadn't dared to enter the crew compartment. I had put the bottle of wine on my knees and tossed my jacket over it. I looked around at the passengers. Each time I had looked back, two people seemed to be watching me steadily—a stewardess sitting in one of the rear seats, and a man of about fifty sitting in front of her. Maybe they really do watch the passengers who choose to sit in the forwardmost seats in the cabin. But maybe it just seemed that way to me. My nerves were taut. I felt those two pairs of eyes on the back of my neck.

The plane began to descend. The stewardess left her post for a minute to announce over the microphone that we were going to land. The man in the seat in front of hers was looking at me. But I decided, the hell with him. It was then or never.

I got up and took the two steps to the door. I pressed on the handle and pulled the door toward me—and it opened. I entered the short corridor, quickly closing that door behind me. To the right was a door into the tiny space where the stewardess goes to get whatever is needed during the flight. And in front of me was another door—to the flight compartment. Through its frosted glass I could see a dull red light. Four steps, two jumps, from one door to the other. It would take two seconds. Was the forward door locked or unlocked ?

I took the four steps and pressed down on the handle of the door, aware as I did so of my agitation. The handle yielded easily, just as the first had. Thank God—both doors had been closed but neither was locked. The door to the flight compartment was not bolted shut from inside, probably because the crew members went in and out of the cabin during the flight.

I found myself facing the backs of the heads of the four crew members. In front of them was the instrument panel and the wide, glazed nose of the plane. The evening lights of Riga were visible through the front window of the plane. It was about a meter and half from the door to the two rear crew seats—two steps, one leap.

As I closed the door behind me, one of the crew members looked around and then immediately jumped up and came toward me. I offered him the bottle of wine and in the name of the passengers thanked the crew for a pleasant flight. For the sake of propriety he started to refuse, but then he smiled and took the bottle. The pale stewardess had followed me in and was already dragging me from the compartment by the arm, dressing me down for my nerve. I don't know if she had finished her announcement when she saw that I wasn't in my seat. But surely it was her responsibility to watch the conduct of the passengers during the flight—especially those who were sitting in the front part of the cabin!

After the plane landed, I got off and went into the terminal, then turned to observe what was going on around me. It didn't seem as if anyone had followed me. I didn't see the man who had been sitting in front of the stewardess. The other passengers walked past, and then about ten minutes later the crew went by. I didn't see the stewardess. The plane had been positioned so that it could be refueled. That was good to know—it meant that if we could not hijack a plane on the way to Murmansk, we could try on the return route and be reasonably sure that there would be enough fuel in the tanks to make it to Sweden.

After about half an hour in the waiting room, studying the technical aspects of the TU-124 and TU-135 planes that flew to Murmansk, I went out to catch a bus. Everything seemed to be all right. The crew probably wouldn't mention the incident—it wouldn't look good for them!

In Riga, the only people I knew well were Aron Shpilberg and Silva Zalmanson. Aron was one of the founders of our Leningrad Zionist organization. After he married Margarit and moved to her place, he handed the group over to Tolya Goldfeld. I decided that it was not wise to talk to Aron. If he came to the conclusion that the operation was not desirable or necessary—and there was a good chance of that—he would do everything he could to disrupt the project. Silva was different.

Silva loved our Lileshka, who called her "Auntie Silva." She was a friend of Eva and of our whole family. When Silva came to Leningrad, she stayed with us. I felt that I knew her well.

All of the Zalmansons—Silva's family—were Zionists. This was particularly true of Silva and two of her three brothers—Wolf, the oldest, and Israel, the youngest.

Silva had twice submitted an application for an exit visa. The first time she went through all the bureaucratic requirements and then was refused. She waited the required time and then applied again. The second time, OVIR, the prosecutor's office and the moped factory where she worked contrived a circuitous trap. OVIR refused to accept Silva's documents without a character reference from the factory. The factory refused to provide a reference without a request from OVIR. OVIR would not issue the request. And the prosecutor refused to interfere, commenting: "Your departure to Israel is your personal affair."

I was aware of all this. I knew that Silva was frustrated, even desperate. She would participate in the operation. And she would know others who would want to participate. I called her from a telephone booth.

"Hello. You're not likely to recognize me—we haven't seen each other for a long time. The last time we met was at a dance."

"Who is speaking?"

"My name won't help you. You've probably already forgotten it. Let's meet and stroll around Riga. All right?"

"Wait a minute. Your voice is familiar." And then, after a long pause, "Is that you, Hillel?"

"It is, Auntie Silva. Greetings."

"Greetings. I have some news for you. I've gotten married, but it's still a secret. All right?"

"Fine. But we must meet on the street. I have something important to discuss with you."

"Where are you?"

"The devil knows."

"Look around and tell me."

I peered out of the phone booth and described the surroundings to Silva, and soon she arrived. Since I was very hungry, we stopped at a cafe for a snack. There we talked about common acquaintances and about her marriage.

The man Silva had married was Edik Kuznetsov, a thirty-year-old Muscovite. Two years earlier he had been released from prison after serving a seven-year term for anti-Soviet propaganda and agitation. Kuznetsov had begun to serve his time while he was still a young student . After his release from prison, he was denied a permit to live with his mother in Moscow. So for a while he had lived in the provinces working as a teamster. He studied English, and now he was working as a translator in a psychiatric institution in Riga.

Not until we had left the restaurant and were walking along the street did I talk to Silva about the operation. I stressed that this project was not being undertaken just as a matter of personal salvation—we had to place the whole issue of the *aliyah* of Soviet Jews before the world in a dramatic way.As I had expected, Silva accepted the plan without hesitation. But, she said, "I'm afraid that I may not be strong enough. You know what kind of heart I have."

I knew that Silva had a weak heart. But I also knew that it had not prevented her from spending long hours typing our materials, from maintaining the link between Zionists in Riga and those in Leningrad, from participating in signing open letters. I was confident that Silva would hold up. And she did.

There was not much left that we had to talk about. It was time to go home.

"What do you think, Silva—will Edik go along?"

"I think so. He is very brave."

"Can I speak with him openly?" I couldn't bring myself to say that I had doubts about her hasty marriage. Perhaps this fellow simply wanted to use the marriage to get a foothold in Riga and then to leave the USSR. Getting an exit visa was easier from Riga than from other places.

"Yes, you can trust him. He's a good fellow. You'll like him."

"Which of us should speak to him about this?"

"Let me prepare him, and then you can talk to him."

Late that evening I made my way to Silva's house, and she introduced me to her husband. He made a good first impression with his smiling blue eyes and strong build.

Even before I met Edik, I had felt friendly toward him. A man who at the age of twenty-two had begun to serve time for anti-Soviet behavior inspired respect. And when I saw how calmly and confidently he behaved, I thought: "This fellow was created to participate in the hijacking. If a youngster isn't broken by the difficult conditions of a labor camp, but instead becomes a man, that means he has backbone."

The next day Edik and I went to Rumbula, a suburb of Riga, the site of the mass shootings of Jews in December 1941. I had long wanted to visit there. For years I had heard about how the Zionist group in Riga had searched for the site, how after they found it, they spent all their free time restoring this neglected, gigantic cemetery without individual graves.

They leveled the ground, laid out flower beds, planted the flowers, and erected a six-pointed star made of barbed wire. And then the local authorities showed up. The star disappeared. In its place appeared a stone on which the words "To the victims of Nazism" had been carved in three languages—Latvian, Russian, and at the very bottom, Yiddish. Under the earth in that cemetery were tens of thousands of Jews, only Jews. Yet the inscription on that stone ignored the reality and the horror of what had happened at Rumbula on December 8, 1941. When those who still remember are gone, no one will know what happened on that terrible day. We went by foot from the bus stop. Even though it was February, the day was warm and sunny, almost as if nature had grown tired of waiting for spring. The blinding snow gleamed under the bright sun. It was difficult to imagine that at this spot, under these beautiful pines, once lay heaps of clothing, children's shoes, old people's canes, and thousands of bodies.

The path that wound among the snowdrifts unexpectedly ended in front of a swept square with a stone monument. This is where it had happened. Here. We faced the monument and doffed our hats.

Edik and I talked things over on the street. I was impressed by him, and Silva's opinion carried weight. Nevertheless, I presented to Edik the version I used for people I did not know well. When I had finished describing as much as I intended to, I asked him if he was ready to take a risk in order to escape from the USSR. Edik asked whether we would cross the border on foot, by sea or air. I told him that what was important was not the details but the principle. He asked whether the others were trustworthy, and I told him we were trying to be sure we selected trustworthy people.

"Is it possible to meet them?"

"Eventually. But not yet."

Edik stressed the importance of picking brave and trustworthy people. He felt that we had to be very cautious. What he said was reasonable and logical. But how can one be safe? I too, would rather be rich than poor, and prefer being safe to leaping in the dark.

I did not tell Edik everything I had told Silva the previous day. They were different people. In Silva's hierarchy of values the word "Israel" occupied first place. In Edik's hierarchy, the word "freedom" was in first place. Silva had typed and disseminated *Homeward!* and *For the Return of the Jewish People to Their Motherland*. Edik had typed and distributed *The Memoirs of Maxim Litvinov* and Shub's *Russian Politicians*. In the same home and on the same typewriter. The Zionist and the dissident. And so I did not tell Edik that we conceived of the operation as a way to achieve freedom of emigration for Soviet Jews.

If Silva was desperate to emigrate to Israel, it could be said that Edik was three times as desperate simply to leave the USSR. He was disenchanted with the dissident movement and with the slavish behavior of the Russian people. But his ties to Zionism were tenuous. Edik's father was a

Jew, and although Edik had not known his father, he found himself drawn to a people he could call his own, the Jews. But he was still far from being a Zionist.

Edik hated autocracy. He had a creative nature and an observant, analytical mind. He knew that he was capable of being more than a translator in a psychiatric hospital. But all other paths were closed to him—the Soviet regime never forgives its political opponents, whether they are in prison or out. And so at the end of our conversation Edik said firmly:

"I am ready to cross the border on land. I'm ready to take part in hijacking a ship or a plane. I'm ready for any escape plan that has a chance to succeed."

"Do you have friends who can be trusted?"

"There are two men who served time with me. Reliable men. And I think they would go for this. Neither of them has a chance here. I can get in touch with them."

I promised that he would hear from me soon.

CHAPTER NINE

Plans for Operation Wedding

At the beginning of March 1970, Mark Dymshitz, Sasha Halperin and I watched the famous television press conference of the "fifty-two." This program was the culmination of an anti-Zionist campaign by the Soviet government and it featured a staged press conference at which fifty-two prominent Soviet Jews proclaimed that "Zionism expressed the chauvinistic views and racist ravings of the Jewish bourgeoisie." The group of fifty-two "persons of Jewish nationality" included generals, artists, writers, actors, dancers, scientists, engineers—among them Veneamin Dymshitz, Deputy Chairman of the Council of Ministers (the highest ranking Jew in the Soviet government, and no relation to Mark); Maya Plisetskaya, prima ballerina of the Bolshoi Ballet of international standing; Arkady Raikin, outstanding satirist and actor; and Elina Bystritskaya, a first-rate dramatic actress.

Watching the performance of Deputy Chairman Dymshitz, with his nervous tic, I could not help but contrast his manner to that of Mark Dymshitz, who was sitting next to me, his face showing cool contempt. Here were two Jews, two Dymshitzes. One was following in the path of those Jews who 3,500 years ago escaped out of Egyptian slavery to face hunger and to wander in the desert, enduring wars to reach freedom in the promised land. The other descendant of those same Jews preferred to remain in Egyptian slavery, as long as he got food and shelter. Among the fifty-two who sold out for the "pottage of lentils" were two persons I had respected since childhood. How could Arkady Raikin and Elina Bystritskaya let themselves be dragged into this disgraceful performance? Perhaps the KGB pressure could not be resisted. Perhaps they had to choose—to participate in this political circus, or to lose the privilege of continuing their artistic careers.

That press conference clearly demonstrated to those who were willing to face reality that, for the Jews of the USSR, there was no hope but mass *aliyah*. Jews who wanted to remain in Russia had to renounce their brothers in Israel, and they had to give up the study of modern Hebrew language and literature as well as Israeli music and dance.

This television farce convinced us that we were on the right path. Preparations for the hijacking continued.

Even though we discussed the operation only on the street, we decided to take the added precaution of using a code name for our plan. I proposed calling it Operation Wedding. That name and the idea behind it solved many problems. I realized that it might become evident, even before we boarded the plane, that all the passengers on the flight were Jewish. And it would be obvious that many of the passengers arriving at the gate knew each other. The crew might well become suspicious. Where, they might wonder, would all those Jews be going together, and why?

Another factor that we had to deal with was that something might prevent us from hijacking the plane on the flight to Murmansk. If that happened, we would have to stay overnight in Murmansk, then buy one-way tickets and try to implement the operation on the return trip to Leningrad.

How could we explain why a large group of Jews would fly to Murmansk, stay overnight, and then fly back? We could say that we were all going to attend a wedding in Murmansk. Nothing would completely satisfy the KGB. But I decided that the wedding story would satisfy the merely curious.

Misha Korenblit was to be the "groom," and Polina Yud-Borovskaya would be the "bride." Polina studied at the ulpan, typed for the organization, and was an ardent Zionist. They were both single, and they knew each other. Why shouldn't they get married?

The wedding of Misha and Polina did take place, but not in Murmansk. After the arrest of her "fiance," and in an atmosphere of intense anti-Zionism, Polina decided to challenge the authorities while demonstrating her solidarity with Misha and the rest of us. She and Misha were married in the KGB investigative prison. Their wedding lasted just a few minutes. Then the young husband was taken back to his cell on the fifth floor of the prison with his hands bound behind him.

Theirs was not the only prison wedding among the members of our organization. Viktor Boguslavsky would also receive permission and register his marriage in prison. But the first prison marriage in the group was the remarriage of Mark Dymshitz to the woman he had already chosen once, twenty-two years earlier. Mark and Alya, divorced for a year, were married again after Mark was arrested in connection with the hijacking.

We had a "bride," a "groom" and "guests" for the planned operation. But we did not have a date. It was Mark who demanded that we set a date.

Mark, Misha and I decided that the "wedding" would take place on the second of May. This seemed like good timing. It left a month and a half—enough time to complete preparations, but not enough to create psychological stress. Moreover, it would be easy for the participants to gather on the off-days of the May holiday, and to return to work unobtrusively afterward if the "wedding" did not happen.

We hoped that on the day after the May Day celebration we would benefit from a holiday mood in the anti-aircraft defense forces. The radar operators might not be as vigilant as on an ordinary day, and the officers might not be sober enough to make quick decisions. All we needed was five to ten minutes of delay and we could be over Finland.

It quickly became evident that Mark had been right to press for a deadline. The target date added an urgency to our preparations. Misha flew to Riga to inform Edik Kuznetsov of the newest details and to call him to Leningrad so that we could all talk. And then Misha made preparations for his trial flight, from Leningrad to Kishinev.

The time would come when the Soviet press would proclaim that the hijackers were "Zionist murderers" armed with pistols, axes, knives, ropes. The press would assert that their primary goal was to murder unarmed pilots, that flight to Israel was merely a secondary goal. Yet I do not believe that there has ever been a hijacking in which the attacking side tried so carefully to deprive itself of its offensive advantages.

The means were an important part of our goal. If we reached Stockholm but spilled blood—and not ours—in the crew cabin, then our method would have become an obstacle to our goal rather than the means to achieving it. We had to be sure that only we could become the victims. This determined our attitude toward carrying arms.

Edik Kuznetsov offered us an automatic pistol. Boris Azernikov—a member of our organization and a potential participant in Operation Wedding—could have obtained hand grenades. But we voluntarily rejected weapons. For quite a while Misha Korenblit could not reconcile himself to this. He thought we were being unconscionably stupid to go unarmed when we knew that the crew would have loaded pistols. Misha believed that we would be depriving ourselves, even before we entered the plane, of the possibility of emerging as victors in any struggle with the crew.

From the very beginning I opposed taking anything onto the plane that could be used to threaten the life of any member of the crew, or to injure anyone. After I learned from Mark that the crew kept their pistols in the navigator's bag, not on their persons, I was firmly resolved that we should not carry weapons. Mark and Edik supported me, at first cautiously, then energetically.

We knew that we would have to deprive the crew of both the will and the ability to resist. Each crew was made up of at least four healthy men who had been trained to take risks and make quick decisions. How do you instantly incapacitate such a group without hurting anyone?

Viktor Shtilbans, a young pediatrician who was a potential participant, suggested using a wad of cotton soaked with liquid nitrous oxide (a light anesthetic preparation used in Russia during childbirth) to be held against the nose and mouth. When nitrous oxide is inhaled by a person, he becomes unconscious and stays that way for several minutes—and that was all we would need to tie up the members of the crew. But we would have to take the crew so completely by surprise that they could not offer any resistance to this odd-smelling substance.

I had another idea, which I discussed with Edik. It came to me from memories of my distant childhood, when all the boys had admired the film actor Peter Aleinikov. In the film "Behind Enemy Lines," Aleinikov had played a Soviet spy who infiltrated the rear guard of Finnish ground forces and was caught by the Finns. The entire audience exploded with joy when Aleinikov threw a handful of tobacco into the eyes of a Finnish guard. While the guard was blinking and wiping his tearing eyes, the spy got on his skiis and took off. Should we try the same thing? Again, we would have to catch them by surprise, before they could even blink.

We needed to be "psychologically armed"—to give the crew the impression that we were armed. If we entered the flight cabin with an unloaded but cocked pistol, that should intimidate the crew without creating a situation in which anyone could be hurt.

When I began to explore this possibility, I found that there were a number of options. First, we had Mark's pistol. If we took out all the cartridges, the gun would fire a blank shot. Then Hillel Shur told me about an army pistol with a filed-off pin. You couldn't even shoot a blank from it. But it was a standard army pistol and presumably the crew would all recognize it as an authentic and lethal weapon.

Boris Azernikov came up with the best idea—he suggested using a starter's pistol. It looked like a real pistol and was the same size. The sound of the shot—loud enough to reach all the seats in an enormous stadium—ought to be convincing.

You needed a special permit to buy a starter's pistol. But somehow Boris managed to buy one and brought it to Leningrad. Boris and Vladik Knopov, a member of the Organization and a potential participant, tested the pistol and decided that the sound was excellent. Now we were "armed." We had a weapon with which to intimidate.

But what if the crew was more frightened by the idea that they would be held accountable if they did not resist, even if their assailants were armed with a gun? How could we prepare for that possibility? At the factory I made six clubs out of a heavy, rubber-coated electric cable.

On March 29, Edik Kuznetsov arrived in Leningrad from Riga. The weather was inclement, unsuitable for an outdoor meeting. So for the first time (except for the Committee meeting at my father's apartment), we discussed Operation

Wedding inside a dwelling, albeit a "kosher" one. A neighbor went out for the evening and left me the keys to her apartment. Taking my guitar so that I would look as if I was going to a party, I went to meet Mark, Misha and Edik. We found that my neighbor had almost no chairs. So we took off our shoes and sat cross-legged on the pushed-together beds.

At this meeting we began to make some final arrangements. Misha Korenblit conceded on the issue of arms, and we reached unanimity in our decision not to take with us any weapon that could shoot and kill. We decided that I would supplement our "arsenal" with instruments of intimidation of my selection. We confirmed the date: the "wedding" was set for May 2, 1970.

At the end of April I was to assemble all those intending to participate in the May 2 Leningrad hijacking for a dress rehearsal. My responsibility was to arrange conditions similar to those we would encounter on the plane.

I was to speak again to those who had agreed in principle to participate but did not yet know the details of the operation. It was obvious to me that I should not talk to these people more than forty-eight hours before the time of departure—so that no one would start to sell property, buy up gems, or do anything else that could betray our plans. It was important to remind all the "guests" that on May 2 we were to leave our apartments as if we were going out to a wedding.

I had to be sure that I talked to everyone before the end of the final work day just before the May Day holiday. Otherwise some of the participants might leave town—and then we would have to go find them.

At that meeting on March 29 we agreed on how to handle the purchase of tickets for the flight. The people in the Riga group would order in advance some tickets for the Leningrad-Murmansk route. And those of us in Leningrad, using false surnames, would buy tickets at various places. In

1970, you did not have to present a passport in order to buy an airplane ticket. The names for all the tickets were to be of indefinite gender, so that it would be easier to sell extra tickets to whomever we chose.

At last the "party" was over. We left my neighbor's apartment and went out into the courtyard. Mark and Edik left for the airport, where they were to study the timetables and select our route. I took the guitar and went home.

Later—too late—I realized that it was on that evening that I lost control of Operation Wedding. That night, as Mark Dymshitz and Edik Kuznetsov traveled together to the airport, they exchanged addresses. After that they were able to communicate directly with each other—and independently of me. Neither of these men were members of the Organization, and they were not as concerned about its interests as I was.

Mark told me that our flight was to leave at a few minutes after 4:00 pm on May 2. We were to go on the last flight to Murmansk that day. I called the Aeroflot office to double-check the time of the flight. The clerk told me that after the summer schedule went into effect on May 1, the last flight would be a few minutes after 1:00 pm.

Since Mark and Edik had gone to the airport and selected the flight together, and Edik was to purchase tickets, I had to alert him about this schedule change. Silva answered the phone when I called Riga. I asked her to tell Edik not to buy the shelf for 16 rubles (16:00 hours, or 4:00 pm on the timetable), but instead to get the little one for 13 rubles and a few kopeks (13:00 hours plus a few minutes, or a little after 1:00 pm on the timetable)—that it was much better.

Then I called Lev Korenblit—a member of the Committee and a man whose opinions I valued—and arranged to meet with him. Lev is ten years older than I am, and he has a doctorate in applied physics. In his native Rumania, before the war, he was a member of Gordonia, a Zionist society. During the war he had been imprisoned in a Rumanian camp, then had escaped and crossed the front lines.

Most of the members of our Organization's Committee were temperamental, emotional, often uncompromising. But not Lev Korenblit. I was attracted by his cool calculation and his preference for calm, unhurried analysis. He applied the same methods to the Organization's affairs that he did to physics. Lev could, when it was appropriate, reduce to naught all the secondary problems that seemed important to other members.

Back in January of 1970, Korenblit had been one of the first people I talked to about Operation Wedding. His reaction then had been encouraging—restrained, but clearly positive. Lev considered joining us but couldn't figure out how he could get his wife on board the plane.

"If Rita didn't know what she was getting into, you wouldn't be able to drag her onto the plane. And if you did tell her, everyone in the airport would know from the expression on her face what was going on," he said.

I understood what he meant—I was facing the difficult task of telling Eva.

I called Lev Korenblit to ask his advice about the "instruments of intimidation" that I was to provide, so that we would not appear unarmed and thus invite defeat.

Lev met me and we walked along the street as he listened to my explanations. He agreed with my reasoning and with the logic of the compromise about weapons, and said he would go shopping with me. We went along the shopping arcades and into many stores, carefully evaluating all likely objects. For example, we saw a gun used for underwater hunting. Easy to carry on the plane. But what if you shot it? The arrow would kill a fish, we were assured. But what would it do to a man, we wondered. No, we would not take that gun.

Eventually we bought a camping shovel and a kitchen mallet—a meat tenderizer, with thick protrusions. Only when you held it in your hand did you realize that it was very light. It was aluminum and couldn't even have been used to drive a nail into a wall. But the metal gleamed threateningly and surely would, for at least a few precious moments, intimidate and paralyze even a strong and brave man. And that would be enough time to tie up the crew and perhaps even gag them.

On the way back we stopped at Lev's place and he added a long toasting fork to the collection. Then we were fully "armed."

It should have been simple to purchase the tickets for the Murmansk flight. But it was not. In the USSR in 1970, you could not buy tickets for a particular flight until a specified number of days before the day of that flight. We wanted to prevent people who were not in the escaping group from purchasing tickets on "our" flight, to avoid the inevitable complications of having strangers and innocent bystanders present. But we knew that the central Aeroflot office kept records of all tickets sold in all their offices. If Aeroflot personnel saw that, on the very first day they were available, all the seats on that particular flight had been purchased, they would be astonished—and probably suspicious.

Acquiring the money with which to buy the tickets was somewhat simpler, but still not easy. Only a few of the prospective passengers were to know about the flight more than forty-eight hours in advance. Since we were not telling the others the details, we could not ask them for ticket money. Yet we had to buy all the tickets in advance. So we had to raise the money—a substantial sum—for most of the tickets.

Some time earlier, Boris Azernikov had told me about a family of Georgian Jews—the Kozhiashvilis—with whom he had vacationed one summer. That family, which included three grown sons, was willing to do anything to emigrate to Israel. According to Boris, the Kozhiashvilis had a great deal of money. I talked again with Azernikov and with Vladik Knopov, who also knew the Kozhiashvilis. And then I decided to call the most militant of the sons to Leningrad. Otary Kozhiashvili soon flew in.

Our conversation took place in the Victory Park in Leningrad. Spring had just arrived and big puddles had formed in the spongy, dark snow. It wasn't easy to take a stroll through the slush, but it was even more difficult to converse with Otary. Later in my life I would speak in broken English and fractured Hebrew. But never again did I encounter such broken Russian. It was difficult to believe that Otary had completed medical school in the Russian city of Kalinin.

Speaking slowly and repeating some words and phrases, I presented the version of Operation Wedding that I used with people I did not know well. Otary strained, but he seemed to understand most of what I said. He said he would, with my permission, talk it over with his parents and then come back to Leningrad with his answer. In any event, he said, he deeply respected us and was ready to extend material help to our cause. "Could you spare a few hundred rubles—perhaps even a thousand?" I asked brazenly.

Otary responded, "Five thousand." He said that he would send the money to Azernikov, whether or not the Kozhiashvilis decided they wanted to be passengers. When we parted I was not at all certain that he would send the money—it never arrived.

On April 3, Eva and I returned late from the celebration of the second birthday of young David, son of Shalya Rozhanskaya and Grisha Zlotnik. Two years earlier Shalya and Grisha had chosen us as godparents of their firstborn, and we were delighted with this honor. We felt close to the joyous, optimistic parents of young David. Those two were always willing to offer a shoulder or an ear or a helping hand to someone with a problem.

That night, as always at Shalya's, everything was simple and delicious. We drank a little in honor of David's birthday. And we were in a good mood as we walked home. I decided that it was time to begin to prepare Eva.

The woman in a family is the guardian of the home. I knew that what I was going to tell Eva would be a blow. Our life together had not been easy for her. We didn't have a normal family life. She had worked so hard for both of us while we were students in the Technical Institute. In the evenings I was almost always at the Committee, with the group, or at an ulpan. Eva was always waiting. And now I was going to make life even more difficult for the person dearest to me.

We walked through the underground passage below the Nevsky. Several times I was about to begin and several times my resolution deserted me. Finally I set myself a marker, and when we reached it I began talking.

I said that a split life, when the soul is in one country and the body in another, was unworthy of us. I said that we might soon have a chance to take a risk and end up in Israel, and that we must take this opportunity. Eva interrupted:

"Vladik too?"

"No."

"And who says 'yes'?"

"Silva, for example."

There was a long silence. I knew that Eva considered

Vladik Mogilever to be a model of caution, reason and attentiveness toward family. I decided that I had said enough for one day. Eva might not ask any more questions right away, but she probably would not sleep that night.

Vladik and Yulya had built their family nest before my eyes. They met when Vladik began to give private Hebrew lessons to the eighteen-year-old Yulya, and they were married after several months of "intense study."

I have been to many weddings, but the wedding of Vladik and Yulya was the gayest. Their many friends were both joyous and funny, and there was much laughter that day. When Eva and I arrived almost all the guests were already there. Dissidents and Zionists mingled—Vladik Mogilever's past and his present. Yulya's father Isai, surrounded by young people, sat at the piano and played and sang. Everyone was smiling.

Then we were all invited into the dining room, where Sasha Blank was in charge. He delivered a flowery Georgian toast in honor of the young couple. Then a tape recording was turned on and we all listened as the "presidents" of various countries congratulated the newlyweds. The radio call signals of Israel came through with a crackling noise. Finally we heard the voice of the "Israeli president." It was difficult to make out what he was saying, but a few words came through clearly—*batim*, *ganim*, *yeladim*.

The voice of the "president" was familiar, but at first I couldn't figure out whose it was. And then I realized that it was Yulya's father. The "president," whose entire Hebrew vocabulary came from a few lessons in the basic textbook *Elef Milim*, seemed to think that all real Hebrew words ought to end with "im."

The gaiety was infectious and delightful. We read poems and told stories and laughed. The memory of that wonderful, noisy, happy, Jewish wedding stayed with all of us for a long time.

Vladik and Yulya had rented a room beneath our apartment. I remember how we all bustled around when it was time for Yulya to go to the hospital, and I remember when they brought that helpless little bundle home. Vladik and Yulya asked Eva and me to be his godparents, and I held the boy during the circumcision. Even before little Ilyushka could crawl, he had learned to point to Jerusalem on the map and say "laim"—the end of the word "Yerushalaim." Eventually the Mogilevers moved away but we remained close friends.

At the beginning of April 1970, I went to visit Vladik, to give him all the Hebrew material I had. He was a Hebrew teacher and could use every scrap he could get. That day I took to him all the books and journals and grammars that it had taken me so long to collect, piece by piece. When he saw what I had brought, it was clear to him how far things had gone, how close we were to departing.

Operation Wedding had not been discussed in the Committee since the meeting at my father's apartment. Once, at Solomon's apartment, David asked a question about the "wedding." But apart from that instance I had refused to discuss the matter inside a building. I was concerned about security, true. But I used security as an excuse because I did not want to discuss the plan. The attitudes of Committee members had begun to change, from cautiously positive to cautiously negative. I did not try to convince anyone to participate. I did not try to influence the decisions of those who hesitated. It was absolutely essential to me that all who participated would do so voluntarily, fully aware of the importance of the operation in general and of their participation in particular.

Edik and Silva chose Iosif Mendelevich as the first person in Riga to be asked to participate. Mendelevich accepted the proposal in principle, but then decided to try to find out if the plan was the work of a provocateur. David Chernoglaz learned about Iosif's investigation and became alarmed, for he realized then that we were preparing, energetically and seriously, for the hijacking.

And so David actively began to dissuade the others. Solomon grew cool. Tolya Goldfeld stopped mentioning the possibility of participating, and then he began to try to talk the Kishinev people into withdrawing their support. Vladik Mogilever's initial, cautiously positive attitude became cautiously negative, then sharply negative.

Vladik Mogilever and David Chernoglaz told me that they wanted to meet with Mark Dymshitz. They didn't know his name but said they wanted to talk with "the pilot." I did not want them to try to shake Mark's determination to go through with the plan—the second of May was not far off. So I refused to put them in contact with Mark. Nevertheless, they hoped that the plan would be aborted.

Now, when I appeared at Vladik's door laden with Hebrew materials, he understood that my visit meant that the "wedding date" was approaching. We went in for a few minutes. Vladik put the books and papers away, and we talked of inconsequential things while we had a cup of tea. When I stood up to say good-bye, Vladik indicated that he would go down to the street with me. As we walked down the stairs he asked,

"Are you all ready?"

"In principle, yes."

"When?"

"I'll let you know in advance. You'll have time to get all the 'unkosher' stuff out of the house."

"Do you understand what you are doing? The Bolsheviks will shoot you down without any hesitation."

"If they knew who the passengers were, perhaps they would. But they won't know. And if they do find out, they will arrest us before we get on the plane."

"If you do manage to get to Sweden, do you realize what will happen here? The Organization will be destroyed. The ulpans will be shut down. There will be searches, arrests."

"That's possible. But the goal of the Organization is not to exist for as long as possible. The goal of the Organization is to implement our program. It is not enough for us to educate people. We need to achieve *aliyah*. Our flight should break down the barriers. Do you realize, Vladik, what an explosion this will be, what a bang it will make?"

"Yes. But you can't decide for others. It is also possible that the result will be the opposite—that Jews will no longer be allowed to work and study at the institutes, for example. A wave of anti-Semitism may flood the country. Think about the people you are leaving behind."

"We can't wait for generations, fearing that our 'bad' circumstances could become 'very bad'. We must take a risk."

"Hillel, think of my Yulka, of Ilyushka. You don't have the right to decide their fates. Hillel, perhaps I'll go with you on the bus?"

"Never mind. It's late already. Be well."

I jumped on the departing bus. My heart was heavy.

"Think about my Yulka, about Ilyushka. . ." Vladik's final words pierced my heart. I want only the best for Yulya and Ilyushka. . .I want only the best for Eva and Lileshka—my dearest in the whole world. . . Vladik, I am not deciding the fate of your wife and son. You decided it before you knew

Yulya, even before Ilyushka was born. You decided it on that cold windy day in November of 1966 when we together chose the road, not only for ourselves but for our loved ones.

I could not fall asleep for a long time that night.

CHAPTER TEN

April Conference

By the spring of 1970, three and a half years had passed since the founding of our Organization. We had grown in numbers, but our program and bylaws remained unchanged. And so the Committee decided to convene a conference of representatives of our disparate groups. Two issues to be discussed were our program, with Vladik Mogilever as the presenter, and our bylaws, with David Chernoglaz as the presenter.

My group was responsible for arranging the conference. There was to be one delegate for every three group members. The members of the Committee attended the conference independently of whether they were selected by their own groups. In addition, several members of the Organization were invited to the conference as individuals.

I began making the arrangements by choosing an apartment. It had to meet the following two requirements: the owner had to be a person who would not arouse the suspicion of the secret police; and the apartment had to be sufficiently spacious, comfortable, and secure.

Misha Korenblit knew of such an apartment. One of his friends was Valya Smirnova, a Russian woman who worked in the Aeroflot dining room. Valya lived alone in a separate apartment in a new building on Slava Boulevard.

Misha told Valya that on Saturday, April 4, he wanted to have a "day with the boys" and he didn't want his aunt to know about it. Valya gave Misha the keys to her apartment without asking him any questions—she never refused him anything.

Our group of eight was entitled to two representatives; Misha Korenblit and I were selected to attend. About an hour before the conference was to begin, we arrived at Valya's apartment and prepared places for the thirteen participants. At each place we put a pencil and a pad of paper. As camouflage we had collected several empty and half-empty wine bottles. Vladik Knopov and Viktor Shtilbans from our group were to keep a lookout outside during the meeting. They went to the store for some food—we expected the conference to last for the whole day, and we would all get hungry.

I had warned the Committee members that the representatives were supposed to arrive on time, enter one by one, and not speak to anyone on the steps or in the courtyard. The group gathered in a disciplined fashion. Each person was met at the entrance to the building and directed to the elevator, and when he came to the apartment door, it opened before him, so that no one needed to ring.

Soon everyone had arrived. In addition to Misha Korenblit and me, the others at the conference were Solomon Dreizner and Lassal Kaminsky (from the Dreizner group), Vladik Mogilever and Hillel Shur (from the Mogilever group), David Chernoglaz and Ben Tovbin (from the Chernoglaz group), Tolya Goldfeld and Venya Grossman (from the Goldfeld group), and Lev Korenblit representing a group of three people. Two others were invited as individuals—Grisha Vertlib and Lev Yagman.

I greeted everyone in the name of the Committee, told the group how the conference would work, and requested that everyone speak as briefly as possible—we wanted to meet for only one day. Actually, if we had had dire need of the apartment for a second day, we could have kept the keys on Sunday, but that was not desirable.

At the end of my opening remarks, I reminded the men of our security rules: if someone knocked at the door, all papers were to be given to the secretary of the conference and he would lock himself in the bathroom. If the visitors proved to be "uninvited guests," the secretary would destroy all the papers. We would say that we were celebrating the birth of David Dreizner, who was then three weeks old (Eva and I were his godparents, too). When I finished speaking, I gave the floor to Vladik. He gave a report on the program of the Organization.

The report and the debate on the first agenda item were brief. Vladik said that there was no need to change the program (the one adopted in the fall of 1966). Everyone agreed. It was easy to remember. There was no need to write it down.

Debate on the bylaws took all the rest of the time, until late that night. Each point of each article was considered accepted if at least two-thirds of qualified delegates voted for it. It wasn't easy to get nine votes for each point. David Chernoglaz proposed a basis for the discussion. And then, unexpectedly, Ben Tovbin introduced a rival plan.

The first intense argument arose over the question of who should be considered a member of the Organization. This issue hinged on who was considered a Jew. The discussion of this issue echoed the dissension in Israel on the same subject. Our decision, however, was more liberal than the one in the Israeli Knesset. We decided that if either of one's parents was a Jew and one acknowledged oneself as a Jew, one could be a member of our Organization, regardless of one's membership in other organizations and parties. Thus, we did not require that an individual leave the Komosomol or the Communist Party. We recognized that to leave the Party a member had to submit a declaration of resignation. Such an act would have been an extraordinary occurrence and would have created problems and aroused suspicions.

The bylaws that we adopted that day in the name of the

Organization differed considerably from the old ones. We decided that henceforth such conferences of group representatives would function as the governing body of the Organization, that conferences would be convened periodically and would determine our general strategy. We also decided that the Committee was to serve as the executive body of the Organization. Henceforth, the Committee was to direct the associated groups, theoretically and practically, as well as coordinating their activities. The decisions of the Committee, accepted by a simple majority, were to be binding on all.

Although I did not understand it at the time, this last point was directed against Operation Wedding. I realized that only when a crucial question—something not on the original agenda for this conference—was brought up. But before that, there was discussion of whether the conference should continue.

In the evening, when the discussion of the bylaws was coming to an end, we were startled by the sudden ringing of the doorbell. I had seen a film about Anne Frank in which the director had arranged a similar soul-shaking sound in the scene when the Gestapo came for the hidden Jews. That night in Leningrad I did not go to open the door.

I reasoned that if a friend of Valya's had come to visit her, that person would ring and, getting no answer, would then leave. But the rings became more insistent and longer. Well, we did have a story prepared. Tolya Goldfeld, secretary of the conference, gathered all our notes and notebooks and locked himself in the bathroom. Then I opened the door. There was no one in the hall outside the apartment, no one in the stairwell. The elevator was motionless. No steps were audible.

Vladik Knopov and Viktor Shtilbans, our guards, went downstairs, circled the courtyard, and went out into the street. It looked to them as if everything was in order. They saw that a car with an antenna was parked near the entry to Valya's apartment. But there were cars, some with and some without antennas, near most of the entries. So we decided to continue the conference. And that is when the key question was brought up, by David, with support from Vladik Mogilever:

"Our Organization now stands at the edge of destruction. If we don't take decisive measures today, our Organization won't survive much longer. This is because of the activity of a member of the Committee, Hillel Butman. He is now preparing for a deed that could result in the arrest of members of the Organization, searches, cessation of all of the Organization's activities. Hillel has spoken to some of us privately about this operation, and he has gotten from each of us the promise not to speak to anyone about it. Now there is only one way out. Hillel must renounce this destructive plan and he must influence those who support it so that they, too, will decide not to go ahead with the operation. If that is not done, catastrophe awaits us."

Until David spoke these words, the conference had been proceeding smoothly. Now the discussion took an entirely different direction.

With many of the participants of the conference I had talked about Operation Wedding in advance. And they were now bound by their promises not to say anything, anywhere, about it without my consent. Those men were silent. But others at the conference knew nothing about Operation Wedding, and they became agitated—as might be expected. As members of an illegal group, they all lived with perpetual tension. Now one member of the committee was planning an adventure that threatened to destroy the Organization. He had to be stopped, they believed, before it was too late.

Ben Tovbin fumed first: "If Butman doesn't stop, I'll go to the KGB . . ."

All of us had known Ben for a long time, and we understood that his threat was just an expression of frustration and not realistic. But Ben's words intensified the atmosphere of anxiety in the room.

At that moment there was a banging at the door. Again Tolya gathered all the papers and notebooks and went into the bathroom. When I opened the door, Eva rushed into the apartment. She was panting so hard that she couldn't speak for a few moments.

I took her aside and asked, "How did you get this address? Who is with Lileshka? What has happened?"

Still gasping for air, she said, "Solomon called. He gave me the address. He said he thinks he has been 'poisoned by canned food.' He said you should be very careful—otherwise you could be 'poisoned,' too. Do you understand?"

"I understand. Wait for me in the kitchen with Vladik Knopov. We'll go home soon."

Solomon had left earlier. His wife was in the hospital and he had left his three-week-old son with his mother. Apparently Solomon thought he had been tailed on his way home. Perhaps it had only seemed that way, but probably he really had been followed. Solomon would not have called Eva without good reason.

I went back to the others and told them what Eva had said and what I believed it meant. What were we to do? I said that I thought that if it was already too late to prevent the KGB from being aware of our conference, then it made sense to continue working and to finish the conference as we had intended.

We decided to complete our discussions, end the meeting, destroy all compromising papers, and then leave singly or in twos and go in different directions. If KGB agents were aware of the conference and were waiting outside to tail us, they could only go after the first ones to leave. We repeated that we would tell them we had been celebrating the birth of Solomon's son. If we were taken in and interrogated, we would not answer any questions.

Then I was given the floor. I responded to David's challenge about Operation Wedding.

"Yes, we are planning an operation that is intended to get attention focused on the issue of emigration, so that we can get *aliyah* moving. That is one of the goals of our program. I am not going to talk here about this operation. The work of planning and carrying out such operations under the old bylaws is the concern of the Committee and not of this conference. When this plan first came into being, it was discussed in the Committee and there were no objections to it on principle.

"It is true that the Committee then gave approval only for preparatory work that would clarify the technical possibility of preparing for the operation and implementing it. But until now the Committee has only coordinated the activities of the groups, and its decisions were not binding. If the new statute—that decisions of the Committee are binding on all groups—is in force from today on, and the decision of the Committee opposes this operation, then my supporters and I will leave the Organization and will carry the operation to fruition."

"Right! We'll leave," said Misha Korenblit.

If those of us who supported the idea of Operation Wedding were to leave the Organization, that would mean its breakup—and no one wanted that to happen. Lev Korenblit and Lassal Kaminsky spoke, expressing the same thoughts: end this debate on the plan which had not been on the agenda, had been brought up without any preliminary discussion, and refer the issue for future consideration by the Committee. Those present agreed, and the conference ended.

Eva, Misha, and I left last, after cleaning up the apartment. Everyone appeared to be calm. True, Misha seemed somewhat shaken. The conference had been a strain on everyone's nerves. But the majority had remained silent.

What, I wondered, would Grisha Vertlib, Lassal Kaminsky, Lev Korenblit and Hillel Shur have said if they had not promised me that they would be silent? When I had first told them about Operation Wedding, each of them had been enthusiastic about a favorable outcome. Only the practical Lassal had said, "They'll shoot you down." But none of them had spoken about the danger to the Organization. This was understood to be part of the risk. We believed that our sacrifices would be justified if we managed to get *aliyah* moving.

CHAPTER ELEVEN

_____

Shadows of Doubt

During the week following the conference, events were crowded together like passengers on a bus during rush hour.

Aron Voloshin flew in from Kishinev. He brought me 120 rubles for three plane tickets to Murmansk and back. He was confident that we were right to go through with our plan. We walked for a long time through the streets of Leningrad, talking about possible options for our actions on board the plane. When we parted, we shook hands firmly. Aron had the strong hands of an athlete. They would be valuable during the hijacking. His visit was for me a breath of fresh air. I was becoming more and more isolated and felt smothered by the daily psychological pressure; it was becoming impossible to breath.

Most of those who supported Operation Wedding were not only outside the Committee, they were outside the Organization and were scattered all over Russia, communicating with each other through me. Those who opposed the operation sensed that the crucial date was approaching and did everything they could to persuade me to withdraw from the project. This could only be done by implanting the worm of doubt in my soul, to eat away at my insides.

I asked Misha Korenblit and Pinhas Shekhtman to come over on the evening of April 8. We were to prepare training and accommodations for the hijacking group. I thought that Misha would find encouragement in Aron Voloshin's visit and had asked Misha to come a little earlier than Pinhas, so that I could tell him of my conversation with Aron.

124

But when Misha arrived, I knew immediately that a crack had formed in his resolve to participate in the operation—a crack that was widening by the minute. He couldn't sit still, kept jumping up and pacing around the room, sitting down and twirling a pencil, then tossing it down and getting up and wandering around again. When I told him that the Kishinev group had sent money, he was a little calmer for a few minutes, but that did not last.

Pinhas Shekhtman arrived and we went out on the street to talk. Pinhas had a dacha on the outskirts of Leningrad, in Ozerki. We planned to use this house for our support base on the eve of May 2. There, at the very end of April, we would assemble all the "passengers" from Kishinev, Riga and Leningrad. I would bring the rubber clubs I had made, as well as other "weapons," and we would arrange chairs just as we believed they were arranged in the crew cabin of the plane. And then, with four of us seated in the chairs as "crew," we would carry out a simulation of what we expected to do on board the plane. And God grant that on May 2 we would not need to use the rubber clubs.

As Misha and Pinhas and I walked along the streets, we worked out the last details. Pinhas said he would have the little house in Ozerki ready by the end of April. When we had settled everything, we headed back to my home. As we approached the entry, we saw in the twilight that another group was approaching from the other side. Gradually I began to distinguish faces—Vladik Mogilever, David Chernoglaz, Grisha Vertlib, Lassal Kaminsky, Solomon Dreizner. Were these five really all of one mind? Misha and I said good-bye to Pinhas and went to meet them.

Their gloomy faces revealed anxiety. We sought a secluded spot so that our conversation would not attract curious onlookers. As we walked it became clear to me, from fragments of conversation among the five, that they had just come from Solomon's apartment where they had met, discussed the situation, and formed ranks. Nearby we found a kindergarten courtyard away from the street and went in there to talk.

"You spoke openly about this in Solomon's apartment?" I asked in astonishment.

Their silence made it clear that anxiety and despair had made them forget their promises and the need for security, and had robbed them of all common sense. My last illusion about their support vanished.

Operation Wedding, they said, would mean the death of the Organization. It would give the authorities an excuse to take retaliatory action against Zionists and against such activities as the ulpans and distribution of literature. The authorities would turn the screws, as they had during Stalinist times. They would create the fear that produces silence and inaction. People would burrow into their holes, afraid to talk or read or sign open letters requesting permission to leave.

The realization of their feelings revived the seed of doubt that I had carefully buried when the planned operation was brought up at the conference, and after I had taken the Hebrew books to Vladik.

Solomon and I were linked by a quarter of a century of friendship. Our fates had become intertwined when we were still boys. I knew that Solomon was decisive, bold, devoted to the cause. When I had first told him about the plan for hijacking an airplane, he did not doubt that it was a good idea. He was the first person I introduced to Mark Dymshitz. And now he was against the operation—categorically.

Grisha Vertlib and I had finished the institute together, had been unemployed together afterward, had been together in the Organization from its first days. Grisha was honest and always said what he thought. When I first told

him about Operation Wedding, he had reacted sympatheti-
cally. Now he was against the plan—categorically.

I had brought Lassal Kaminsky into the ulpan at Lisy
Nos, then into the Organization. Lassal was a group leader at
the planning institute where he worked. He thought logi-
cally. And now he was against the operation—categorically.

It was past midnight and soon the buses would stop
running. But this was not a discussion that could be
postponed.

I believed in the worthiness of Operation Wedding. I
believed that it was justifiable to jeopardize our Organization and our fates, even our lives, to start the exodus of
Soviet Jews. But standing there in that school courtyard, I
realized that my faith in the operation was no longer as
unconditional as it had been. For the first time, I allowed
myself to think that I could be wrong. And that thought
became the ally of my co-conspirators as they struggled to
convince me that I was wrong.

I was struck by the realization that all of them, my
comrades in the struggle, men I respected, men to whom I
was bound by years of shared risk, had come to the opposite
conclusion from what I believed to be true. They were no
more stupid than I. Did I have the right to take responsibility
for a decision that would have consequences throughout the
country? How easy it is when you have no choice! How
difficult it is when you have choices but cannot possibly
predict the consequences! If Operation Wedding turned out
to be ill-conceived, it would crush the destinies of thousands
of people. On the other hand, if it was a solution to our
predicament and we did not go through with it, we would
miss our chance and I would never be able to forgive myself.

By one o'clock in the morning, the last buses had gone.
A few passersby hastened home, glancing at the strange men
behind the kindergarten fence. We were at an impasse, each

insisting that he was right. And then Grisha Vertlib made a suggestion.

"Let's ask Israel. Whatever they say, we'll do. If they say yes, I'll do everything that you need, even if I don't participate, and the others will do the same. Agreed?"

I looked at Misha. Before he opened his mouth and said "I agree," I could see that "yes" was written all over his face. "Yes" was written on almost all of the other faces. "Yes" was the only way out of this war of nerves. "Yes" to the only arbiter all of us would listen to. "Yes" as the way to save the Organization.

Only David Chernoglaz's face did not say "yes." David had become an irreconcilable enemy of Operation Wedding. No matter what Israel might say, David could only say no. But David was silent. For him it was enough that the "wedding date" would be postponed.

That postponement frightened me. The "timing mechanism" on our "bomb" had already been set for May 2. Ten days in advance of May 2 we had to start buying tickets for our flight. We didn't have a link with Israel—we would have to find one. Even if we were able to send our inquiry quickly, how fast would the reply arrive? Three years earlier we had queried Israel about the issue of the open letter, and we had never received an answer.

This was a much more serious matter. I knew that this time we would receive an answer—but when? Clearly, if I agreed to this compromise, the "wedding" would not take place on May 2. The terrible psychological stress already felt by those who had agreed to participate would be prolonged. Would we all be able to hold up under such pressure?

"If I agree to this compromise, and the answer from Israel is that we should go ahead with the operation, are you prepared to do everything that is necessary for the success of the 'wedding,' without regard to the possible consequences?"

"Yes! Yes! Yes!" The shadow of a smile appeared on each of their tense faces. Perhaps this compromise could end the crisis. Only David remained silent.

"Good. We'll think about it for forty-eight hours. The day after tomorrow we'll decide."

We shook hands all around. Each of us felt like a sick person who has passed through a medical crisis and knows now that he will live. And then we parted, to meet again in two days. Why the forty-eight-hour delay? I needed time to think carefully. To weigh all the pros and cons. To sit alone and think without the pressure of the presence of the others. I believed that they all thought that in two days I would say "yes." What would I say?

Misha left with the other five—an act that was, even if unintentionally, symbolic. For him, the compromise would mean salvation from the doubts within.

I had that night, the next day, and yet another night. For a week straight I had barely slept. Eva didn't sleep either. She didn't ask questions. Occasionally she would say, "Try to fall asleep. Try, and maybe you'll succeed."

But it didn't work. The only one who slept was Lileshka. We could hear her even breathing in the quiet night. For the first year and a half of her life she almost never slept. And we stayed up with her. Now she was asleep, and again we were not.

"Try and fall asleep, try."

I tried and seemed to succeed. I fell into a kind of semidelirium. I saw the burning remains of a downed plane. Doubled up bodies were lying about. I saw a small corpse. I rushed toward it. My heart thumped with a terrible premonition. Lileshka, my darling daughter. I destroyed you. . . Colored flames flashed. I woke up and felt tears rolling down my cheeks. I was glad that it was dark and Eva couldn't see me. Or hear the palpitations of my heart. But she sensed everything. I heard her stir.

"Try to fall asleep, try."

Finally the night ended. I got up, exhausted. I could still feel my heart pounding. My left eyelid had a tic. What a terrible responsibility, this decision. Especially for a young man untested by life or battle. For Edik Kuznetsov everything was clear: You go forward without hesitation, without reflection. The more you think, the more your head hurts. Forward and farewell. Another chance will not present itself. For David Chernoglaz everything was clear: backward, without hesitation. The goal does not justify the means. The world will condemn the act of piracy. The Organization will be crushed, the ulpans closed, the screws tightened. Each of them was confident that he was right.

CHAPTER TWELVE

The Compromise

On April 9 I waited impatiently at the factory for the bell that marked the end of the work day. Lev Korenblit had called the day before and I agreed to meet him that evening. What would he say? At the April 4 conference he had been silent. A few day earlier he had gone shopping with me and helped to select "weapons of intimidation," and he had given me a toasting fork to add to the "arsenal." He was a decisive man, and courageous. In 1944 he had fled from a concentration camp and made his way alone to the front—and with his nearsightedness, even the loss of his eyeglasses would have meant the end.

When we met he told me, "Hillel, you must agree to a compromise. The Organization is the most valuable thing we have. Operation Wedding would mean the end of it. You cannot assume responsibility for that. You must agree to the compromise."

"But that will delay the operation. Do you realize what that means?"

"Yes, but you have no alternative."

The next day—April 10—four of us agreed to an oral compromise—Lassal and Vladik for the opponents of the "Wedding," Misha and I for the supporters. The compromise consisted of three items. First, if we received a "yes" from Israel, all the opponents would help with the preparations and with the execution of the project. Second, if we received a "no" from Israel, all the proponents of the operation would refuse to take part in it and would try to prevent it from taking place. Third, until we received an answer, the opponents would do nothing that could prevent Operation Wedding from being carried out in the future, and the proponents would cease further preparations. Vladik Mogilever and I were to take responsibility for the inquiry to Israel.

On April 11 I met Mark Dymshitz and informed him of the compromise. He repressed his annoyance, but not easily. Mark was in the most difficult situation of any of us—he had left his job and thrown himself into preparations for the "Wedding." His wife Alya had refused to endanger her daughters, and so they had separated. He was living in a rented room, his entire being focused on May 2. I could understand his reaction.

At the next session of the Committee, the compromise was confirmed by a majority—only David Chernoglaz voted against it. The crisis had been avoided, and we sighed with relief. The next step was to transmit our query to Israel quickly by way of a reliable messenger.

Vladik phoned and invited us to spend Passover with him and Yulya on April 22. Eva stayed home with Lileshka, but I went. At the Mogilevers' home, the modest seder table was already set and Yulya was finishing her preparations for the meal. Before I could even sit down, Vladik said, "Listen, we just met a tourist at the synagogue. A Jew from Norway. A doctor. He speaks Hebrew fluently—lived in Israel and has family there. I invited him to the seder. Would you go out and watch for him near the house. He could get lost here, among the new buildings. His name is Rami Aronson."

I went back out to the street. At that time Vladik and Yulya were living in the Okhta district, on Telman Street. The buildings had twin courtyards, twin apartments, twin entries, and even a native might have had a hard time finding his way in that large, architecturally homogeneous neighborhood.

In the 1950s you could tell a Soviet man by the flare of

his trousers and by his short haircut. But things had changed. By 1970 Soviet citizens were dressing quite decently. Which of those fashionably dressed young men was the stranger for whom I was waiting? A stream of long-haired, mustachioed, bearded men flowed by, in jeans, sweaters, leather jackets. And then I saw a man who was somehow different, somehow un-Soviet. He was bearded and wearing jeans and an imitation leather jacket, but he was not quite the same as the others. As I watched him, he walked past Vladik's house, stopped abruptly, reached into his pocket and took out a piece of paper, studied it, and then turned sharply into the courtyard.

I overtook him and greeted him joyously:

"*Shalom u-Vracha!*"

He was startled by my greeting and turned around.

"Hillel."

"Rami."

"I've been waiting for you. Let's go in."

We began the seder late and ended after midnight. Rami took charge. It was evident from his ease at handling the wine, matzos, charoseth, and other parts of the meal, and from his speedy reading of the Haggadah, that he was familiar with the Passover ritual. He seemed to be what he said he was—not a KGB agent, but a Jew. A Jew who had lived not only in Norway, but in Israel. Should we send our inquiry through him to Israel? We had no choice, no time to check. We had to take the risk.

After the seder was over, Rami and I left in a taxi. I was going home, he to the Hotel Rossiya. We agreed that the three of us would meet the next day.

I met Vladik near the entrance to the Victory Park subway station half an hour before Rami was to arrive.

"Vladik, the inquiry is our responsibility. And neither of

us has yet found anyone more suitable and less risky than Rami. In my opinion he's one of ours. Let's try to send the inquiry through him."

Vladik mused for a few moments, then said,

"All right. Let's try."

"Good. But let's agree to the following. I have a greater interest in this conversation than you do. But your Hebrew is better than mine, and if you do the talking, I may not understand everything. So, I will talk and you will listen. If there is something that I can't explain so that he understands it, you will tell me how. All right?"

"Agreed. But you will give both sides of Operation Wedding? And I will have a chance to talk, too."

"Fine."

Rami arrived on time. We checked to see if we were being tailed, then walked along Basseinaya Street near Victory Park. I spoke.

"Rami, listen carefully. What I am going to tell you is very important, and no one must know about it until you leave here. We don't know you well, but we feel instinctively that we can trust you and that you won't let us down. Can you understand my Hebrew?"

"Yes."

"Listen carefully. In Leningrad there is an underground Zionist youth organization. Vladik and I are its representatives. We have no link to Israel, but now we need one, right away. Do you understand?"

"*Beseder* (all right)."

"Our organization is preparing an operation. I am one of the proponents of this operation, and Vladik is one of the opponents. This is a serious operation, one that will have important consequences. But we cannot predict what the consequences will be. I believe that the operation will lead to the free *aliyah* of Soviet Jews to Israel. Vladik believes that the operation will lead only to the destruction of the

Zionist movement in the USSR. We need an arbiter. Do you understand?"

"*Beseder.*"

"Only Israel can be this arbiter. We want the opinion of those at the highest level in Israel. It doesn't have to be the opinion of the government of Israel. But it must not be the opinion of one individual, even a highly placed one. Is that clear?"

"*Beseder.*"

"Now to the heart of the matter. A group of people are preparing to hijack a Soviet plane in the air, to fly it to Sweden, then go on to Israel. They have their own pilot, who will fly the plane if the crew refuses to take it to Stockholm. We are talking about a large airliner, with about 50 passengers. And the passengers will all be ours. Only the crew will be theirs. From Sweden our people will go to Israel on a commercial flight. Do you understand everything, Rami?"

"*Beseder, Beseder.* All the people are yours. Understood."

"We will not have any firearms aboard. We will use only psychological force against the crew or, at worst, rubber clubs. In Stockholm we will hold a press conference for foreign correspondents and we will talk about all the complex problems connected with the situation of Soviet Jewry. We will stress our despair about how impossible it is for Soviet Jews to leave for Israel. Is that clear?"

"*Beseder.*"

"Rami, is it clear to you that we are not undertaking this operation for ourselves personally? A flight of several dozen people is only a drop in the sea. We are thinking about the fate of hundreds of thousands. We must provoke world discussion of the issue of free emigration of Jews to Israel. Can you imagine what turmoil would ensue if we were to succeed in carrying out this operation? The Soviets would no longer be able to deny that they are preventing Jews from emigrating. They would have to start letting people out. And if they were to arrest us and news of that got out, the uproar would be no less, and that too would produce results. Do you understand that for us the important thing is the uproar that this would cause, and not the flight itself?"

"*Beseder.*"

"Now, there is another point of view. If we carry out this operation, it is possible that the whole world will brand us as air pirates and the Soviets will crush our Organization— close the ulpans, twist the screws, intimidate Soviet Jews, and not let anyone out. You must be aware of both points of view."

"*Beseder.*"

"Well, that's the story. Now, tell me. Will you be going to Israel?"

"No. But I have a friend who will be flying to Israel soon. He's a reliable man. He will do everything that needs to be done."

"When can we count on an answer? Can we expect it in a month?"

"That's difficult to say. Perhaps yes."

"Now, about the technical side of transmitting the answer. There is a Dr. Asher Blank who lives in Israel. He is a member of our Organization who left the USSR last year."

"Dr. Asher Blank? I have heard of him."

"The answer must come through him. He knows that the doctors found that my mother-in-law has cancer. We spoke to him about the medicine. Now he is supposed to call and tell us whether the doctors in Israel recommend that she take this medicine, or not. If they recommend the medicine, that means that we should go ahead with our operation. If the doctors say she should not take this medicine, that means we should not go ahead. Agreed?"

"*Beseder.*"

"Today is April twenty-third. We will wait for a call on

the twenty-fifth of each month. The first time we will expect a call is the twenty-fifth of May."

"*Beseder.*"

"Rami, tell me. Which answer do you think we will receive?"

"I think it will be a negative one. It is true that your goals are positive—but the method. . .you understand. That's my personal point of view."

"Now Vladik will speak and I will listen."

"Let's suppose that the answer is negative," Vladik said. "Then we would try other methods to achieve the freedom to emigrate. We have thought about this. There are at least two other ways we could pressure the Bolsheviks to allow Jews to emigrate. First, we could organize a demonstration in Moscow or Leningrad to demand freedom of emigration. We would alert foreign correspondents in advance, so that they could arrive in time to cover the demonstration and report it in their newspapers. Second, we could simply hold a press conference for foreign correspondents on the emigration issue, as a counterbalance to the press conference of the fifty-two in March."

Vladik went on, talking about the plan of action that would be needed if we received a negative reply from Israel. Vladik and I had discussed the idea of a press conference while we were waiting for Rami, and I found it particularly attractive. Such an event would be especially effective if we could assemble exactly fifty-two participants. Fifty-two against fifty-two.

Rami listened carefully. Occasionally he nodded his head to indicate that he understood, or agreed. And every so often he repeated "*Beseder.*"

We were approaching my house. I summed up what had been said and agreed upon.

"So, Rami. We will wait for a call from Asher Blank. He must inform us of the opinion of "Israeli doctors" about three medicines for my mother-in-law. Medicine No. 1—hijacking an airplane. Medicine No. 2—a demonstration. Medicine No. 3—a press conference. Yes or no. One other thing. If someone from your office should come to Leningrad in the future, would you ask him to call me? Remember the telephone number: 996-681. You only need to remember the number nine. First, two nines. Then you turn them upside down, and in the end you multiply them by each other. Can you remember?"

Rami moved his lips, memorizing the number. Then he repeated it correctly out loud.

"All right. Now, one last thing. What will your man say when he comes to Leningrad and calls—how will I know that he comes from you?"

"He will say the first line of the Bible—'In the beginning God created the heavens and the earth'—in Hebrew."

"Good. And now I would like you to come to my place for a visit. My wife has been waiting for us. After all, today is Passover. And we have invited several other guests."

Rami was the first to get up to leave. He did not want to arrive late at his hotel again. He said good-bye to everyone and we walked out to the entry. Rami put on his jacket, shook my hand firmly, and turned toward the door. Just before he reached it, he suddenly turned around and came back and hugged me. As the door closed after him I called out, "Have a good journey, friend."

In a few days, God willing, he would pass the checkpoint at the Leningrad airport. And we would wait for the reply from Israel.

"*Leshana habaa b'yerushalayim* (next year in Jerusalem)" I had whispered to Geula Gil at her concert in Leningrad in 1966. If only we could know what was being prepared for us *hashana hazot* (this year).

CHAPTER THIRTEEN

The Wedding Is Cancelled

On May 1 Edik came in from Riga and met with Mark and me at the open lot near my house. They had come to clarify the prospects for Operation Wedding.

"When do you expect an answer from Israel?"

"No earlier than the end of May."

"And what if the answer is 'no'?"

"Then according to the conditions of the compromise we made in the Organization, Operation Wedding will be called off."

"And what if we do not submit to this? After all, we're not members of your Organization."

"Of course, I can't prevent you from going ahead. But in that case you would be carrying out your own operation, and Jewish ears shouldn't stick out from it."

"What do you mean?"

"The participants should not all be Jewish. Moreover, once you get to Sweden you should not arrange a press conference without the advance consent of the Israeli embassy. And you must warn us in advance."

That was a very difficult conversation. Operation Wedding was to have taken place the next day—May 2. But once we had agreed to the compromise, it was postponed, indefinitely.

Perhaps the most important thing about that meeting was that I felt that a wall of alienation began to grow between me and them. If Israel's response to our inquiry was "no," I knew that the "wedding" participants who were Organization members would follow me—they would withdraw. But what about the others—what would Mark and Edik do? I did not know. I realized that I had lost control over the operation.

May dragged by slowly. Finally the twenty-fifth arrived, and an answer came. The first medicine was categorically unsuitable. The second medicine was unsuitable. The third medicine was to be used with discretion.

The answer from Israel did not surprise me. After our conversation with Rami Aronson, I had begun to prepare myself for a negative reply. The word "categorically" surprised me. Was David Chernoglaz really right in saying that Operation Wedding would have irreversible, unfortunate consequences? Was the advantage of the operation—which I had believed to be so obvious—really only an illusion?

It did not matter. The answer was "no." Sasha Blank had spoken clearly over the telephone, saying that "the best medical authorities had been consulted." The hijacking had been rejected. So had a demonstration. Only a press conference was deemed acceptable, "with discretion." So often we had heard the accusation that Israel was using us, the Zionists, as a fifth column in the Soviet Union. But actually the opposite was true. Israel was restraining us. Surely, if the Soviet Union had been in Israel's place, the answer would have been "yes."

I had told Mark that he could telephone me early on the morning of May 26, before I left for work. He called and we agreed that he would come to the entrance of the factory during my dinner break, and that I would go out to meet him.

I was resolved to implement the conditions of the compromise, to prevent Operation Wedding. I sympathized with Mark and realized that I was delivering a blow to the solar plexus. But it was difficult for me, too. We had conceived Operation Wedding together, and now we had to kill it. As I walked toward Mark, I remembered Sasha's words: "Categorically no." But I need not have been apprehensive about Mark's reaction, which expressed both resignation and bitterness.

I had barely managed to say that the answer arrived, "categorically no," when Mark interrupted me. I did not need to worry, he told me. All the plans we had considered turned out to be unrealizable—they all reached an impasse. For most of us it meant a pitiful existence to the end of our days in the Soviet Union. Even if the authorities would let some people go, they would never release him—a former air force pilot.

I listened to Mark and understood his bitterness. But I did not understand his pessimism about emigration. By nature Mark was an optimist; so am I. I do not believe that good fortune is a pause between two misfortunes. I could not live without faith and hope. If Operation Wedding was not possible, we would act in a different way. Our goal had not changed. One path to that goal—the path we had thought best—was closed. But there were others.

"Listen, Mark, all is not lost. We'll succeed in emigrating some other way. We'll escalate the campaign of open letters, arrange a press conference, request many invitations from Israel."

"Even if they let you emigrate, they will never release me."

"Why? Solomon served in the air force, where you did, in the Zabaikal region. If they let him go, they would probably let you go, too. And he is asking for an invitation."

Mark's only response was a curse.

"I am an officer, too," I said. "And the interior ministry has its secrets. I am going to ask for an invitation from Israel.

And the others who had pinned their hopes on Operation Wedding are going to search for 'relatives' in Israel. Do you want to receive an official invitation?"

"I don't have any relatives in Israel."

"Don't worry about that. Give me the data on yourself."

Mark was willing to dictate to me the information I would need when requesting an invitation for him. And when he had finished giving me the information about himself, Mark began to give me the data for his wife, Alya, and then for his daughters Liza and Yulya. Only then did I learn that he had already returned to his family, and that he had begun to look for work.

The only thing in that conversation with Mark that I was not pleased about was his motivation for rejecting Operation Wedding. Those of us in the Organization abandoned the operation unconditionally because the response from Israel was "no." He and his friends had rejected the operation because they had decided that it was impossible to carry it out. What, I wondered, would Mark and his friends do if they figured out a way to hijack a plane and escape?

I expressed my apprehensions. I told him I needed to have a clear and final answer to one question: "Do you renounce Operation Wedding in principle for the future as well as for the present?" Mark said that he would think carefully about this, and that he would come to visit me that evening to give me a definitive answer.

My sense, from our conversation, was that Mark's answer would be "yes." He had left his family only because his wife had refused to go with him to the "wedding," and now he had returned to her. He had left his job so that he could give all of his time and attention to the operation, and now he was looking for a job. And he had agreed to receive an official invitation from Israel—an act that would immediately make him suspect in the eyes of the KGB and would have other serious consequences.

I believed that Mark would say "yes" that evening. But I wanted to do whatever I could to ensure that response. As we talked, I thought of a way to strengthen his commitment to abandoning the operation.

A few days earlier in northern Israel, Arab terrorists had attacked a busload of Jewish children from Moshav Avivim and sprayed them with bullets from Soviet-made automatics. Misha Korenblit and I had decided to send a telegram to Avivim, as an expression of condolence and solidarity with the grief-stricken parents and the entire country—and also as a gesture to the members of the Organization who had opposed Operation Wedding. During the entire time that preparations for Operation Wedding had been underway, none of the members of the Organization who were to participate in the operation had signed an appeal or an open letter—we had stayed in the shadows. By sending a telegram to Avivim, we would be making it clear that we had abandoned Operation Wedding, and that we felt it was time to emerge from underground.

I suggested to Mark that he sign the telegram to Avivim. Again he replied that he would think it over and give me his answer that evening. We agreed to meet at my house, and then we parted. I went back to the laboratory, where I had a lot of work to finish before the end of the day—the next day was the first day of a three-week vacation. I did not know that I would not be returning to work after the vacation, or after a year, or ever.

The day before a vacation is always a little crazy, with many unfinished tasks that have been postponed and have piled up and need to be done before you can get away. But May 26, 1970, was especially frantic. In addition to the usual personal matters, I had other responsibilities as well.

Immediately after work I met Vladik Mogilever and

made arrangements with him to submit requests for invitations to Israel—for Mark's family as well as for mine. Then I dropped in on Lassal Kaminsky. After I left him, I met with Misha Korenblit and Boris Azernikov; the three of us went to meet with Solomon Dreizner. I told each of these men the same thing: "The pilot has requested an invitation!" These words told them, more eloquently than any others could have, that plans for Operation Wedding had been abandoned, that the decision from Israel would be implemented, that the threat of a schism had been avoided, that we could again join hands and march along the knife's edge.

It was late at night by the time we made our way toward Solomon's house. And I still had to go to the international telegraph office to send the telegram to Avivim. I realized that I would not get home in time for the meeting I had arranged with Mark. True, the important talk had been the one that morning. In principle everything had already been decided. I did not doubt that he would have a positive answer to the first question—and the other question was secondary in importance.

I decided to telephone home. Eva answered and said,

"Mark is sitting here waiting for you. Will you be home soon?"

"No, not soon. Give him the phone."

Mark's calm voice came over the line:

"It's like this. The answer to the first question is 'yes,' the answer to the second is 'no.' "

"Good. Be well."

I hung up and turned to the others.

"Everything is all right. The answer to the first question is 'yes.' He doesn't want to sign the telegram, but that's his business. And now we will send the telegram to Avivim."

Much later I would see a copy of that telegram on the investigator's desk. It was considered evidence—not that we had rejected the hijacking plan, but that we were "inveterate Zionists."

That night I slept calmly. In the morning I wrote a letter to Sasha Blank in Israel: "The recommendations of the medical consultants were accepted." Then I got on the train and rode to Siversky, to begin my first normal vacation since I had finished the exhausting years of night school. Three weeks of carefree life with my family—Eva, Lileshka, Annushka and Mama, who were already there waiting for me.

For months I had been under the stress of the merciless responsibility for Operation Wedding. Now that was in the past. The burdens of life seemed to slip from my shoulders as I sat looking out the train window. Forests and thickets flew by, grass was coming up, and the first flowers bowed under the light breeze. I noticed for the first time that summer had already arrived.

Only once during that vacation did I travel to Leningrad. A meeting of the Committee had been scheduled for June 9 at Lassal's apartment. We were to make preparations that day for a two-day conference of the All-Union Coordinating Committee, to be held on June 13 and 14. The Leningrad members were to organize that conference, at which groups from new cities were to become members of the AUCC.

That meeting, on June 9, 1970 was the final one for our Committee. We did not know it then, but we had only six days left to live "in freedom."

Afterwards, I traveled back to Siversky, looking forward to another delightful week. I would be able to spend as much time as I wanted with my little friends. I had managed to get Howard Fast's *My Glorious Brothers* from Lev Korenblit after the Committee meeting. The sun was shining. Life was good. Does an optimist for whom the absence of misfortune is good luck need much in order to be in a cheerful mood?

My Glorious Brothers—I would recall that book often in the years ahead. And each time with a tickling in my throat.

Lev Korenblit had asked me to return the book as quickly as possible—I had the only copy, and reproduction could not start until I brought it back. So on the morning of June 10 I went to Aunt Sonya's room and began to read. But I didn't get far. Soon I heard light steps in the corridor—someone was opening and closing all the doors. My young friends had gotten up and were looking for me. I barely managed to get behind the door when it burst open and in came Lileshka. She looked around the room quickly, and then closed the door, her little fingers struggling to reach the knob, and then I heard her footsteps recede as she went away.

I decided to seek a safer refuge. Eva's parents were using a room on the second floor of the dacha, and they had gone out. The two small girls never used the tall, steep spiral staircase that led from the first floor to the second. I crept quietly up to the second floor, opened the briefcase containing the pages of Fast's book, and tried to concentrate.

Before I could read even a single page I heard footsteps again, and again outside my door. Once more I repeated my trick and again Lileshka, opening the door, concealed me behind it. But this time she stood there for a long time.

"Daddy, dear, where are you?" she finally asked in her small voice. And then she left.

Her words startled me. The hell with the book! I rushed into the hall after her, wanting to pick her up in my arms and hug her. But she had already started down the steep steps and I was afraid that the unexpected sound of my voice might frighten her.

"Daddy, dear, where are you? Daddy, dear, where are

you?" she repeated as she went down the stairs, and her voice floated back up to me. Then she was hidden by the twist of the spiral steps, and I went back into the room and began reading again. How could I know then what irreplaceable minutes I had lost. . .How could I know then how often during the sleepless nights of the years ahead I would be tormented by the memory of that small, beloved voice asking "Daddy, dear, where are you?"

CHAPTER FOURTEEN

The Big House

The black Volga moved along the city streets and turned onto Liteyny Boulevard. I remembered this route—when I was arrested in 1960 I had been taken along the same streets. Just before the bridge across the Neva, at the very beginning of Liteyny Boulevard, we came to a large, gray, barracks-like building. It had an illustrious history for such a dull-looking building. At the end of the previous century "the great leader of the world proletariat" had sat in cell 193 and written his revolutionary works using milk as invisible ink. And almost half a century later, at the end of the thirties, in these same cells sat his followers who had not succeeded in keeping in step with the "general line of the Party." The citizens of Leningrad call that building "the Big House," and they cross the street rather than walk in front of it.

The driver turned the car onto Kalyaev Street and stopped in front of the gates at the side entrance. Leather jacket jumped out and soon returned. Then the gates opened, the car moved into the inner courtyard, and the gates closed behind us. I did not hear them clang shut.

The men who had accompanied me in the car took me to an office with barred windows on the second floor. Those windows must have opened out onto Kalyaev Street—I could hear the sounds of traffic. There were two writing tables arranged to form a T. Behind one of them sat a thin, elegant man of about forty, wearing a gray uniform. He indicated that I was to sit on a stool that stood at a writing stand near the door. Both the stool and the stand were bolted to the floor.

When I was seated he said, "I am going to conduct your

case. My name is Kislykh, Gennady Vasilyevich. Sign here that you have familiarized yourself with this decree stating that you are involved as a suspect in a very serious crime against the state."

What? Had they gone out of their minds? "I am going to conduct your case." That meant a case already existed. It seemed that this time everything was much more serious than the last time and that I would not just be detained as a witness. Had they really decided to start the case against the members of the Organization? Would they really dare to try us for this as for organizing ulpans and distributing Jewish literature, as if we had committed a particularly dangerous crime?

Kislykh went out of the room, leaving me with the men who had accompanied me. They sat silently, looking at the portrait of Dzerzhinsky that hung on the wall behind the investigator's table. We waited quite a while, and my guards grew impatient. Leather jacket was the first to give in. He picked up the receiver and dialed a number.

"Comrade Colonel, Senior Lieutenant Vedentsev speaking," he began. "Comrade Colonel, we have been on our feet since they woke us at two in the morning. And we haven't had anything to eat, not even a crumb. Comrade Colonel, permit. . ."

But "Comrade Colonel" evidently cut him off. Leather jacket now only listened, from time to time interjecting "O.K." and "Yes, sir." Finally he hung up with a bang, and then the room was silent.

I was astonished and puzzled. They had been on their feet since "two in the morning"? I didn't have any idea whether the authorities had known about our activities for years or had learned about the Organization only within the previous twenty-four hours. But either way, why were they now in such a rush—why had they roused these men at two in the morning? And what had these men been doing since then—they had not gotten to Siversky to pick me up until about one in the afternoon. Had they arrested anyone else? What was going on? And why?

At that moment I knew only that I had been brought in to the Big House and that there was a case against me—which I assumed was based on the activities of the Organization in starting ulpans, disseminating literature and so on. I did not yet know what the case was really about. I did not know then that after I met with Edik and Mark on May 1 at the empty lot near my house, they had continued with preparations for Operation Wedding. I did not know that after May 1 the base for the operation was shifted to Riga, and that from that day on the driving forces behind the operation were Mark Dymshitz, Edik Kuznetsov and Iosif Mendelevich. I did not know that on the morning of June 15, 1970—just hours before I was arrested, those three and their supporters had assembled at the Smolny airport near Leningrad for their own version of Operation Wedding!

Iosif Mendelevich was a twenty-three-year-old Zionist from Riga. He had dreamed since childhood of living in Israel. He and his sister began to participate in a Zionist youth group while they were practically children. The members of that group were inexperienced and naive, but they burned with enthusiasm, and they acted.

The group wanted to create in Riga a cultural center that would be used to communicate Zionist ideas to other Jews. Iosif suggested that they "seize" a cafe to use as their headquarters. Several long years later, in a cell in Vladmir prison, he told me about his plan for seizing the cafe—and couldn't refrain from smiling as he recalled his method and his innocence.

His plan was simple. The group was to pick a cafe. Then members and their supporters were to go there and occupy all the seats at all the tables, day after day, until the people who usually ate there understood that it had become a Jewish cafe. Then non-Jews would stay away, and it would become a center for Jewish life in Riga. One thing those youngsters failed to consider was the reaction of the waiters. Day after day the Zionist students sat at the tables. They ordered no more than tea and a roll. The cafe was not meeting its quota, and the waiters were not getting any tips. That was too much—the waiters soon put an end to this Zionist occupation. But Iosif was not defeated.

He was still a member of the Zionist group in Riga in 1970 when he wrote articles for *Iton*, helped to print it and, with Boris Mafzer, represented the Riga group at All-Union Coordinating Committee meetings. After I talked to Silva and Edik about Operation Wedding, Iosif was the first person they recruited to participate. He left his job, and the escape plan became the focus of his life.

For Iosif, Operation Wedding became what self-immolation was for Vietnamese Buddhists. From the very beginning Iosif believed that the escape would fail, that the participants would be killed or would spend the rest of their lives in prison. But he believed that the attempt had to be made, that the flame had to burn, to light the way for those who would follow.

Few people are capable of self-sacrifice, and Iosif's attitude did not evoke enthusiasm in Edik or Mark. But in spite of their differences, the three worked well together. They created a new version of Operation Wedding, with a different "guest list." One of their guests was Aryeh Khnokh, a twenty-six-year-old electrician who had grown up in the small town of Daugavpils in Latvia. Aryeh was a Zionist, a stubborn man, and the new husband of Iosif's eighteen-year-old sister Meri. The couple risked not only their own lives but also the life of their unborn child—Meri was pregnant when she was arrested on June 15, 1970, and little Yigal came into the world in January 1971, soon after Meri was released from prison. All the defendants were soon lovingly referring to the unborn baby as their "little co-defendant."

Another participant in the new escape plan was Tolya Altman, a jolly Odessan who was working as a woodcutter at a kolkhoz near Riga. Tolya was born in Kharkov in September of 1941, during the battle against the Germans on the outskirts of the city. Tolya's mother, a refugee from Chernovitsi, then fled immediately to the Tambov region. For many years Tolya's life was a continuous journey, through cities and professions. In Odessa he was a lathe operator, chauffeur, filing clerk, engineer, engraver, sailor—even a geography student. When he heard rumors that "they were letting people out" from Riga, he went there and joined Mark and Edik. I met Tolya in the Mordvinian camps. He was with me during my first stint of fifteen days in a punishment cell there. And he was with me in a punishment cell during my last detention of fifteen days in the Urals.

Vulf Zalmanson, Silva's older brother, Edik's brother-in-law and an officer in the Soviet army also agreed to participate. So did Izrail Zalmanson, Silva's youngest brother, a fourth-year student at the Riga Polytechnic Institute. I would spend a year with Izrail Zalmanson in the Ural camps.

A twenty-four-year-old artist-designer from Riga, Boris Penson, also signed up. My brief acquaintance with Boris would occur in Mordvinia.

Another participant was Mendel Bodnya, a thirty-three-year-old worker at the No. 3 bread factory in Riga. Mendel knew of no other way to reach his mother, who was living in Israel. He became the tenth member of the escape group. None of us ever met him in the prisons, or camps, or in the convoys.

The group also included two non-Jews—Alik

Murzhenko and Yura Fedorov. When the Soviet press was denying charges of anti-Semitism in connection with the trial and imprisonment of the "airplane group," the presence of these two men made it possible for the press to write that "in the group, along with others, there were also people of Jewish nationality."

Edik had met these two men during his first imprisonment, and he involved them now because he knew they were trustworthy and he could rely on them, not because he wanted to make Jewish participation less prominent. Why, though, did Murzhenko and Fedorov—neither of them Zionists—join the group?

The Ukrainian Murzhenzko was born in the same place as Dymshitz, at Lozovaya Station in the Kharkov region, but fifteen years later. At the age of twenty, Alik was sentenced to six years of imprisonment for anti-Soviet agitation and propaganda. When he left prison after serving the full sentence, this talented lad was convinced that his record blocked all roads. He had studied five foreign languages independently and dreamed of becoming a translator. But he was sure that he would not be accepted at the Institute of Foreign Languages or that, if he was accepted, the authorities would kick him out when they learned about his past. He could not get a permit to live in Kiev with his wife, and his family life was difficult. In short, he suffered the typical fate of most released political prisoners: he had no life.

Fedorov, twenty-seven in 1970, was only eighteen when he was convicted of anti-Soviet agitation and propaganda. He served four years of a five-year sentence and then, after his release, was forced to work in a cable factory. He knew that, with his past, that job was his present and his future—his life sentence.

Alik Murzhenko and Yura Fedorov were guilty of wanting to be citizens, of not wanting to be subjects. They would be judged as "particularly dangerous recidivists" and would be sent to a special camp with cell-like barracks, isolated from the rest of us. Yura's wife in Moscow and Alik's wife in Kiev would have a long wait for their husbands.

Mark Dymshitz's group of twelve met in Shmerli Park, in the school stadium, or in other places in Riga to discuss their version of Operation Wedding. Silva Zalmanson made copies of topographic maps. Others made rubber clubs and gags. Preparations for "Wedding Number Two" were underway.

The author of this version was Mark Dymshitz. He had come to the conclusion that the superfluous passengers on a large airliner created too many unpredictable factors that would have to be dealt with during a hijacking. Mark proposed to this group that, instead, they should hijack a small plane, a twelve-seater AN-2—and not in the air, but on the ground at a small, local airport. The AN-2 was not a fast plane, but Mark had had experience navigating it during the time he worked in Bukhara. He could fly the plane close to the ground, to avoid radar detection. The Finnish border was not far, and God willing, there would be no disaster. Edik agreed to the plan, and Mark brought it to the group for discussion.

If the group was to hijack a small plane on the ground, they would have to find an airport where the small planes were not well guarded. On the evening of May 23 Mark and Edik arrived at the small, local Smolny airport, about twenty kilometers from Leningrad, toward the Finnish border. They knew that the first secretary of the Leningrad regional Party committee, Tolstikov, kept a plane there, in a state of constant readiness. This plane was the right size and always had a full tank of fuel. But Mark and Edik found that it was guarded by men, dogs and searchlights: at night the area around the plane was as light as day. Later Silva telephoned her older brother, Vulf. "We didn't rent the dacha," she told him. "There's a vicious dog in the courtyard."

An atmosphere of heavy despondency hung over the group. Mark began to look for work. It was three days after that when he met me near the entrance of the Elektrik factory and I told him that the answer from Israel had been "categorically no" and that Operation Wedding could not be carried out. His bitter words reflected accurately his feelings that day. Neither of us realized on May 26 that just five days later version number three of Operation Wedding would be created.

Mark could not reconcile himself to the thought that he would never be allowed near the controls of a plane. And so it is not surprising that when he began to look for work he again rode out to the small Smolny airport. On June 1 he was again at the "dacha" that on May 23 he had not "rented" because of the "vicious dog." While he was there Mark noticed something that radically changed his plans. A new route, Leningrad to Priozersk to Sortavala, had been added to the timetable as flight 179. This route was ideal for a hijacking—the little town of Sortavala was right next to the Finnish border. And the intermediary landing, in Priozersk on the shore of Lake Ladoga, also offered some advantages.

Instead of going to the personnel department to apply for work, Mark bought a ticket for the new route and took a test ride. That evening when he got home, Mark called Edik to Leningrad, and Edik came with Yura Fedorov. The two of them listened to Mark's description of his day's flight and his plan, and accepted this new proposal at once. Again their hopes brightened, like an ember that unexpectedly bursts into flame.

On June 8 the three of them flew to Priozersk. There Mark showed Edik and Yura exactly what he had in mind. In addition to the group of twelve who were to participate in this version of the "wedding," four others were to go along—Mark's wife and two daughters, and Meri Mendelevich, Aryeh Khnokh's wife. But only twelve tickets could be purchased for seats on the little AN-2. Mark suggested that a foursome—Silva Zalmanson, Boris Penson, and Aryeh and Meri Khnokh—leave Leningrad the night before the hijacking and go to the airport at Priozersk. There they would set up a tent at the edge of the forest near the landing strip and wait until flight 179 arrived, with the other twelve aboard. At the moment the plane landed, the participants on board would tie up the crew, stuff gags in their mouths, drag them from the plane, and put them in sleeping bags in the tent. Great care would be taken to ensure that the crew would not catch cold or get wet if it rained before they were discovered. Then, with all sixteen of the participants aboard, the plane would take off for the little Swedish town of Boden on the Finnish border .

Mark, Edik, and Yura decided that this "wedding" would take place on Monday, June 15.

On June 10 the Riga participants of this version gathered in Shmerli Park. There they adopted an "Appeal to Soviet Jews" written by Iosif Mendelevich. The appeal began with the words of the prophet Zechariah, used in an epigraph: "Flee from the northern country. . . . Escape, O Zion, that dwellest with the daughter of Babylon" (Zechariah 2:10-11). It ended with a postscript that was not taken note of by the court during any of the trials: "It should be emphasized that our actions pose no danger to outsiders; when we take the plane up in the air, only we shall be on board." Before Iosif left for Leningrad he gave the appeal to Lev Eliashevich. After much delay the appeal would later reach Israel but it would not be published.

On June 11 all the participants in this "optimistic tragedy" (the title of a 1932 play by Vishnevsky, in which per- . sonal tragedy is overshadowed by the optimistic future of the Revolution) began to assemble at Mark's apartment in Leningrad. Prior to this date, Mark's fifteen-year-old daughter Yulya had completed a test flight along the entire route. That day Mark and Edik, using false names, bought all of the twelve tickets available for flight 179 on June 15.

At the same time that the group began to assemble, the Committee of our Organization was beginning preparations for a meeting of the All-Union Coordinating Committee, to begin on June 13. Delegates from cities not previously represented in the AUCC were to attend that meeting, which would focus on tactics for the struggle to achieve free *aliyah*.

And so it was that while I was relaxing serenely in Siversky, two groups—participants in this latest version of Operation Wedding and the AUCC group—were, unbeknownst to each other, meeting in Leningrad, pursuing the same goal but along different paths. The two halves of my divided soul.

On June 12, the day before the AUCC conference was to begin, Misha Korenblit suddenly showed up at Mark Dymshitz' apartment to get Mark's signature on an open letter. The Committee in Leningrad was collecting signatures for an open letter to United Nations Secretary General U-Thant on the problem of *aliyah*. Since Mark had asked for an official invitation from Israel and had, in effect, thus emerged from the underground, it seemed reasonable to ask him to sign the open letter. Misha did not get Mark's signature that day—what Misha saw at Mark's apartment made him forget the purpose of his visit.

The usually hospitable Mark was cautious and unfriendly when he opened the apartment door and saw Misha. He immediately led Misha into the kitchen and closed the door behind him. But in the moment that Misha had to glimpse into the living room, it seemed to him to be full of people who had fallen silent and did not speak during his visit. And there were, he realized, many coats hanging in the entryway—too many for Mark's family. A terrible suspicion came to life in Misha's head. But Mark's face revealed nothing except that he was anxious for Misha to leave.

Misha did manage to get Mark to promise that if he was, indeed, going to go ahead with "that," he would warn Misha by calling and telling him "Marusia is going to the doctor in X hours"—X to be the number of hours left before the start of Operation Wedding. Those hours would be all the time the Organization would have to prepare for the consequences of the operation. Misha left Mark's apartment in complete confusion—and without Mark's signature for the open letter.

Misha then went to see Lassal Kaminsky and told him about his visit to Mark, and about his suspicions. But Lassal had little time; knowing Misha to be emotional and suspicious by nature, he did not try to determine if this time Misha's suspicions had some substantial basis in fact. In the meantime, the hours ticked by. "Marusia" was just about ready to go to the doctor.

The AUCC conference ended on June 14. Those who had attended began to disperse. At dawn on June 15 the telephone rang: "Marusia is going to the doctor in three hours." But Mark phoned my apartment, not Misha's. I was at the dacha in Siversky—only Eva was in the apartment. She was surprised by such an early call from the usually punctilious Mark. Moreover, she realized that the sentence was clearly one that had been prearranged. When Eva told Mark that I was away, he asked her to convey the message to Misha Korenblit, which she did immediately.

When Mark left the phone booth from which he had

made the call, he joined a group carrying rucksacks, and they set out in the direction of the Finland Station. The plane for Sortavala via Priozersk was to leave from Smolny at 8:35 am, in less than three hours.

In the group that Mark joined there were three women—his wife Alya and their two daughters, nineteen-year-old Liza and fifteen-year-old Yulya. Alya had capitulated. She had decided she was willing to pay any price so that the family could be together—at what she realized might be its final hour.

They arrived at Smolny with time to spare, and joined the participants who had spent the night in the forest near the airport. Tolya Altman had spent the last few days and nights wandering along the Leningrad quays, dazed by the beauty of the former Petersburg. In Tolya's pocket was a ticket, in the name of Sokolov, for flight 179, and three rubles and change.

In the pocket of Yura Fedorov, who stood nearby, was something else—something that would later enable the Soviet press to refer to the group as armed bandits and murderers. In Yura's pocket was Mark's little pistol, the one that we had thought to use as a weapon of intimidation by shooting a blank. During the investigation the experts, with difficulty, managed to produce one shot from that pistol. It took several experts, their tongues hanging out as they strained, to cock the pistol for a second shot. No one was able to get a third shot out.

Given this performance, one can imagine how such a pistol would have performed during a hijacking. That pistol had been barely visible in Mark Dymshitz' palm when he showed it to me half a year earlier as we stood in the entrance of my house. From the moment it was manufactured in Bukhara until it was examined by the experts during the trial, that pistol had produced only one shot—when Mark had tested it on Alya's ironing board. But the quality of that pistol was not mentioned at the trial or in the press.

When, later, I was given an opportunity to read press accounts, I found stories about the band armed with "firearms, axes, brass knuckles, ropes, gags." I couldn't imagine what they were talking about. The expression for "firearms" in Russian does not indicate number, and usually evokes a picture of a pile of automatics, revolvers and grenades. But this expression can, theoretically, also be applied to a single small pistol capable of producing only one shot in its lifetime.

The group did have one set of brass knuckles cast by Silva according to a sketch made by Edik. In Russian there is a precise singular for "brass knuckles," and so the Soviet press had to use a literary device to convey the idea that the group had more than one. The group also had a camping ax, which was to be used to chop wood for fuel if they were forced to land in the woods of northern Finland.

The description in the press of a band of "recidivist criminals who never worked" and who were armed with "firearms, axes and brass knuckles" produced horror in even Jewish readers in the Soviet Union. After all, in the Soviet Union, the people who paraded on Red Square with banners proclaiming "Hands off Czechoslovakia" are considered to be the same kind of criminals as the people who set out at night with crowbars in hand to hunt down their victims.

Months after those reports in the press, when the vise of fear and despair gradually loosened its grip, Soviet Jews began proudly to call the members of the group "our" boys. And that possessive pronoun was the best reward that could have been given to those of us from Leningrad who were arrested that day in June.

CHAPTER FIFTEEN

An Optimistic Tragedy

As the group gathered at the Smolny airport to board flight 179 from Leningrad to Priozersk to Sortavala, Edik sensed that they were being tailed. He warned the others. But by then they were already underway, moved along by the momentum of despair, and nothing could have stopped them. Doesn't it seem to anyone who sets out on such a deed that he is being followed, that danger lurks behind each bush and column? But they were so close to freedom—perhaps tomorrow Stockholm and the next day Tel Aviv. So they went on.

The group that was to wait in the woods near the airstrip at Priozersk had started on the evening of June 14, riding the train from Leningrad. They, too, had sensed that they were being followed, but Boris Penson had said "Better to the noose than backward," and they went on. He tore up his notebook and threw it out of the moving train, along with two rubber clubs. He, Silva, Aryeh and Meri got off the train one stop before Priozersk and went on foot to the landing field.

They arrived at the site of the landing strip on schedule, set up the tent, crawled into sleeping bags and, with one of them on guard, the others tried to sleep. At 3:00 am they were arrested.

The group at the Smolny airport did not know that. When the airport loudspeakers announced the boarding of passengers for flight 179, they hoisted their knapsacks up on their backs and moved toward the plane. They did not know that KGB sharpshooters with police dogs were waiting for them on the grounds of the airport, and that a special group was waiting for them inside the plane, straining in expectation. The KGB officers had been warned, when they were ordered to capture the "criminal recidivists," that "the enemy is armed."

As those twelve took their final steps toward the small plane with number 85534 on its side, they did not know that a second pilot had not even been assigned to flight 179. They did not know that the previous evening a criminal case against them as well as against other members of the Leningrad Organization had been opened; that arrests were already taking place in Leningrad, that my apartment in the city had already been searched, and that Eva had been prevented from going to work. They did not know that Lieutenant General Nosyrev, director of the Leningrad KGB, was reporting every hour to his superiors in Moscow on the progress of the KGB operation.

Two plans clashed at the little airport north of Leningrad, two designs. The Dymshitz group planned to break through the blockade and bring Soviet Jews out of the empire of the northern pharaoh. The KGB counterplan was to capitalize on international concern over air piracy and to represent Zionists in the USSR as "a band of criminals in the service of Israel, a splinter in the body of the Socialist fraternity of nations." The KGB was determined to crush the Zionist underground, to smash the awakening Soviet Jewry and the dissident movement in general. From the moment that the KGB organs found out about Operation Wedding, all their efforts were directed at not letting the plan get bogged down: their interest was as great as ours in bringing it to its logical conclusion. From the point of view of those who planned the counteroperation, the action gave the KGB an ideal excuse for a pogrom, with the attendant silence of the confused and distracted West.

Eventually it became clear that the KGB had known about the plans for Operation Wedding at least a month and a half or perhaps two months before June 15—and did not prevent it. During this time it would have been possible to call in the conspirators, accept their documents and even to give them emigration visas. But this is exactly what Andropov, then head of the KGB, didn't want. On the contrary, sometime at the end of April, Vladik Mogilever, Lassal Kaminsky, Natan Tsiryulnikov and several other active Leningrad Zionists were summoned to OVIR, where it was suggested that they speedily submit documents for emigration. Since these men had already submitted documents and been refused, and the time required before they could reapply had not yet elapsed, this summons and suggestion from the OVIR clearly augured a positive answer. But a week later—at about the beginning of May—they were unexpectedly called in again and told that they need not submit documents. By that time, evidently, the plan had been finalized to use Operation Wedding as an excuse for a pogrom against *aliyah* activists, and to prevent the escape of potential victims.

When Iosif Mendelevich was brought from the Smolny Airport to the Big House, the first question he was asked by the KGB was: "Do you know Butman?" The KGB needed the missing link to connect the attempt to hijack a plane with the Committee of the Zionist Organization in Leningrad. They evidently had been keeping track of us individually, but did not yet have the whole picture.

How did the KGB find out about the plan for Operation Wedding?

In the summer of 1971, after the trial, I was sent on my first transport—they were sending me from Kishinev to Leningrad by way of Odessa, Kaluga and Kalinin. I was in a cell in a Black Maria, waiting while the truck stood in the courtyard of the transit prison in Kalinin. Mark Dymshitz was in another cell of that same truck. After it was loaded, a tow-headed machine gunner from the convoy that accompanied us jumped into the cab, burning with impatience. As soon as he saw my "Semitic face" he asked, "Are you serving for the airplane?"

"Yes, among other things, for the airplane."

"Who informed?"

That fellow's face expressed curiosity, impatience and also, it seemed to me, sympathy. So urgent was his desire to know that he forgot that he was holding a loaded automatic with the barrel pointed at me. He was agitated, and his hands wandered near the trigger—and I wasn't sure that the safety lock was in place.

"Would you please put down your gun and calm down, and I'll tell you everything," I said.

He put the submachine gun on the prisoners' things lying around on the floor. The jolting of the truck could have easily knocked the automatic off its perch and triggered it to give off a round.

"Listen, " I said, looking nervously at the gun, "I have a wife and daughter. I want to live. For God's sake, put your toy away."

He turned the gun barrel toward the door. Only then could I comfortably answer his question.

"There were no provocateurs amongst us—I am sure of that, as much as it is possible to be sure of anything!"

I did not tell the curious machine gunner all of my thoughts on this subject. But what I did say was true. I still believe that there were no provocateurs in either the Leningrad or the Riga group. It could not have been difficult for Andropov's men to learn about Operation Wedding. Too many people knew about the plan—honest, decent, committed people who were not always cautious. How could you not confide in your closest friend if you were preparing for such a crucial hour in your life? The friend's wife is trustworthy and faithful and can hold her tongue. . . But the wife has a friend, someone she has known from childhood and the friend has . . . and so on.

It is impossible to know when the first careless word was spoken. Was it in Leningrad or in Riga? Over the phone or in person? On a bus or on a porch? The only thing that matters is that it was spoken. It is senseless now to accuse those from Leningrad or those from Riga.

I can think of at least two situations that could have engendered the beginning of the end. The first was the conference at the apartment of Valya Smirnova on April 4. When Solomon left that conference, he sensed that he was being followed. A car with an antenna stood near the entrance to the building for some time. Had the KGB known in advance about the conference? Had they managed to "recruit" the owner of the apartment? It is always possible to find "compromising material" against a restaurant manager like Valya. And what if the KGB had been listening in on our conference and had heard the crucial question that David Chernoglaz raised within the walls of that building? They might not have understood immediately what was being said. But once the words would have reached the KGB, it isn't difficult to guess how General Nosyrev would have acted on this information.

The second situation that could have doomed us all was the urgent discussion of the operation that took place at Solomon Dreizner's apartment on the evening of April 8. Solomon, David Chernoglaz, Vladik Mogilever, Lassal Kaminsky and Grisha Vertlib talked inside Solomon's apartment, before they came to me and we arrived at the compromise. Solomon was a member of the Committee. It is likely that the conversations in his apartment were being bugged. No pillows thrown over the telephone could have prevented eavesdropping by the KGB. The men were disturbed. They forgot their promises to me not to speak about Operation Wedding within four walls.

I believe that in Riga things were even worse. When Edik and Silva first proposed to Iosif Mendelevich that he participate in Operation Wedding, they talked to him, in detail, about the plan while sitting in Silva's apartment—even though it is likely that the KGB was aware of Silva's Zionist activities and of Edik's dissident past.

When Edik invited Yura Fedorov and Alik Murzhenko to participate, he also invited other friends from his first imprisonment. The others rejected the plan. But did they value what they were told as a secret to be guarded?

Silva invited Ruth Aleksandrovich, niece of the famous singer Mikhail Aleksandrovich, to participate. When Silva telephoned to ask Ruth for her answer, Ruth's mother came to the phone and said only that Ruth could not go to the "wedding" because her dress was not ready. So she, too, had known about the plan.

Today we can only speculate about what happened. The time will come when the dungeon walls will collapse and freedom will come to Russia. May God grant that the KGB will not destroy its archives. Then it will be possible to know the answer to the question and to let the matter come to rest.

On the green field of the little Smolny Airport, the KGB won the battle—and lost the war. That would become clear only half a year later when the first airplanes would begin to leave Russia, carrying Soviet Jews.

Sitting on the chair riveted to the floor in Major Kislykh's office, surrounded by the hungry men who had arrested me, I did not know any of this.

Earlier that day, as I sat with my little friends in the reading room of the library in Siversky, I did not know that the interrogation of Mark Dymshitz had already begun at the Smolny airport.

CHAPTER SIXTEEN

June 15, 1970—Evening

Finally Kislykh returned. My refusal to answer questions was accepted calmly. Apparently it was expected. Kislykh pressed a button on the table and ordered that I be taken away. The supervisor led me to a room where someone rolled my fingers in dye and made prints on special blanks: all the fingers together, each finger separately, the right hand, the left hand. Then a photograph was taken of me in profile, with my surname and first name printed on the background.

That photograph was placed in the criminal case file that remained in the trial archive. A copy of it was placed in the secret personal file that accompanied me through camps, prisons and transit places. At the end of 1970, I was allowed to look through the material in our case. When I saw that picture, I was astonished at how criminal my physiognomy appeared. In the photographs in those files, all the fellows had criminal mugs. Even the noble and intelligent Lev Yagman looked like an experienced pickpocket.

After my fingerprints and my photograph had been taken, I was led into a small room and told to sit down. A supervisor with the bluish nose of an alcoholic sat opposite me, with a pile of questionnaires and blank forms. He took the top sheet from the pile, put it in front of him, and stared at me—like a boa constrictor staring at a rabbit. After a few moments he leaned over the sheet, underlined a word, and then again fixed on me his unblinking gaze. I lowered my eyes to look at the sheet. He had underlined the phrase "with a hook." Aha, I thought—you are describing my nose.

Well, write, write. I've had a lot of trouble because of that nose, but I wouldn't change it for any other.

What was he underlining? "Average . . . average . . . straight . . ." Look carefully! Do I really have a straight chin? No—mine is recessed. I have hated it all my life, and envied fellows with strong, protruding chins. But never mind. He can underline whatever he wants. Everything average. Nothing special. If I run away, no one will be able to identify me from this description.

The supervisor looked up again and stared at me carefully, gazing at each part of me. Then he underlined the phrase "No special marks" and, with a grunt of relief, put that form to one side. He took the next sheet from the pile and began asking questions.

"Surname? First name? Patronymic? Date and place of birth? Nationality?"

Even before I could open my mouth to answer that last question, I could see him writing "Jew."

"Wife's maiden name? First name? Any children?"

"Yes."

"Sex?"

"Daughter."

"Surname? First name? Patronymic?"

"Butman, Lilya Hilevna."

"Age?"

"Three, going on four."

"Goes to school?"

"She's three going on four."

"Goes to school?"

"No, doesn't go."

Was he an idiot? Or had he already had so much to drink that he didn't understand anything? Or perhaps he was just tired of me.

When the supervisor had finished filling out that questionnaire, he put it with the sheet containing the description of my physical features, looked wearily at the thick pile and took another form from it. Question, answer. Question, answer. Finally the process was finished.

The supervisor got up and came over to me.

"Get up and take off your trousers, jacket, pants—all your clothing. Take everything out of your pockets and put it all here on the table."

I am incapable of changing my ways. After I removed my shoes and socks, I stood on them and looked around for something to put my feet on. The supervisor looked at me with annoyance, but he brought over a piece of newspaper and I stood on it. How many times in the future would I stand naked during a frisk? And each time I would try to avoid, somehow, standing barefoot on the dirty, spit-covered floor. It is hard for the human spirit to die within a human being. With four hands the warden and a helper felt my clothing. They checked the seams millimeter by millimeter.

"You can get dressed now. Metal objects, shoelaces and belt are not permitted. They will be held with your personal things."

Only then did I notice that they had already taken the buckles from my sandals and the hooks from my trousers. I got dressed.

"Hands in back. Follow me."

A guard with a ring of large keys led me. We went up a staircase, then down and along corridors. Some of the corridors ended with partitions made of steel rods, with a door in the middle. Each time we came to one of those, the door was opened for us from the other side, and then we continued our march.

It was irritating to walk with "hands in back." Without a belt, the trousers fall; and without buckles on the straps, the sandals slap about the feet.

Now I was a prisoner, a *zek*, without even the paltry

rights of the "big zone"—the Soviet world outside the prison. And they were letting me know that right away. I had to become accustomed to being a nonperson. I had to become an animal. Then they would believe that I had "started on the road to correction."

The guard went into another corridor, gesturing to me to stop and wait at the entrance. He looked to the left, then to the right, as if he were at a street crossing. After he had made sure that the corridor was empty—and that I would not accidentally meet other prisoners—he indicated to me to come ahead.

Finally he opened a door with one of his oversized keys. We went outside and down some steps, across a walkway, and into a long, wide corridor with high ceilings. On the right side as we entered stretched huge windows, and on the left an endless row of identical brown doors with numbers. Above the doors was a gallery and another row of similar brown doors. In the middle of the building was a small, spiral staircase leading to the gallery.

Another guard was standing near the staircase, peering through the peephole of a cell. The man with me coughed, and the guard lowered the cover of the peephole and walked toward us. A runner on the floor in front of the cells silenced the sound of his footsteps. Before he reached us we heard the low sound of a bell, and a metal flag popped out of the wall right in front of his nose. He pushed the flag back into the wall and said into the door of the cell next to the flag, "I'm coming right away." Then he came over and opened the brown door next to us. I looked at the number above the cell, and went in. The door closed behind me with a light tap.

The cell was fairly large, about 12 square meters, with a high ceiling in a strange shape—neither oblong nor round. The window opposite the door was covered by a Venetian blind and an electric light was burning. By the wall stood a cot of hollow metal pipes with steel strips welded down and across. A night table. Chair. Sink. Bedpan. Everything was bolted down. Nothing could be moved.

Well, I would have to adjust to living here at my new address: Leningrad, the Big House, Cell No. 195. There was nothing I could do about it. I had to remain silent. We had rehearsed and agreed on that during that now long-ago "interrogation" of Grisha Vertlib. I would be silent. In three days, the sanction of the investigations department would end. If there was no proof, he would have to release me.

I went over to the cot, turned and went back to where I had started. It was uncomfortable to walk because of my sandals. I would ask for some kind of string. I went to the door and knocked, and the door of the food trap opened.

"You don't knock here. To call the guard, you have to press the button to the right of the door."

I pressed the button and heard the low sound of the bell and the click of the flag going up. The guard returned the flag to its starting position.

"What do you want?"

"My sandals are falling off, and it is uncomfortable to walk. Could you get me some kind of string?"

"Wait."

In a few minutes the food slot opened and the warden's hand offered me two scraps of cloth, apparently from a floor mop. Even the most motivated and ingenious *zek* could not have hanged himself with those scraps.

I used one of them to tie one of the sandals and tried it out. Not bad. I attached the second to the other sandal. Then it was possible to walk.

I took off the sandals and lay down on the cot. I covered myself with my mother's quilted jacket.

An ordinary summer day, June 15, 1970, came to an end: the first day of a long detour on my road to Jerusalem.

PART 2

A Time to Be Silent and A Time to Speak

CHAPTER SEVENTEEN

I Refuse to Answer

The trap in the cell door opened. The guard said, "Bedtime. Go to sleep." A few seconds later I heard the same words again, but less clearly, and then the sound of the trap snapping shut in the door of the next cell. As the guard went down the hall, I heard the sound of each trap as it opened and shut. And then there was silence. It's a shame, I thought, that I didn't think to count the traps as they shut.

I don't remember if I slept during the night of June 15, 1970, my first night in the Big House. Probably not. I lay on the metal cot trying to analyze my situation, but I couldn't think clearly. Then I realized that I was fantasizing, that I had fallen into a semi-delirium.

When the trap opened in the morning and the guard called "Get up," I couldn't imagine where I was or how I had gotten there. A bowl of cereal was pushed through; I ate a few spoonfuls, without any appetite. No sooner had I returned the bowl to the first guard than another guard opened the trap and asked softly, "Name?"

"Butman."

"Prepare to leave."

What does he mean, "prepare"? Psychologically I was ready. I knew I would remain silent. What else could he mean? Why was he warning me? Eventually I would learn that "prepare" meant "use the toilet while you have a chance."

Now the cell door clanged open.

"Hands behind your back. Come out."

Long corridors. Descents and ascents. Finally we came to

a door. The guard ordered me to stand several steps away, facing the wall. He knocked. Great care was taken so that I would not accidentally meet any of my friends in the corridor or in the interrogator's office, to keep us from communicating with each other in Hebrew, "*Sheket* (be silent)."

The guard was given permission to enter and led me into the room—the same one in which I had been interrogated on the previous day. Major Kislykh signed a form acknowledging that I had been given into his custody, and the guard left.

The room was full of people, some in uniform, some in civilian clothes. They all looked at me sternly but with curiosity. At a desk across from Kislykh sat a pretty woman in a tunic and short skirt. Later I learned that she was Inessa Katukova, a supervising prosecutor and the niece of a famous army marshal. I didn't recognize anyone in the room but Kislykh.

"Hello, sit down," he said. "How did you sleep?"

I sat on the stool bolted to the floor near the door. The barrage of questions was about to begin, but I resolved to remain silent.

The time seemed to drag endlessly. With an effort I was able to withdraw into myself so that I did not hear their words, only the intonation as first one and then another person spoke, questioning, reciting, commanding. Their voices came to me as if through fog, diffused, indistinct.

I became conscious again of my surroundings when someone came up and thrust a newspaper into my hand. It was, I saw, *Vecherny Leningrad* for June 15, 1970. My glance was drawn immediately to the headline "Current Events." Such headlines rarely appear in a Soviet paper and almost always are used to introduce sensational stories. Below the headline were just a few lines of type:

On June 15 at the Smolny airport a group of criminals who tried to hijack an airplane was detained. An
investigation is being conducted.

I could feel the stares of all the others in the room as
they watched to see what my reaction would be. Perhaps, I
thought, there was a KGB psychologist in the group who
would decide, on the basis of my response to what I was
reading, what tactic would be used against me, the carrot or
the stick.

My whole body was on fire. I looked at my fingers and
was surprised to see that they were not trembling. Who, I
wondered, had been "detained"? Was I connected with
them in any way? Could it really have been Mark and the
Riga group? No, I thought, I had seen Mark two weeks earlier and he had said that they were stymied. And everyone,
including the people in Riga, knew about the categorical
"no" from Israel. Mark had said he wanted an official invitation from Israel. No, I decided, it was not Mark who had
been detained. And no one could have done it without him.
So why was I sitting in the Big House?

Katukova spoke first:

"Butman, you are the locomotive in this trial. Your com-
panions are the railroad cars. Your punishment will be the
most severe because your guilt is the greatest. But your
punishment will be determined not only by your guilt, but
also by your conduct during the investigation. Your prison
term may be long or it may be short. And the prison terms
of your friends will depend on yours. If you won't think
about your family, at least think about your friends."

When she finished, Kislykh stood up.

"Hilya Izraylevich, this is a particularly dangerous crime
and your role in it is serious. You understand from Inessa
Katukova's words that you are the chief defendant in the
case. In accordance with Article 64-A of the Criminal Code

you are accused of treason. The maximum sentence for treason is capital punishment."

Kislykh paused a moment, so that I could digest his words, and then he continued:

"Have you heard about the Filimonchik case? No? It took place last year, here, near Leningrad. There were three of them, including a woman, and they, too, wanted to hijack a plane. In that case Filimonchik was the instigator. He is no longer among the living." With that Kislykh threw a pen down onto the table, emphasizing the finality of his words— the end of Filimonchik's life. Again I was aware that everyone in the room was staring at me. Perhaps the blood had drained out of my face. After all, what Kislykh had said was terrifying. In a subdued voice I asked for permission to write down my statement:

> Having familiarized myself with the "Current Events" item in *Vecherny Leningrad*, I declare that I know nothing about the attempt to hijack a passenger plane in the Smolny airport on June 15. And I know nothing about the participants. I refuse to answer any questions as a sign of protest against my illegal arrest and demand my immediate release.

When I had finished writing, Katukova read my statement.

"Well, that's a shame," she said. Someone handed her another piece of paper and, without bothering to read the contents she signed it. Then Kislykh called the guards and I was taken back to the cell.

A bowl of soup, covered so that it would not get cold, had already been placed on the small table. Next to it was an aluminum spoon and some bread. Stirring the soup with the spoon, I saw that it was thick and full of cooked fish. But I had no appetite. A terrible inner tension demanded release. I covered the soup and began to pace around the cell.

Why, I wondered, had Mark and Edik not warned me, if they had indeed decided to try the hijacking? Now the authorities would go after the entire organization. Had my Aunt Sonya understood my parting words when I was arrested? Had she and Mama been able to warn Solomon? If he and the others had learned about my arrest, they would have gotten rid of everything that was not "kosher." Had they been able to do that? And why was I arrested? Apparently someone from that group at Smolny knew me and had already begun to give testimony. Well, the hell with them! After all, I really did not know anything. Sooner or later it would get straightened out. The days of Stalin were over.

For quite a while I paced around the small cell, struggling with conflicting feelings—annoyance at those for whose sake I had been arrested, and satisfaction that apparently someone had tried to carry out the plan that for so long had been my project. I had, in fact, never considered the hijacking to be a worthless idea, had abandoned it only in deference to the compromise agreed to by the Organization.

When the reply came from Israel, I had been relieved— not because the answer was "no," but because it ended the exhausting doubts, internal struggles, and unbearable tension. It also put an end to my isolation from the Committee. I experienced not disappointment but sorrow that we had, perhaps, relinquished our only chance to get *aliyah* moving. And now, along with irritation, I felt sympathy for those unknown people who had been at the Smolny airport.

The trap opened before I had managed to think through the unthinkable.

"You're not going to eat? Hand over the dishes and prepare to leave."

And a moment later, seeing that I was not "preparing," the guard opened the door.

"Hands behind your back. Come."

As we walked through the corridors, the guard rattled his key chain, to let other guards know that we were coming and to avoid an unintended meeting with another prisoner.

CHAPTER EIGHTEEN

Interrogation

June 18. Day three in my new quarters. I had already become a regular *zek*. Sometimes I could even predict what was about to happen and prepare myself.

My refusal to testify did not stop the questioning. All day, from morning to bedtime, with just a break for dinner, the interrogation continued—question, answer, question, answer, question, answer. My response each time was the same: "I refuse to answer the question." And each time Kislykh recorded it.

Most of the time Kislykh and I were alone and I sensed that, for a while at least, the main attack was not directed at me. All the people who had filled the room on the second day were no longer around. They had gone someplace else, to an interrogation where a psychologically sensitive spot had been detected, where there was a chance for a breakthrough, where there was a weak link. The relative quiet in my room meant a desperate struggle in a neighboring one.

Sometimes Karaskov, one of Kislykh's superiors, dropped in to the office, sat down at the second desk, and, pretending that he was listening carefully, tried to doze a little. In those days he, too, was not sleeping nights: he had a lot of work to do.

Once, emerging from his half-sleep because of Kislykh's loud voice, Karaskov decided to take part in the interrogation. Perhaps he deluded himself with the thought that he, Karaskov, would succeed where Kislykh failed.

"Listen, Butman, here you are a Zionist, but I'm sure that

you didn't read everything written by your leader—Herzl's his name, if I'm not mistaken." He flashed his knowledge, looking at Kislykh victoriously. "Tell me, do you know that even Herzl toward the end of his life reevaluated his attitude toward socialism and the Soviet regime and even welcomed the great October Revolution?"

Insofar as this was a question about the spirit rather than the substance of the case, I decided that here I had the right to deviate from my refusal to answer all questions.

"Tell me, when did he say that? Somehow I really don't remember such statements by Herzl."

Hearing my response, Karaskov immediately hastened to add:

"Yes, yes, he said it, you can believe me, only I don't remember exactly what year, sometime right after the great October Revolution."

"That seems a little strange to me," I began in a serious voice, but with a shade of doubt. "In order to express this thought Herzl would have had to rise from the grave. He died in 1904."

Kislykh's cheeks puffed up from the chortle that he had difficulty suppressing. A joyful spark glinted in his eyes, but he knew better than to show such disrespect in front of his superior: a mere smile would cost him dearly.

The embarrassed Karaskov in the meantime was seeking a way out of the blunder that he had committed out of ignorance.

"Guess you cannot believe the western press. I got this information from the newspaper Daily. . .Daily. . .Daily." I remained silent. Karaskov looked with a pleading glance at Kislykh, but the latter was also silent.

For the next five minutes Karaskov sat as if on burning coals, and then suddenly left the room. Kislykh was finally able to allow himself a light laugh.

"Well, what do you want, Hilya Izraylevich? Of course, in this matter you were, so to speak, the hot-shot expert with better qualifications than prosecutor Karaskov."

In dealing with me, Kislykh avoided direct lies. Even when he spoke to me on the second day about the death of Filimonchik, what he said was not a brazen lie. Filimonchik had, in fact, died. But he had not been shot at the order of the court, as Kislykh's words of warning had implied. Filimonchik was seriously wounded when he was arrested, and he died in the hospital soon afterwards.

So Kislykh had not lied. But he used that trick well. I tried, after that, not to think that they could shoot me. But Kislykh's words made me aware of that possibility. They disturbed my subconscious and influenced the decisions I made.

My third day at the Big House was coming to an end. They could keep me in prison for only three days without the approval of the prosecutor. If they were going to release me, they would do it today.

I felt my isolation acutely and wished that I could exchange even a few words with any one of my friends, to find out how the others were conducting themselves. How had they evaluated the situation? How had they chosen to behave? Were they remaining silent?

Apprehensive, tired, even clumsy, I accidentally knocked over the empty supper bowl. It was made out of some heavy metal alloy. I saw that on the bottom the Russian alphabet was engraved, with the same number of letters on each line.

The sight of those letters reminded me of a system of tapping messages from one cell to the next. I ran to the wall of the cell and managed to tap out a few letters before the trap opened and the guard warned me that I had better stop.

Later I learned that the other fellows had also tried to break the isolation and somehow communicate. Lev Yagman had tried to use a mug. First he knocked lightly on the wall, to attract attention. Then he pressed the mug tightly against the wall, grasping it on both sides with his palms to extend the length of the "pipe" he was creating, and pressing his mouth against his hands. Through that improvised pipe he sent his first words:

"Allo! *Shalom!* Who's there?"

In answer, Lev heard a knock. Quickly he turned over the mug, transforming his portable transmitter into a receiver. Muffled sounds came from the wall, then something like words, but he couldn't understand them. It was clear, though, that even through the thick walls of the Big House it was possible to speak with the help of no more than a mug.

Lev could hardly control his excitement. He turned the mug over again and began to scream into it. Then he turned it over again and rapped on the wall. And again he heard some indistinct speech. Then, suddenly, what he heard improved sharply. Lev turned the mug again and began a joyful conversation. A few moments passed before he realized that even though the mug was in the transmitting position, he could clearly hear someone speaking to him. Slowly he removed the mug from the wall and looked around the cell. And then he understood why he had been able to hear the other half of the conversation so clearly—the trap was open and the guard's head protruded into the cell.

"Yagman, I've been talking to you for some time now. If this happens again, you'll be sent to the punishment cell."

In the nine years between 1970 and 1979 I passed through dozens of prisons. Nowhere did I see a system for isolating prisoners from each other that was so well thought-out, or guards with such iron discipline as at the Big House in Leningrad. During the investigation no two of us ever sat in the same cell. Nor were we ever put in adjacent cells—that eliminated any opportunity for communication by tapping. And we could not have exchanged written notes: we were forbidden to have pens or pencils, and constant searches made it impossible to hide anything.

Each time I was summoned to an interrogation, the guards went through the same ritual. The trap would open, and a guard would point a finger at one of the prisoners in the cell. The guard would ask, almost whispering: "Name?" If he had pointed at the wrong man the first time, he would point at another prisoner.

At first I thought this procedure was an example of bureaucratic stupidity, but before long I realized that this was just one element in a carefully devised system. The guard never spoke the name of the prisoner who was to be taken from the cell. So even if a guard had opened the trap of the wrong cell, he would not reveal to any of the prisoners the name of the man he was seeking—and so the prisoners' sense of isolation was preserved.

At the Big House we had absolutely no contact with administrative staff. We did not see or hear anyone except our cell mates, the guards who led us to and from our cells, and our interrogators. As the guards led us through the corridors, they clicked their tongues, snapped their fingers, or rattled their keys to warn other guards that we were approaching. Before each turn in the corridor they held us back until they had peered around the corner to be sure the next hall was clear. Before we started down a staircase the guard would stop and make noises until, from somewhere far away, another guard called up: "Go ahead."

The guards were responsible for maintaining the system of isolation at all times. And it worked without fail.

For three days I had not read a newspaper or heard the radio. For three days I had had no idea of what was going on in the Middle East.

In an attempt to break this isolation, I tried to trick the guard. I asked him for toilet paper and, as I had hoped, he brought me some newspaper that had been cut into small pieces. I put the dozens of pieces on the cot and, matching them by their shape and by content, slowly put together the jigsaw puzzle of that newspaper article. It was a boring piece about successes in industrial construction, and not even recent. Ordinarily I would have done no more than glance at the headline. Now I read the whole article.

And then the trap door opened.

"Get ready, with your things. Take your mattress and pillow with you."

Where was I going? The third day was almost over. Was I to go home? When I got out into the corridor, the guard opened the door of the adjacent cell, number 196. I was not going home. Then I knew what Katukova had signed. I was no longer a suspect: I had become a defendant. The only way I would get out of the Big House would be by transport to another prison. In the USSR, political prisoners are never acquitted.

I entered the new cell 196 and saw that my solitude had ended. A sympathetic-looking fellow in a sports outfit and a fashionable haircut sat on one of the cots with his legs folded under him. Volodya Veselov, my first cell mate.

Until bedtime I listened to Volodya's story. Volodya was a crane operator at the Leningrad docks and, like me, he was under investigation. He was accused of currency operations with foreigners. The KGB was conducting his investigation, and so he was in the Big House, not in the criminal prison, Kresty. This was not Volodya's first arrest, and he was afraid that he would end up in the striped uniform of a dangerous recidivist.

Later I would hear many more such tales. I didn't talk about myself to others, but I always listened with curiosity.

The next evening I returned to the cell from the interrogation and immediately began to pace around the small room, trying to dissipate the terrible tension I felt.

"Relax, Hilya, don't get upset. The questioning will go on. You'll get used to it. Tell me, have you read *Secrets of the Parisian Monastery?*"

"No."

"What a book! About the nuns, and the kinds of games they played. Translated from the French. An old book, apparently. It got torn to pieces—several guys must have tried to read it at the same time. I somehow got hold of a piece, very sexy . . ."

Volodya wasn't a bad fellow. But I had gotten it into my head that my first cell mate would be a stool pigeon, and that made it difficult for us to be friends.

A few days later the cell door was opened and a prisoner entered. A tall, strong man of about fifty-five. His head had been shaved and he wore a *zek's* uniform—he had come from a camp. He threw his mattress and pillow on the cot and turned to introduce himself, shaking my hand firmly.

"Izrail Natanovich."

What joy! A Jew! Well, now we'll live. Life is full of surprises!

A week later they took Volodya Veselov away and

moved Izrail Natanovich and me up to a cell off the gallery. When the door closed after us, we looked joyfully at each other. It is no accident that a popular Israeli song tells of how good and pleasant it is for brothers to "sit together"— in Russian "to sit" also means to serve a jail term.

CHAPTER NINETEEN

The Pressure to Testify

The third week of uninterrupted interrogations had ended. I was still giving the same answer to each question: "I refuse to testify." But more and more often I asked myself, how long can this go on?

It was only at the end of those three weeks that I understood the price I was paying, in nervous tension, for my silence. Only then was it clear why the investigator had spent long days interrogating me, even though he knew that my answer would not change.

He needed me to hear the questions, for the questions conveyed information even if my answers did not. Each question started with an assertion:

"Suspect M.D., at an interrogation on [date], testified that . . . What can you say about his testimony?"

"I refuse to testify."

"At the interrogation on [date], suspect S.D. testified that . . . What can you say about this testimony?"

"I refuse to testify."

Kislykh wrote it all down meticulously. I signed it. Then he put his pen aside.

A little break. A "free conversation" began.

"Hilya Izraylevich, I'm not surprised by your behavior. We have talked with your friends, and we know about your stubbornness. You know that your former classmates at the law school, Groshev and Konokotov, work for the KGB. We asked them about you. Hilya Izraylevich, you are digging yourself a deep pit. I have told you many times that the severity of your punishment will be determined not just by your actions but first and foremost by your attitude about what you did—by the sincerity and the depth of your repentance."

"Have you heard about the case of Nikolay Braun? I conducted that case, just before yours began. The main defendant was the son of the famous poet Braun and the poetess Komissarova. Nikolay Braun fell under bad influences and formed an anti-Soviet organization. It included Jews, even though it was an organization with a fascist and anti-Semitic bias. During shooting practice they used a photograph of a Jew as a target. There was a lot of filth in Braun's group, including drug addiction and homosexuality."

"I don't want to compare you with them—I have no doubts about your personal decency. Anyone can make a mistake. But you must understand your mistakes in time and repent. In Braun's group, not everyone reached the same conclusions. And the results were sad for some of them. One member of the group, whose actions had been serious but who sincerely repented, was given a sentence of only four years. Another, whose deeds were less reprehensible but who did not repent, was given seven years, plus exile."

"Hilya Izraylevich, you're not a stupid man. Reach the correct conclusions before it is too late. Think about your wife and daughter—I know that you care about their fate."

At this point the "free conversation" was over and Kislykh returned to the desk. He began to record the next question. Occasionally, other investigators dropped into the office and talked for a few moments with Kislykh. As they left, each one looked at me, as if looking at an incorrigible fool.

In my opinion, Major Kislykh was one of the best, if not the best, investigator in the Leningrad KGB at that time. It seemed to me that he was personally decent, but was used as a tool by the KGB to wreck my life. Even today, I don't hate him.

Some of the KGB investigators in Leningrad were jaded cynics who believed in neither God nor the devil. They were prepared to serve whomever offered the best deal. In my opinion, Kislykh served not out of fear but because of his conscience. He believed in the justice of the Soviet order. He believed that the men he investigated were enemies of that order, and that all means could be justified in serving the ends of the Socialist regime.

Another investigator entered the room carrying a thick pile of papers—the transcript of someone's interrogation. He bent over to speak to Kislykh, holding the papers behind his back. I could see the top piece of paper, the fact sheet about the person being interrogated. The investigator shielded me from Kislykh, so I was able to move a bit, trying to read what was on that sheet. But it was too far away, and the name was a long one. I could see that it ended in "i"— was it an Italian name? Then I saw that the name ended in "shvili"—that is how Georgian names end. How could that be? There was not one Georgian Jew in our Organization. But what about Kozhiashvili—the one I spoke to in Moscow's Victory Park, the one who promised to send money? Just before the investigator moved the papers to his other hand I managed to make out the capital letter "K" and what looked like an "o" after it. Yes, Kozhiashvili—there could be no doubt.

When the investigator shifted the papers I could see the transcript from the other side, well enough to see that after each short question there was a long answer. If someone refuses to speak or answers evasively, the questions are longer than the answers. Clearly, Kozhiashvili was talking, telling everything that he knew, and perhaps more. (At the end of the investigation I was permitted to read the colorful tales told by Otary Kozhiashvili, about how I influenced him to "betray the Socialist motherland" and how he courageously resisted.)

Finally the investigator left, taking his transcript with him. And I wondered—had his "carelessness" in letting me see those pages been accidental? Or was it part of a carefully thought-out scheme of psychological pressure? Perhaps it had been meticulously planned and rehearsed at a strategy session to trouble me with the thought that my silence served no purpose.

When they took me back to my cell I paced around the room, trying to unwind and to analyze my situation. The first week of July had passed. They had been forcing the members of the Committee to talk, one after another. And the "plane people," too. The questioners had long since stopped reading to me the testimony of "suspects." Now they were reading the testimony of "defendants." It became clear to me that all the members of the Committee had been arrested—and also Mark Dymshitz, Edik Kuznetsov, Silva Zalmanson, and many others. Only Misha Korenblit had not, so far, been identified as either a suspect or a defendant.

At first I thought that there must be some mistake, but later I found out that the KGB had chosen a terrible tactic to use against Misha—they *did not* arrest him. Instead, every morning a car bringing a KGB investigator drove up to the clinic where Misha worked, and an exhausting cross-examination was carried on, without any protocols. Later these interrogations were transferred to the Big House. When that began, Misha left home each morning as if he was going to work. Each day he hoped that he would not return, that he would finally be taken into custody, along with the rest of us. So each day he took a small suitcase with a toothbrush, a change of underwear, and went to the Big House for an interrogation. And each day they sent him home. Every evening as he descended the stairway of the Big House heading for the exit, he was terrified that he would meet our wives, that he would have to pass them and see in their eyes the unspoken question: "Why are you walking free while our men are sitting in jail?"

Day after day Misha went through that torture. Why don't they arrest me, he thought. How am I worse than the others? You see how I come with a suitcase to your interrogations. Arrest me, please!

They did, finally. But not until they had him put through four months of torture, not until the end of the investigation, on October 17, 1970. That may have been the happiest day of his life.

CHAPTER TWENTY

An Old Camp Wolf

I walked and walked. Four paces to the door, four to the window. During those weeks I came to understand why the guards watched carefully, to be sure that there was nothing in a cell that a man could use to stab or hang himself. Thank God I was not alone. After the arrival of Izrail Natanovich I had the companionship of another Jewish soul.

Izrail Natanovich was born in a suburb of Kiev, grew up believing in the "glorious new order," married and had a son. When the Germans attacked in 1939, he was mobilized and served in the tank corps. His unit retreated to Stalingrad where he was wounded. In the field hospital he met a doctor, a Jewish woman, and they fell in love and were married—he had lost track of his first wife because of the war. At the end of the war he was stationed in Manchuria as a commander of a tank battalion in the war with Japan. When that war was over, he became director of the department of art sales for the artists' organization of the USSR. In his new career, he drank and rubbed shoulders with the lions of the Soviet art world and achieved a reputation as a connoisseur of painting and sculpture.

Such good luck was soon followed by misfortune. Izrail Natanovich was arrested and charged with violation of ten articles of the criminal code of the RSFSR (Russian Soviet Federated Socialist Republic). The crimes for which he was convicted included embezzlement of state property and he was serving his sentence in a camp in central Russia. When I met him in Leningrad, he said that he had been brought from the camp to the Big House to serve as an expert witness in a trial that involved fine art.

Izrail Natanovich also liked to "run" around the room. But as soon as I returned from an interrogation, he would yield the right-of-way to me. When I had let off some steam, he would seat me at the table where he had prepared a meal for us. From the very beginning we shared our food—we put everything we both had together and divided it equally.

When Izrail Natanovich first came to the Big House, I had not yet received any packages. On the second day that Izrail Natanovich was my cell mate, at his request some of the provisions he had brought with him from the camp were delivered to our cell. We were not permitted to have anything made of glass or tin in the room. So the guard unpacked everything and transferred the food to plastic containers. As I watched, I was amazed to see boxes and cans on which the labels were printed in French, English and Italian, canned meat and fish—including my favorite, sprats—and butter, cheeses, canned pineapple, plums.

Izrail had already told me that one of his four sons had married an Italian Jewess who had kept her Italian citizenship and occasionally traveled to Italy. And this son and daughter-in-law did not lack for the foreign currency certificates needed to shop at Moscow's special Beryozka store. Izrail Natanovich explained that one of his sons bribed someone on the outside and that he—Izrail—used his old connections to pressure the political director of the camp from the inside. And so it was that he got a suitcase full of provisions from Beryozka to take with him when he was transferred to the Big House in Leningrad. That was the food he shared with me during those weeks of interrogations.

I did not tell Izrail Natanovich about the facts of my case—not because I did not trust him, but because I did not tell anyone. I preferred to listen. I sat for hours as he told tales about the desperate situations he had been through during the war. Gradually he came to his camp experiences and he, the old camp wolf, gave me, the cub, some rather patronizing advice about how to live in a camp.

"I don't want you to be afraid. In my opinion you're not a coward," he began. "But you must know that a camp is a terrible place. Only the strong survive, the ones who know how to take care of themselves. Sometimes you must be merciless toward others, or you won't survive.

"I don't mean that you will die physically. But the man in you will not survive. If you can't manipulate and get yourself into the crew servicing the camp, the camp authorities will transfer you to general work. You'll never be able to meet the standards there, and then your ration will be reduced to that for nonperformers. And of course you won't even get all of that—the cooks gobble up everything that is tasty and nourishing, or they sell it. Do you know how meat is cooked in a camp kitchen?"

"No, how?"

"Each day you are allotted one piece of meat. But you will never taste it or even see it unless you have an arrangement with the cooks. They put the meat they get into cheesecloth and put it in the soup kettle to give the broth some flavor. When the meat is cooked, they remove it from the soup, take it out of the cheesecloth, and eat it or sell it.

"If you don't have some meat or fish in your diet, you will develop a protein deficiency. From that you will get an ulcer, your teeth will begin to fall out, and your whole body will gradually deteriorate. You will be a goner, and nobody cares about a goner. You will become increasingly vulnerable in every way. Thieves will take away your parcels. And, God forbid, you will be abused sexually.

You'll go around in rags, work like a slave, and sleep opposite the latrine.

"If you don't guard your health from the very beginning, you'll come out a useless invalid—not a breadwinner, but a burden to your family. If you don't think about yourself, no one will. The problems caused by the years added to your sentence because of your foolish behavior during the investigation will be compounded.

"Yes, your behavior is foolish. You tell me yourself that your friends have already begun to testify. Each one of them is thinking about himself. Stop being noble and think about yourself. I'll teach you, dear Hillel, how to live. Only fools learn from their own mistakes. The smart ones learn from the mistakes of others.

"Listen to me, an old Jew, and believe me. I want only what's good for you. When you arrive at camp, try right away to get on the council of the collective—it is the social organization of the camp. Become chairman of a section— for example, cultural-educational activities. Then you can put out a paper on socialist competition, you can write any kind of nonsense, because no one will read it. You will be the political director's right hand—he'll arrange easy work for you on the service staff, you'll be allowed to spend more money at the camp store, you'll be allowed to receive packages and printed material, sometimes more than the rules permit. Sycophants will gather around and do your bidding. When you leave the camp you will be healthy, and you will soon forget the whole nightmare. And when they start letting people emigrate to Israel, we shall meet there, my son," he added in a half-whisper. "My Boris will go first, he's a nationalist, just like you."

"But what other sections are there in the council of the collective?" I asked, sensing that the price Izrail Natanovich was describing for preserving my health might be too high.

"If you don't want the cultural-educational section, then take physical education. There all you'll do is make up lists of all kinds of competitions and register participants for rounds of checkers or chess."

Well, that's a horse of different color, I thought. But even so, that conversation with Izrail Natanovich left me with an unpleasant aftertaste.

CHAPTER TWENTY-ONE

A Step Backward

I walked and walked. Four paces to the door, four to the window. I had so little time in which to think, and so much to decide. I was playing not only with my own fate but with Eva's and Lileshka's as well. If I didn't think about them, who would? And who would think about me?

From the "questions" that Kislykh had asked me, it was clear that the KGB knew about the hijacking plans. Somehow they had even found out about Kozhiashvili—a man with whom I had had only one conversation—and had dragged him from Tbilsi to answer their questions. But it seemed that they were unaware that after the answer came from Israel, I and the fellows from Kishinev and Leningrad abandoned Operation Wedding. And they did not seem to know anything about my last conversation with Mark Dymshitz.

It was not clear to me whether the KGB understood the structure of our Organization, whether they knew who was a member and who was not, whether they knew who was on our Committee, or anything about the relationship—and the lack of relationship—between the people arrested at Smolny and the rest of the people taken into custody on June 15. Also, it was not clear how much they knew about the involvement of any one individual in the plans for the hijacking, in the almost-attempted hijacking, in the Organization or in the Committee.

Perhaps even more important was that I did not know where the KGB had gotten the various pieces of information that were conveyed to me in Kislykh's questions. The source of a piece of information was almost as important as its content. If information had been obtained in a way that made it inadmissible in court, then the KGB sought to get the individual being interrogated to state, admit to, confess the accuracy of that information—because what the individual said during interrogation *was* admissible in court. So, as I listened to Kislykh's questions, I might decide that the KGB already knew something and then I would corroborate it, only to learn later that mine was the first admissible testimony and that I had, with that testimony, increased the punishment of a friend.

But there was also the possibility that information conveyed in a question had been provided by another individual in an earlier interrogation. So, I might deny something I thought they had obtained from an inadmissible source, only to learn later that it had come from someone else's testimony—and that I had thereby increased my own punishment.

I was being interrogated as a prime defendant in what had happened at the Smolny airport on June 15, even though I was not there and knew nothing about what took place. Perhaps, I thought, someone had dumped the whole burden on me and I would have to carry it for a long time. And that would mean that Eva and Lileshka would have to bear the consequences as well. Who would think about them if I didn't?

Only I knew the whole story from my point of view. Only I could explain the nature and extent of my involvement. Only I could explain my absence from the Smolny airport on June 15. But we had decided that we would remain silent. If I started to talk about the plane, it would be difficult to stop. Each night I lay on the iron cot tormented by my thoughts, trying to untangle the questions Kislykh had asked from the questions in my mind, trying to determine, somehow, the wisest thing to do.

Finally I asked Kislykh to give me paper and pen and send me back to my cell so that I could write my testimony about the plane, and only about the plane. Kislykh understood immediately that his complex strategy had been successful. With ill-concealed pleasure he gave me a dozen sheets of blank paper and ordered that I be given a pen and taken back to the cell. As I was leaving he said, "You will see, Hilya Izraylevich—as soon as you start to give testimony, you will feel better."

When I got back to the cell, I sat on the cot and tried to concentrate. It seemed to me, from the carefully worded questions I had been asked, that the KGB knew a great deal. The main question that faced me, it seemed, was whether to tell them about the people with whom I had spoken about the escape plan. If those names were known and I concealed them, then the KGB would start to introduce evidence to catch me and gradually lead me to a confession. Then, in their eyes and in my own, I would be an irresponsible, pitiful, cunning and cowardly man, someone they had trapped and put in his place.

Because I could not foresee what anyone else would say or how anyone else would act, I was at a great disadvantage. Who, for example, would have thought that the KGB would seek out Kozhiashvili and bring him from the Caucasus? Or that he would give such elaborate testimony?

The most intelligent tactic, I decided, would be to name those who were known by someone besides me to have participated in Operation Wedding, and to convey the idea that all of those to whom I spoke about the general possibility of escape to Israel—except for the ones who had participated actively in preparations for the "wedding"— had categorically rejected the idea of a hijacking. In that way I could avoid putting my burden of responsibility on others and could present matters in such a way that the people I did name could not be made liable even for non-informing. The latter was particularly important because noninforming always refers to some concretely dangerous crime, not to an abstract idea. It was repugnant to me to mention any names. But since I had decided to give testimony about Operation Wedding, I had to say something.

Also I did not want to drag Israel into our case, because I did not want to give the KGB a pretext for raising a hue and cry about ties with Israel and alleging that we had acted under the control of and at the instructions of the Israeli secret service. In fact, our early attempts to make contact with Israel had failed. When we sent an inquiry about Operation Wedding, the answer we received from Israel was a categorical "no." The KGB could use the mere fact of a reply—even a reply that restrained us—for their propaganda.

And so, in my written testimony, I balanced on the border between half-truth and lies. I wrote that we had wanted, as quickly and painlessly as possible, to turn all potential participants away from Operation Wedding. And so we had spread the rumor among them "as if" we had asked Israel, and that after some time had passed we informed them "as if" we had received an answer from Israel—the categorical "no."

The next morning Kislykh read my handwritten testimony carefully. Then he looked up and said, sharply:

"All of your 'as ifs' will cost you dearly. Moreover, you have not written anything about the three medicines."

Besides the messenger to Israel and the people to whom he had spoken there, only two of us had known about the three medicines—Vladik Mogilever knew and I knew. That meant . . .

Kislykh's trick worked. With those two words—"three medicines"—he convinced me that Vladik Mogilever had, during an interrogation, told the KGB about the "three medicines," the three facets of our question to Israel, and of the response we received.

I was, then, still a green *zek*. What seemed to me to be a leak in the form of testimony from Vladik might have been something very different—to this day, I don't know. Eventually I learned that that particular trick of interrogation was called "aiming the cannon." Later, when I had begun to give testimony, there was discussion of the shovel and the meat tenderizer that Lev Korenblit and I bought to use as possible weapons of intimidation. When I declared that these had been acquired at the Gostiny Dvor Department Store, I added to the list the toasting fork that Lev Korenblit had given me to be used for the same purpose. Kislykh interrupted me immediately:

"Tell us exactly how this toasting fork wound up in your hands."

I decided that there was no sense in hiding what, apparently, they already knew from Lev Korenblit, and so I told the truth—that when we had gone back to his place after buying the shovel and the tenderizer, Korenblit had given me the toasting fork to add to our "arsenal" of weapons of intimidation. After the investigation, when I was permitted to read the testimony of others, I realized that I had been tricked into being the first one to corroborate this piece of information, and that in so doing I had seriously undermined the testimony of my friend.

This strategy of "aiming the cannon" is very effective because it strikes at the rational sense of the person being interrogated. He is likely to think, "What use is there in hiding what had been a secret between two people if the other person has already revealed it?" The defendant does not know that the other person has not revealed the secret to the KGB, that the KGB in fact got the information from a completely different source. Information gathered by illegal means cannot, by law, be used as proof in court until it has been corroborated by the official testimony of one of the defendants.

Kislykh worded his questions and accusations very cleverly. I was under pressure to respond, isolated from my friends and concerned about myself and my family. Too late I realized that the KGB could have learned about the three medicines by eavesdropping on the telephone conversation between Sasha Blank in Israel and Vladik Mogilever in Leningrad on May 25. Or they could have gotten it from a stool pigeon, a cellmate, or in some other way.

While one individual was being interrogated, it was not unusual for an investigator who was conducting another, related interrogation in a nearby office to drop in and relate, loud enough for all to hear, what had just been "learned." This created the impression that others who were being interrogated had responded freely. And it had the effect of increasing one's vulnerability to "cannon fire" questions.

According to law, the investigator is obliged to first write in the protocol the question that was asked of the person under interrogation, and then to read the question aloud. But "cannon" questions are delivered orally and do not appear in the protocol.

A similar strategy was used by the KGB when they tried to get Eva to talk. For several months she had refused to give any testimony. Then she was told:

"Your husband, the accused Butman, Hilya Izraylevich, at an interrogation indicated that he informed you about the plan to hijack a Soviet passenger plane. Why do you refuse to confirm your husband's words?"

I found this lie recorded in the protocol. When I protested to Kislykh, he explained:

"Your wife was interrogated by a young, inexperienced

investigator who was sent from the Lithuanian Republic to provide us with temporary help. Since the Party's condemnation of certain defective methods of investigation from the period of the cult of personality, the Leningrad Department of the Committee of State Security has not used such methods."

Indeed, after our arrest the KGB brought in dozens of investigators from all over Russia. None of them had the experience of Kislykh and the other Leningrad investigators. The provincials worked like clumsy bears. The methods of their Leningrad colleagues were more refined.

CHAPTER TWENTY-TWO

A Time to Be Silent
and A Time to Speak

At the end of the written testimony that I prepared for Kislykh about the hijacking, I made a declaration. It was a statement that although I had agreed to tell what I knew about Operation Wedding, I refused to testify about my friends with whom I engaged in Jewish cultural activity, because that activity was not criminal.

When I made that statement, I did not anticipate the effect on my future behavior of having given that first written testimony. Having taken one step backward in the beginning to give testimony only about Operation Wedding, I had to take yet another half-step and start to speak about the Organization. With some shame I write here that after I had made that written statement, it was much easier for Kislykh to convince me to give additional testimony.

From the time of my arrest until the day I asked Kislykh for paper and pen, I had answered all questions during interrogations by saying:

"I refuse to testify."

Then, on the morning of July 16, a week after I had asked for paper and pen, Kislykh started the interrogation by asking:

"Do you know Mogilever, Vladmir; Chernoglaz, David; Dreizner, Solomon; Goldfeld, Anatoly; Korenblit, Lev; Kaminsky, Lassal; and Yagman, Lev?"

To his amazement, I responded:

"Yes, I know them. They are my friends. At various times

they joined me in the Committee of the Organization. We engaged in teaching Hebrew and Jewish history to Jewish youth who had no other way of acquiring this knowledge. Our Organization was not anti-Soviet and never had as its goal the subversion or weakening of the Soviet regime."

A flicker of irritation showed in Kislykh's expression, his response to my last words. But he recorded them accurately and read them back to me. At that moment the important thing for him was that I was finally beginning to talk, and he wanted to encourage me. What I said was less important than that I continue talking.

He put down his pen and came around from behind his desk. I could see that he was bursting to share his triumph with someone, even me.

"We have been waiting for you to start to testify. Everyone starts sooner or later. You worked on the police force, Hilya Izraylevich, and you know about psychology. We have watched you and your . . . co-defendants [he wanted to say friends, but stopped himself] very carefully. We observed you at the time of your arrest, when you were searched, when you entered the cell. We watched to see how each of you reacted to all this. After all, fear can be seen in the eyes. And then we knew how each of you would act during the investigation.

"Well, never mind. Now it will be a lot easier for you. I have already spoken to you about that. You are lucky," he said, smiling as he returned to his desk.

"For quite a while we were undecided about which trial to put you in—the trial of the airplane group, or the trial of the Committee. Now we have decided to put you in the Committee trial. You realize, Hilya Izraylevich, that if you had been put on the first bench in the hijacking case, your lot would not be an enviable one."

I sat on the bolted stool near the door and watched as Kislykh took up his pen again. And I thought, No, dear citizen investigator, you did not put me in the trial of the Committee because you are kind and humane and took into consideration that on June 15 I was not at the Smolny airport. You put me in the Committee trial so that through me you could drag the Committee and the Organization into the case of the airplane. Long before you arrested us you decided to use the hijacking as the instrument of reprisal against the entire organized Zionist movement in Russia, so that you could present the Zionists to the world as a band of criminals. Of all the members of the Committee, I was the only advocate of the hijacking. The others were, in the end, opposed to it. And yet you are going to put all of us on the same defendants' bench.

And so I began to give testimony. The tactic of silence, I decided, made sense only when everyone was silent, only if each of us was completely silent. But once any one of us began to speak about any one subject, that inevitably led to another subject, and another. Once we started to talk, the entire KGB apparatus was arrayed against us. They compared my testimony with that of the others, interrogated additional witnesses, searched and counted and cross-examined. For example, during the investigation one member of the Committee said that membership dues were 128 rubles, another that dues were 129 rubles. For several days Kislykh and the other investigators questioned and questioned, until the one-ruble discrepancy had been explained. Such matters were not what was important. Once we had begun to talk, the crucial thing was not to allow ourselves to be sidetracked.

There is a time to be silent and a time to speak. Once I started to speak, I realized the importance of not renouncing our ideals. It was up to us to turn the investigation and trial into a continuation of our struggle against forced assimilation and for free emigration.

It is easy to be honest, noble and courageous when those qualities are not being tested. Of all those tried for participation in the hijacking, only two people refused to testify throughout the investigation. Yura Fedorov began to speak only at the trial. Hillel Shur is the only person I know of who was silent throughout both the investigation and the trial. Hillel was a member of our Organization and the brother of Kreina Shur. All the days of the trial Hillel Shur sat on the defendants' bench, doubled up with pain from a stomach ulcer, pale, weak, but never speaking—not one word.

At the end of the day when I began to testify, I was as usual returned to my cell. Izrail Natanovich was waiting for me, with supper all ready. He knew that I had begun to talk, and he was beaming. We sat down and began to eat. I no longer felt the tension that, even the previous day, had been consuming me.

I felt miserable, but relieved. Kislykh had been right.

CHAPTER TWENTY-THREE

Optimism Eases the Way

The tension was gone. No longer did I have to face each day with the cursed choice—to be silent or to speak. Now the important decisions were about how to answer each question.

I hate lies. I also hated appearing to be a scared Jew trying to escape from the brave Russians who were determined to teach me a lesson. It was clear to me that we had to wage our struggle not in the area of facts, but rather in the area of interpretation. Thus, I believed that it was important for me not to get entangled in questions about how many copies of *Exodus* the group had had, or about who distributed them or who received them. It *was* important to give an objective account of the book as the courageous struggle of the Jewish people for their independence, and to point out that the USSR recognized Israel immediately after its proclamation of statehood.

I did not see any sense in concealing the statutes and program of the Organization. Those were known to dozens of its members. It was important to stress that we were struggling for free emigration, to which we were entitled under the United Nations Declaration of Human Rights. Emigration was not forbidden by domestic legislation but, in practice, it was not permitted. Should I try to conceal the ulpans? It was important to emphasize the striving of Jewish youth to know their language and history.

Was it necessary for me to present the plan for Operation Wedding as an irrational activity that I deeply regretted? No, quite the contrary; it was necessary for me to say honestly that I thought of it as a desperate means of attracting the attention of the entire world, and especially of the USSR, to the question of the free emigration of Jews from the Soviet Union.

I was sure that summaries of our investigations were being sent to Moscow, to be analyzed and reported at the highest bureaucratic level. I felt that the Soviet government was on the threshold of making important political decisions—decisions that could be influenced by our responses to questions during the interrogations, and by whatever commotion was being raised in the West in response to our arrests. The goal of Operation Wedding had not yet been achieved, but it had not been abandoned by like-minded people who were demanding, *Let my people go.*

The constant dilemma of whether or not to remain silent had generated in me a tension that had obscured my awareness of all aspects of my environment. Now that the tension had dissipated, I was able to look around and see more clearly where I was and who was with me. I realized that the situation was not as awful as it had seemed when I was first brought to the Big House.

First, Kislykh had long since ceased suggesting that I might be shot. And he had indicated that I was better off for having been placed in the trial of the Committee, instead of in the trial of the airplane people. There was, of course, still the possibility that I would end up in a uranium mine somewhere in Siberia and gradually lose my health. But I would still be alive.

Second, it was evident that, although the KGB had arrested some individuals besides the airplane group, many members of the Organization and others among our friends and families were still enjoying their so-called freedom. Kislykh continued to give me regards from Eva, and judging from her words, she still had not been fired from work.

And third, I was sitting in jail with a Jew for a cell mate, a man who had been a tank officer and who guarded me as if I were his son. So, things were not so bad, especially if you are inclined to see the bottle as half full, rather than half empty.

The interrogations were less exhausting than before. Kislykh was satisfied now that I was talking, and recorded exactly what I said. When I got back to the cell each day, Izrail Natanovich shared with me his white bread and milk. As a prisoner under investigation I was able to receive each month a five-kilo package of provisions from Eva, and these were now arriving. I had the right to spend ten rubles in the prison store each month. And the food at the Big House was good. Kislykh often said to me, "When you go to a camp, Hilya Izraylevich, you'll remember the food in Leningrad."

Someone who had not served in the army might have been bored with the constant soups and cereals. But our stomachs were kept full. And sometimes, after the regular food distribution was over, the trap would be opened and the guard would offer second servings. The first time that happened I nearly refused. But Izrail Natanovich managed to get to the trap before I did. He took the bowl of millet porridge and as soon as the trap closed, he dumped the porridge into the latrine.

"You are still a green *zek*," he told me. "But live with me and you will learn. An experienced prisoner never refuses food, not even if he is full. True, today all they offered was a second serving of porridge. But tomorrow it might be fish. And once you refuse, the guard will not again offer you seconds. Understand? Learn from me while I am alive!"

On the wall of each cell was a list of rules. We learned those. But it was even more important that we came to understand the exceptions to those rules. We also learned to differentiate the guards—we gave each one a nickname that referred to his essential characteristic. We knew that if "Cupboard" was on duty, we could lie on our cots during the day. But not if the militaristic "Commander Chapaev" was the guard for the day. If the head guard, "Intellectual," entered the cell, he would demand a report. But "Sport" would only ask if we had any complaints. Or he might just open the cell door and then close it immediately, without even coming into the cell. If the stuttering "Lumumba" took you to an interrogation, you would have to keep your hands behind you all the way from the cell to the interrogation room. But the simple "Immigrant from Vologda" would ask solicitously whether you had had time to go to the latrine, and would require that you place your hands behind you only when an officer was coming.

The monotonous days in the Leningrad Big House dragged on in unnatural silence. Soon my cell mate and I had said everything we wanted to say to each other. We sat and waited for some break in the routine, some unusual activity.

Once each day we were allowed to walk in the small prison yard. Once in ten days we were permitted to take a shower. Once a month the bandy-legged Masha brought books from the prison library and we got to see a woman's face through the trap door (we knew that she was bandy-legged because once she came into the cell).

We knew in advance the day for a shave and the day for a haircut. Those offered a little variety, and even a kind of contact with other *zeks*. On those days you could see your own face in the mirror, and over in the corner you could see the pile of swept-up hair. Once I saw, reflected in my mirror, the back of a head of wavy female hair with gray streaks, and realized that it was Silva Zalmanson and that she was beginning to turn gray.

In addition to these predictable breaks in the routine, there were some unpredictable ones. Searches, for example. We knew that there was nothing in our cell that was forbidden, so the searches did not scare us. On the contrary, they broke the monotony.

One day "Pillow" opened the cell door and came in with a young, unfamiliar guard. Pillow was carrying a powerful lamp and dragging a long cable behind him—there were no electrical outlets in the cell.

"Well, confess," said the good-natured Pillow. "What forbidden objects are you hiding in the cell?"

"A revolver and two daggers," we answered in chorus.

"Where are you hiding them?" Pillow asked, going along with our joke.

"There." We nodded toward the side of the sink.

"Well, then, we'll look." He dragged the cord to the sink and began a clumsy but thorough search of the walls, floor, ceiling. He was familiar with the furniture—two cots, the small table, two stools, sink, latrine. He had checked and felt each piece many times before.

"A revolver, you say, and two daggers." He moved the bright light slowly across the walls. "We'll look, and perhaps we will find . . . two daggers."

The beam stopped at a ventilation grid above the floor, near the sink. A yellowed piece of paper had been glued over the grid. That is how we found it when we were put in the cell, and we accepted it as something given, without asking ourselves who had sealed the ventilation shaft, or why.

Pillow bent down and began tearing off the paper. We sat on our cots, watching him work. The mouth of the opening, after he got the paper off, was covered with a thick layer of dust and spider webs. "Well," he said to his assistant, "go and get a piece of wire or some kind of stick."

Then he pushed the wire through the screen and began to fish around. At first all he pulled up were spider webs and clumps of dust. But then we could see from his face that he had come upon something. Cautiously he began to drag it out. And at last he pulled up a long package wrapped in newspaper. When he unwrapped it, we gasped.

While we watched, Pillow unwound something that resembled a folding ruler, a long narrow strip, perhaps a hoop taken from a barrel. Also in the package were five cigarettes and two large nails with sharp points. "A revolver and two daggers," muttered Pillow. He took the wrapping and the contents and left the cell.

No one suspected us, though. The newspaper wrapping was dated 1969. That incriminating package had been lying behind the grid for about a year, unnoticed despite dozens of searches.

CHAPTER TWENTY-FOUR

More Pressure, More Tension

Gradually the atmosphere of the interrogations became tense again. I suddenly noticed that Kislykh had stopped recording my testimony accurately. At first the inaccuracies were inconsequential. I clenched my teeth and let them pass. It was somehow uncomfortable to correct the man who, every day, brought me greetings from Eva, expressed concern about my health, and asked if the room was warm enough and if I had received the liver tablets I had requested. This man would determine my future and also whether Eva would end up unemployed with a hungry child.

But the day came when I could no longer write the standard phrase at the end of the transcript, stating that I had read it and that it was recorded correctly. I began to add corrections that we then both had to sign. Now the transcript was followed by my many additions and commentaries on how my testimony was to be understood.

At first, naively, I believed that nothing terrible was happening. But then I began to wonder. Why had Kislyhk written "assemblage" when I had said "meeting"? After all, in Russian, "assemblage" has a clearly scornful, negative connotation, whereas "meeting" is positive or neutral. At that stage in the investigation a subtle war of words was being waged, a war based not on facts but on interpretations. Now that they had gotten me to start talking, they had to get me to say what was needed. Kislykh again began to talk about sincere repentance, and about the price that was paid by those who did not hasten to repent.

One day he read to me what he said was someone else's testimony. The individual being interrogated described our organization as a nationalist-terrorist group and said that its goal was to subvert and weaken the existing order in the USSR.

"This is the honest and sincere evaluation of a man who recognized his mistakes, completely repented, and is helping the investigation with his honest testimony," Kislykh began. "You ask me why we attach such importance to your trial. Isn't your Organization's programmatic document, 'Our Goals,' a plan to create a massive anti-Soviet Zionist party for the struggle against the existing Soviet order, with the support of an overseas imperialist base?"

The document "Our Goals" that Kislykh was referring to was a single typed sheet that was found during the search of my apartment in Leningrad (while I was away at Siversky). The KGB, in the presence of witnesses, had found it in an inner pocket of my suit. Kislykh read to me some terrible quotations from that sheet of paper. In those quotes there was talk about the need to create an All-Union Zionist party, an illegal organization with local cells throughout the country, with the object of a struggle against the existing order, with the support of a foreign center.

The sentence for any individual found to be a member of such an organization was capital punishment. For several days I was in fear, not only for myself but also for my co-defendants. From the report Kislykh showed me of the search of my apartment, it seemed that this terrible piece of paper had not been planted during the search, but that it had actually been found in my suit pocket. Yet I had no memory of it, nor any idea what it was or how it had come into my possession. I had had time to size up Kislykh's tactics and did not think that he would try a forgery. But he coldly ignored my statements that neither I nor any member of the Committee had ever seen or discussed the contents of this provocative document.

I was not able to understand what had happened. Then Viktor Shtilbans—a member of our group in the Organization who was arrested on August 20—began to testify.

Some time before we were arrested, while reading the journal *Za Rubezhom*, Viktor had stumbled across an article titled "Lenin in Prague." The author analyzed Lenin's role during the Prague conference of the RSDWP (Russian Social-Democratic Workers' Party) and, in particular, the role of the program of action for overthrowing the tsar set forth in Lenin's article titled "Our Goals." Viktor was, at that time, secretary of a Komosomol organization and, unlike most of us, was not totally alienated from Marxist methods. After he read that article, he used Lenin's format to express the goals of our Organization. Viktor wrote his thoughts out on a piece of paper, and at the top of the sheet he wrote "Our Goals."

At the last meeting of our group before June 15, Viktor had thrust that piece of paper into my hands and asked me to read it and tell him what I thought of the ideas it contained. Without taking the time then to even look at it, I folded it up and put it into the inner pocket of my suit—and immediately forgot about it. The next day I changed jackets. During the days that followed I was busy, not just with work and family but also with the responsibility and strain of participating in the Operation Wedding compromise. Without wearing that jacket again, I left for the dacha at Siversky—where I was taken into custody.

When the members of the KGB read the piece of paper that had been taken from that jacket pocket, they became excited. It looked as if they had evidence of participation in a capital crime. As they saw it, what had been wise and courageous for the great democratic Lenin was, in our

hands, defined as a programmatic document of a nationalist-terrorist organization. What had been permissible for the
Communist Zeus was forbidden—indeed, potentially fa-
tal—for the nationalist ox.

Kislykh's interrogation became an attack.

"You say that your Organization was not a terrorist
group. But you spoke against the Middle East policy of the
USSR. You expressed doubts about the correctness of the
policy of the Party and the government on nationalities.
And you aroused nationalist feelings and a desire for emigration among people of Jewish nationality. Did you not in
those ways cause harm to the Soviet order?"

"It is possible that we caused harm. But our goals
were not anti-Soviet. Only the indirect results of our activities may have caused some harm to the Soviet government."

"Aha! That means that you understand that indirectly
your Organization was anti-Soviet, if not by direct intention,
then by the results of its activities. Do you agree?"

"Yes, to some extent you could say that."

Kislykh sat at the desk, rapidly recording our exchange.
He had taken another small step in a direction known only
to him. I was happy that I seemed to have gotten rid of the
description "nationalist-terrorist." After that, when I was
reading through the transcriptions, I watched to make sure
that after the words "anti-Soviet" he always wrote "in the
sense that objectively it caused some damage, although
such goals were not directly pursued."

Apparently, I was more exhausted from the daily interrogations than I realized. A few times I signed transcripts
after doing little more than leafing through them. When the
indictment was brought to me at the end of the investigation, I read that I had acknowledged that I was a member of
an illegal, anti-Soviet, Zionist organization. They had kept

the words that suited their purposes, and had taken out
the rest.

Each day I returned to the cell from my daily "work"
feeling exhausted and annoyed, and the annoyance did not
dissipate. Although Izrail Natanovich was just as caring and
attentive to me as before, everything he did irritated me. He
chomped his food when he ate; he rustled the paper when
he sat writing poems for the wall newspaper that would be
displayed in his camp after he returned there; and when he
sat on the toilet, his bare thighs hung over the sides. He was
just an ordinary man, I told myself, with the usual collection
of irritating habits. It was not his fault that we had been
placed together in a public toilet. I was, I realized, tense
from the investigation and venting on him all the anger and
fear that had accumulated inside me. I was never alone,
never had a chance to think everything through. During the
day I was with Kislykh, and in the evening with Izrail Natanovich.

And then one day a simple incident opened my eyes and
I understood that my seemingly irrational irritation with
Izrail Natanovich had been well founded. He had written
another poem for the paper and asked me to read it. Like his
other poems, it was pitiful in form and pathetic in content—
it called upon the tortured *zek* to increase his productivity
and hasten his reeducation. And suddenly I realized what it
was about Izrail Natanovich that drove me crazy. I understood why he had been on such good terms with the political director of the camp. Why he was permitted to bring a
whole suitcase of foreign delicacies with him to the Big
House. Why every two days he received gorgeous, crusty,
white bread and fresh milk. Why he was allowed a personal
meeting with his wife in prison, a visit that lasted for a day
and a night, without any witnesses. Why he had tried to

persuade me to become a member of the council of the collective at the camp.

We clashed with a bang and then separated. His delicacies had long ago begun to stick in my throat, and I had been looking for a reason to refuse them. Now I had one. All relations between us came to an end, and I ceased talking to him. Earlier, I had been silent in Kislykh's office and had spoken in the cell. Now, ironically, the situation was reversed. The cell became two cells, albeit without a physical partition.

Several times Izrail Natanovich tried to draw me into conversation, to explain, to appeal to my solidarity as a Jew. But I was so pleased with my inner independence that not even sprats could entice me out of it. A few weeks later he was removed from the cell. As he stood at the open door, holding his tightly bound bed-roll in one hand, he extended the other hand to me.

"Forgive me if I did something wrong. It is not easy to sit in a cell with another man for half a year. All kinds of things happen. Don't remember me badly . . ."

Silently he held out his hand, but I could not bring myself to shake it. Then the door closed behind him.

Several months later, after the trial, I was placed in a cell with Lev Yagman. When I told him about Izrail Natanovich, he said immediately,

"He was planted there."

"Do you really think so?"

"I don't think so. I'm sure."

Autumn ended. The first snow fell on October 31. I walked in the narrow courtyard and watched the blue-tinged snowflakes fall onto the double screen overhead. The screen formed a barrier so that messages could not be passed between the prisoners who were walking in different courtyards of the prison. At first, the snow melted as soon as it hit the ground. But then enough remained so that we could write messages in the snow—no need for pencil and paper. But the guards were thorough—as they led us away from the exercise yard, they carefully rubbed out our inscriptions in the snow.

CHAPTER TWENTY-FIVE

Laughter

On my birthday, Kislykh handed me a little post-
card written in Eva's hand.

"My dear. . .Congratulations. . .We wish. . .we believe
that you will always remain the same honest and brave
person we know and love. Yours, Eva, Lileshka."

My eyes filled with tears. That was the first and last note
I was given from Eva during the investigation. That was all
that she was permitted by the investigator to write. It meant
so much to me—to know that somewhere in the world at
least two hearts, a big one and a little one, were beating in
unison with mine.

And then Kislykh began the day's conversation.

"Hilya Izraylevich, I need to tell you something that has
been very unpleasant for us. Your wife is behaving badly.
She refuses to testify, even though her actions evidently
include some that are criminal. It is now being decided
whether to hold her criminally responsible. Only Sima Kaminskaya is more defiant than your wife."

"My wife knows nothing, about the Organization or
about the airplane. For the sake of her well-being and peace
of mind, I did not tell her anything. She has nothing to tell
you even if she does testify. I assure you of this, Gennady
Vasilevich." As always happened at such moments of great
agitation and tension, I felt heat enveloping my body. My
voice trembled and faltered.

"Are you sure of that, Hilya Izraylevich?"

"Yes, I am sure."

"Do you want to speak to Eva on the telephone?"

"Yes. Yes! I will tell her to testify."

"Only that."

And so it was that after all those weeks I was able to hear Eva's voice. For a long time we were too excited to actually start our conversation. Finally I forced my voice to behave. Then I spoke, it seemed to me, calmly and firmly and confidently.

"Listen, Eva, your refusal to testify doesn't make any sense. You can tell all you know and you will be absolved of all guilt. Eva, testify. You won't betray anyone. The investigators know a lot more than you do."

Eva had difficulty waiting until I had finished before she replied. As soon as I stopped speaking I heard her staccato speech answering.

"I know nothing. And you know nothing. Why do you slander yourself? You didn't do anything. You're not guilty of anything. . ."

I heard a click and the conversation was cut off. Apparently Eva had been speaking from a nearby room, and her investigator had decided that there was no sense in allowing the conversation to continue.

After I was returned to the cell, I thought about how the arrested and the unarrested live in different worlds, and how difficult it is for them to understand each other, even if they are man and wife.

The investigators hurried. The trial of the airplane group was set for December 15 and ours was set for December 23. The court session was to be closed. They offered to find lawyers for us. I declined, to save Eva the cost. The value of an attorney at a Soviet political trial is nil.

But my refusal was not acceptable. How could they leave a Soviet citizen without a defense? One of the articles of the indictment was a capital crime, punishable by shooting. And so, they explained to me, I didn't have the right to decline a defense, not even if I was a lawyer. If I didn't have the money, the state would pay for the lawyer.

The hell with you, I thought. Go ahead. At least Eva won't end up in debt.

And so I met with the public defender, in the investigator's office. No one else was present, but each of us was aware that we were not alone. The lawyer was a pleasant Jew, tired, with a slight tremor. He had never before defended a political prisoner, but the rules of the game were clear to him. He tried to be as helpful as possible—once he even brought me bread and sausage from Eva. But he understood his limitations.

We agreed that he would defend me as he saw fit, as long as he did not defame what was dear to me. And during the trial he observed that part of our agreement. Not once did he slander or revile either Zionism or Israel. Instead, he limited himself to a declaration that he could not share the political views of his defendant. It seems to me that, within the limits of what is possible in a Soviet court, my lawyer was the most decent of all the lawyers in our trial.

While the investigators were drawing up bills of indictment and preparing for the two trials, we were permitted to look through the material that had been gathered in our cases. And there was a lot of it—forty-two thick volumes, with appendices. For the defendants, that was an interesting time.

Those volumes contained the testimony of the defendants and the testimony or refusals to testify of hundreds of witnesses and experts in technical fields including graphology and weaponry—material from the investigation of the Committee defendants and from the investigation of the hijacking group. It was during the days I spent reading through those volumes that I learned, finally, what had happened at the Smolny airport on June 15, and who was arrested there. I saw the names of the Zalmanson family, Edik Kuznetsov, and Mark Dymshitz. I also saw many unfamiliar names. Only two of those were names of non-Jews.

During those days I left the cell every morning and returned each evening. But instead of being subjected to interrogation all day, I was reading the volumes of material gathered for our cases. I could, of course, have merely leafed through a few pages and then signed a statement that I had utilized my right according to Article 206 of the Criminal Procedure Code of the RSFSR and had become acquainted with the material. The investigator on duty would have been pleased to make forty-two checks opposite my name with a red pencil. And then I could have rested on my cot, waiting for the trial to start. But I did not do that. I read each volume carefully, one after another, and ignored demands from the investigator that I read faster and skip the less interesting parts. Even so, when I did finally sign the appropriate statement, I was sure that Lassal Kaminsky was reading even more slowly.

As I read through those volumes, I saw the activities of our Organization as I had not been able to before. While we were caught up in our daily lives and activities, we had not had time to sit down and look objectively at what we were doing. Now, finally, we were indeed "sitting," leafing through thousands of pages, reading dozens of reports about hundreds of items published illegally in the USSR or smuggled in from abroad. I could acknowledge with pride that we had not done badly in the three and a half years before our arrests. And there was even high praise, from an expert in copying technology, for Solomon's cleverness in putting together the components of a copying machine.

The transcripts of the interrogations contained hundreds of names, some familiar, some unfamiliar. It was interesting to see who had withstood the pressure to testify, and for how long. And it was at least as engrossing to see who said what during interrogation, when the might of carefully devised psychological pressure was brought to bear.

I read very little as I leafed through the two volumes of my own testimony—I remembered most of what I had said. But here and there I stopped to read a particularly relevant section. One contained the story about a letter from Israel. I had waited for that letter for a long time, but I never received it. This letter had been registered, and so I inquired about it at the post office. There a clerk explained that the letter had been lost, to the great regret of the head of the postal department, of course. He told me that as the postman approached my house carrying a stack of letters a terrible wind tore all those letters out of his hand and scattered them about a vacant lot. The poor postman ran around gathering them up, and found all the letters but one—the one addressed to me.

That letter was now included in one of the files before me. And on that letter was affixed a crudely ungrammatical note ostensibly written by a patriotic citizen who supposedly had found it in the empty lot and brought it to the KGB.

The volumes contained an assortment of documents—pamphlets, sheets of paper, smaller pieces of paper. I came upon a copy of the telegram we sent from the central post office in Leningrad on May 26, expressing solidarity with the parents of Israeli children from Moshav Avivim. And I found an excerpt from an article in the Paris *Herald Tribune*. That story reported that during a search of the Leningrad home of one of the members of the underground Jewish Organization—a police officer—ammunition was confiscated. Aha, I thought, that means that they found those small-caliber cartridges that I stashed away during the reserve call-up, and then forgot. The *Herald-Tribune* was a very popular English-language paper published in France: I seemed to be acquiring international notoriety.

Gradually I began to see what a truly savage method of

psychological pressure had been used against the other members of the Committee, to instill fear in them, and hatred for me. All of those who in the end opposed Operation Wedding were charged, just as Misha Korenblit and I were, according to Article 64-a of the Criminal Code of the RSFSR, with treason, for which the punishment was death by shooting. Only at the very end of the investigation was that charge dropped. What remained were charges of "anti-Soviet propaganda and agitation and organized anti-Soviet activity." Some of us, myself included, were also charged with "unreported concealment of stolen property." As I read, I began to understand more fully what the others had suffered during the interrogations.

Probably the most extensive and despicable testimony was that of Otary Kozhiashvili. Most of the others testified that they "didn't know" or "didn't remember." Our wives remembered only that we were marvelous husbands and fathers and had not engaged in any reprehensible activities. And the memories of our mothers, brothers, fathers and sisters were similar.

I read the transcript of Eva's last interrogation, after she and I had spoken on the telephone, and learned why Eva had refused to speak. She had known something that I did not know, because we had not seen each other on the day of my arrest. She knew about the telephone conversation early in the morning on June 15, when Mark Dymshitz called to warn Misha Korenblit that in another three hours "Marusia was going to the doctor." Eva did not want to give evidence that could be used against Misha Korenblit.

Then I came to the papers related to Sima Kaminskaya, whom the KGB detested, and a pamphlet confiscated from her. And there was a brief note to Lassal Kaminsky written on June 15 by his daughter Lyuba, who came to his office immediately after his apartment had been searched:

"Papa, friends came to see you. Do what you think is necessary."

Gradually, reading the records I pieced together Lassal's story. By the time Lyuba wrote that note, Lassal had already been picked up and taken to the Big House. In his inner jacket pocket was a copy of the last issue of *Iton*. Lassal had taken it to work with him, but had not yet "disseminated" it when the KGB came for him. Fortunately they committed many minor errors that day. When they took Lassal into custody, they forgot to search him. And they left him alone in the investigator's study at the Big House for a few minutes—long enough for him to drop that incriminating copy of *Iton* behind a sofa near a wall.

I began to look for what had been said by those who had not been arrested. Grisha Vertlib was silent, as we had all agreed to be after our "rehearsal." Ben Tovbin was silent. Good for him. I was by then not that well disposed toward Ben. His threat, made at the April conference, to go to the KGB, rankled in my memory. I had also had disagreements with David Chernoglaz. But with him I was always certain that we were marching toward the same goal. Not always in step, but at least along parallel paths. Ben, I felt, was too often on a path that seemed to be at right angles to mine.

And then I came upon the information about Rudik Brud. Rudik, too, had been silent. "How are you, Rudik?" I thought. "We haven't seen each other for a long time, friend. . ." We were in different groups. Although Rudik had been one of the six founders of the Organization, he had not joined the Committee and so we rarely saw each other. Rudik had not joined for two reasons. First, his wife Natasha, unlike the other wives, kept track of what Rudik did and would not let him step over the line into dangerous activities. Also, his phlegmatic nature limited his activities.

Kreina Shur was silent. But she was silent with sarcastic

brilliance. She replied to only the first question by saying "I refuse to testify." Her answer to all the questions after that was, simply, "Look at the answer to the preceding question." Good for you, Kreina. I didn't think of that.

And then I came upon a story that was truly fascinating—and amusing—about Efim Spivakovsky. Efim had gone to the conference of the All-Union Coordinating Committee in Leningrad on June 13 and 14, and on his way home had stayed at a friend's apartment in Moscow for a few days. While he was in Moscow, the apartment was searched. A notebook of Efim's, containing anti-Soviet notes, was found. His explanation of the origins of the notebook was ingenious. Efim had already sat in jail, and had experience with investigations. So what might have been an impossible task for almost anyone else, for him was a simple exercise in sophistry:

"Yes, everything written in that notebook is mine. Why did I write those things? Since childhood, I have been inarticulate, I have had trouble explaining what I was thinking. I could somehow do it orally, but not in writing. So I set myself a task—to learn, at any price, to express what I think on paper. And so I wrote and wrote, trying to express myself clearly on paper. What you have in front of you is one such attempt. Now, reading this notebook, I must say with regret that I was still unable to express correctly in writing what I think. On paper, everything still comes out exactly the opposite of what I am thinking."

I couldn't read calmly any more. I began to snicker. And the more I tried to hold it in, the worse it got. As bad luck would have it, the next thing I came to was also funny. It was the testimony of Boris Azernikov about how he was "recruited," by accident, into the Zionist organization. He described it as follows:

His professional colleague, the dentist Misha Korenblit, promised to help him get a job, perhaps in his clinic. At an agreed-upon time, Boris went to Misha's home and rang the bell. The door immediately burst open and Boris was told to enter one of the rooms. The air was full of cigarette smoke and several young people of Jewish appearance were heatedly arguing about something. Boris was told right away that henceforth he was a member of an illegal Zionist organization and told to sit down. He sat. A vote was taking place just then on one of the issues on the agenda. He raised his hand . . .

My snickering turned into snorting. I pulled out a handkerchief and stuffed it into my mouth. My voice was hoarse, my eyes were tearing and the end was not in sight.

The investigator on duty came over.

"You have a nervous laugh. It is a form of hysteria."

He pressed a button and had me taken back to the cell.

I walked back through the quiet corridors of the most silent prison in the Soviet Union, chuckling wildly. It was an abnormal kind of laughter. All the tension from the long months of the investigation had risen to the surface and was spilling out in that strange mirth.

As we passed No. 195, the cell that had been Lenin's, I thought, "Il'ich, once upon a time behind that door you analyzed the development of capitalism in Russia. If today you could analyze the development of socialism, you would get a glimpse of how merry it has become in the prisons of Russia fifty years after the victory of the Great October."

I was walking in the hands-behind-the-back position, snorting. Nothing could stop that savage, hysterical laughter.

CHAPTER TWENTY-SIX

Theater of the Absurd

There is a joke about a trial that describes Soviet justice in political cases:

A Soviet judge is sitting at a closed political trial, and from the very start is writing, writing, writing, without paying attention to what is happening in the room. Finally, the defendant can't stand it any longer and cries out:

"Citizen judge! What's going on here? The trial is only beginning and you are already writing the sentence. Where is Socialist legality?"

"Don't be an idiot," says the judge, without interrupting his writing. "This is the sentence in a case that will be heard next week."

The trial of the airplane group began in Room 48 of the Leningrad Municipal Court on December 15, 1970. That trial was like a dramatic production—a play that had been carefully planned and scheduled to open at the time most auspicious for the producers, the KGB. The premiere was to be held on November 20, but was postponed to December 15, because by then the United Nations—distressed by incessant hijackings by Arab terrorists—would have adopted a resolution against air piracy.

The roles of the government officials were played by experienced actors who never forgot their lines. It is true that the prosecutor—Leningrad District Attorney Solovyev—was already senile, and, as nasty tongues affirmed, couldn't remember to lower his pants in the bathroom. But he had a trusty helper who never forgot anything—Inessa Katukova. The presiding judge, Ermakov, was a qualified executioner.

He not only followed KGB orders to send heads rolling, but did so with great pleasure.

The people's deputies were named Rusalinov and Ivanov. At the last moment the tragicomic role of people's prosecutor was added. It was to be played by the owner of a triple chin, the pilot Mednanogov, a representative of the northern civil aviation department. It was his first experience as a representative of the people and everything that man did would have been funny if it had not been so sad.

In the USSR, it is customary to hold a preliminary hearing of a case. During that hearing, representatives of the state—the prosecutors and the judges—carry out a dress rehearsal of the trial. When the airplane trial started on December 15, that dress rehearsal had already been held. The lawyers had crammed to learn their parts. Preparations had been completed and it was anticipated that the "play" would be a great success.

The attack by the prosecutors was to be fierce. The sentences were to be harsh. The defendants were to be made to look like a band of cunning Jewish criminals who dreamed day and night of murdering unsuspecting Soviet pilots. In the background would be the future inconsolable orphans and widows. The theme of the production was to be "Destroy the gang. Destroy cursed Zionists, those who were responsible for harming Mother Russia, the omnipresent 'invalids-of-the-fifth-question.' "

Those planning the trial had taken seriously the Soviet refrain that although the Soviet court is strict, it is also just and humane. As expressions of this policy, the wife and two daughters of Mark Dymshitz were found to be the deceived victims of an inveterate criminal and as such were absolved of responsibility. Meri Khnokh, then in the eighth month of her pregnancy, was released from prison—perhaps because of concern that the future Yigal might inadvertently appear during the prosecutor's speech.

Vulf Zalmanson was turned over to a military court to be tried separately. That left eleven airplane defendants. Two others were selected to be recipients of Soviet humanitarianism: Mendel Bodnya and Izrail Zalmanson. Mendel was given special treatment because his parents had been living in Israel for a long time and he wanted to join his family. Izrail was selected because he was a minor.

A dramatic production must have an audience—after all, someone has to applaud. And so courtroom No. 48 was arranged with an aisle dividing it into two unequal parts. There was a large section for those who came to the court to express disapproval of the airplane people, and to applaud the court. And there was a small section for the relatives. I was present at that trial only on December 17, when I was brought to the court to testify as a witness. Then, for the first time, I learned who the defendants were.

In answer to the judge's questions, I said that according to my conception of the plan, the goal of the operation was to show the entire world, as well as the Soviet government, that Soviet Jews who wanted to emigrate to Israel were being prevented from doing so. I said that the press conference to be held in Stockholm was to have served the same goal—to force out into the open the question of the emigration of Soviet Jews to Israel.

Since I did not know what position the defendants in that trial were taking, I used the word "I" rather than saying "we." By doing that I inadvertently gave the court an opportunity to avoid a political appraisal of the purpose of the plane hijacking. The judge was able to declare that Butman's plans applied only to the first phase of Operation Wedding—and to further assert that the defendants who had participated in the second phase had wanted only to achieve their own emigration.

As soon as I had finished, I was taken away. Years passed before I learned what occurred during that trial.

The so-called court and the so-called traitors were in different worlds. There was absolutely no relationship between the replies of the defendants and the conclusions of the court.

The "criminals" asserted that they were not anti-Soviet, that they did not want to cause the Soviet Union any harm, but rather that they felt alien and deprived in Russia and for that reason and "only for that reason" they wished to leave the USSR and go to Israel. Since they had not been permitted to leave legally, as Jews in other countries do, they were not able to emigrate. And so, they said, in desperation, they decided to flee without permission.

And they had not wanted to steal a plane. What would they need a plane for? If the group had flown to Stockholm, then the Swedes, as is accepted and proper, would have returned the plane to the Soviet Union.

In reply, the court said to them: we will be the judge of what you wanted. You wanted to subvert our great motherland, the hope of all peoples. Don't portray yourselves as lambs. Look at you—Kuznetsov, Fedorov, and Murzhenko, all dyed-in-the-wool anti-Soviets who have already sat in Soviet prisons without learning anything. Mendelevich, Khnokh, Altman, and Silva Zalmanson—arch-Zionists, disseminating Zionist material, systematically slandering our Soviet reality. Would such people hijack an airplane without subversive goals? No. And not simply hijack—but steal. Yes, steal! This is thievery on a large scale. And these actions come under the jurisdiction of Article 93, Part 1, of the Criminal Code of the RSFSR. The punishment is execution by shooting.

Mark Dymshitz sat in the courtroom and wondered how they could be tried for what "would have" happened. After all, he thought, the airplane is still at the Smolny airport, the crew is alive and well.

Mark's lawyer, a Jew named Pevzner, did not ask stupid questions. He was the first lawyer to speak, and he set the tone with his first statement:

"We, the lawyers, share the indignation expressed by the state prosecutor Comrade Solovyev. . ."

The lawyer Pevzner should have differed from his defendant at least in his knowledge of the law. And theoretically he should have known that treason, according to the provisions of Article 64 of the Criminal Code of the RSFSR, is "a deed, intentionally committed by a citizen of the USSR, to the detriment of: (a) state independence, (b) territorial inviolability, or (c) the military might of the USSR." If none of those three factors was determined to have been present, then there had been no treason.

But attorney Pevzner acknowledged the definition of the given article by the court as correct. After all, it was not he but Dymshitz who would be shot. And for playing his role in this trial so brilliantly, he might even receive the title of meritorious judicial artist of the USSR.

The lawyers appraised the actions of their respective defendants in different ways, depending on the decency and courage of each lawyer. But they all insisted on one point. The defendants did not want to steal the airplane, they just wanted to borrow it. According to the Tokyo Convention of 1969, Sweden would have been obliged to return the plane to the Soviet Union. And in general, without the intention to appropriate, there is no misappropriation—that is taught in the first year of the law institute.

On this subject, the lawyers were indignant in unison. Since the article on misappropriation had no connection to high politics, on that subject they could display their independence. It is even possible that this charge was included to provide an opportunity to show the independence of the Soviet court from the KGB, and then to remove the charge of misappropriation from the indictment as a demonstration of fairness.

But totalitarian judicial systems are not constrained to prove anyone's guilt; they rely solely on political guidelines. Not one of the lawyers took upon himself the responsibility for contesting the charge of misappropriation. Dymshitz and Kuznetsov, for their alleged desire to steal a plane, received the death sentence with confiscation of property. For the same thing, Bodnya received four years of imprisonment.

When the sentences in the case of the airplane group were pronounced on December 24, no one laughed:

Dymshitz, Mark—capital punishment with confiscation of property;

Kuznetsov, Eduard—capital punishment without confiscation of property in the absence of such;

Mendelevich, Iosif—15 years without confiscation of property in the absence of such;

Fedorov, Yuriy—15 years without confiscation of property in the absence of such;

Murzhenko, Aleksey—14 years without confiscation of property in the absence of such;

Khnokh, Lev—13 years without confiscation of property in the absence of such;

Altman, Anatoly—12 years without confiscation of property in the absence of such;

Zalmanson Silva—10 years without confiscation of property in the absence of such;

Penson, Boris—10 years with confiscation of property;

Zalmanson, Izrail—8 years without confiscation of property in the absence of such;

Bodnya, Mendel—4 years without confiscation of property in the absence of such.

Those sitting in the large area to the right of the aisle greeted the sentences with unanimous applause.

"We're with you, lads!" burst out a solitary voice through the sobs from the small area to the left of the aisle.

After Mark Dymshitz and Edik Kuznetsov had been handcuffed, Mark said as his final words in that courtroom:

"If you think that shooting us will intimidate potential freedom seekers, then you miscalculate. In the future others will go, not with brass knuckles, but with automatic rifles, because they will have nothing to lose."

I understand why Mark was given the death sentence. He was the one who had suggested that it was technically feasible to hijack a plane. It was from that idea that Operation Wedding was developed as a plan to bring Soviet Jews out of the empire of the northern pharaoh. Without Mark, a pilot, as part of the group, I would never have taken on the organization of the operation. From the very beginning we were determined to avoid any coercion of pilot or crew. And that would be possible only because we had a pilot of our own who could take over from a recalcitrant crew. It was Mark's iron will that forced us to set the first "wedding date"—May 2. And Mark did not give in when Edik suggested delaying for a year.

But why was Edik given the death sentence? Had he really participated more actively than Iosif Mendelevich or Silva Zalmanson? Was he so different from the rest of the group that he deserved to be shot? No, I don't think so. Had he been sentenced to die because he was insolent in court? No, for that there is the punishment cell. Was it because he was a zealous Zionist? No—he was not a Zionist at all.

Edik declared at the trial that, in his hierarchy of values, freedom, not Israel, was his first priority. In this he differed from his wife, Silva Zalmanson—for her, Israel was more important than freedom. Edik was a Russian dissident. But he was convinced that he would not live to see the victory of freedom in Russia. He believed that, given an indigenous population that traditionally had been politically downtrodden, and the autocracy of the KGB, dissidents would not succeed in fueling a mass movement. That is why he counted himself among the humiliated and insulted Jewish people. And so, without becoming a Zionist, Edik had decided that he needed to emigrate to Israel.

In his speech to the court, Edik's lawyer, Lurie, said: "His crime is dangerous, but Kuznetsov himself is not dangerous."

But the presiding judge, Ermakov, was no fool. He knew that the other defendants in the plane group were Zionists. He knew that they felt no great love for the way of life in the USSR but were not basically anti-Soviet. The Zionists were not dangerous. Kuznetsov's crime was not dangerous. But in the eyes of the judge and the KGB, Kuznetsov was dangerous because he was anti-Soviet, not just pro-Israel. That is why he was given the death sentence.

This was obvious to everyone in the courtroom. Edik felt a deep hatred of the order that had mutilated his life and the lives of millions of his fellow citizens, and he did not want to nor could he conceal that hatred. It was obvious that if Kuznetsov had succeeded in fleeing, he would have used his exceptional qualities to struggle against the regime that he hated. Edik Kuznetsov had already served seven years in prison, after his arrest in 1962 for anti-Soviet views. And a person cannot be tried twice for the same thing. But at the end of this trial he received another sentence for the same thing—capital punishment without confiscation of property in the absence of such.

Alesha Murzhenko had come from his native Ukraine to

escape with the others to Sweden. He did not know the others and had not participated in planning the escape. He was given a sentence of fourteen years of imprisonment—a longer sentence than was given to many of those who had been actively involved in the planning. Yura Fedorov, who also had served an earlier period for anti-Soviet agitation and propaganda, received a sentence of fifteen years.

At about nine o'clock in the evening on December 24, our corridor in the Big House resounded with the slamming of doors and then with the rising, hysterical sobs of a woman. We knew that this was Silva, they had brought the airplane group back from the trial.

Silva's choking sobs were cut off by the slam of another door. Hysterical laughter, hysterical weeping, burst forth in different ways in different people. But it must burst forth if you are to go on living.

Silva's husband was to be put up against the wall and shot. Her younger brother was to be imprisoned for eight years. Her older brother was facing a special military court, and you could imagine what awaited him if even non-officers and non-deserters from the army had been given such terrible sentences. And she herself was to serve ten years in prison. What would her life be like after that? Would she ever be able to bear children and raise them, like other women? Her health would deteriorate, her beauty would fade, the years would pass. . .

None of us knew, that night, whether any of the sentences would be commuted or reduced. We could only wait.

CHAPTER TWENTY-SEVEN

We Shall Overcome

Long ago, when I was still a not-yet-arrested citizen of the USSR, I read an article about a Yugoslavian who never again slept after he had been shell-shocked during the war by the explosion of a grenade. Not for a day or a night or a year—he had not slept for fifteen years! The article said that the man felt fine for all his lack of sleep. He had at his disposal twenty-four hours a day, and he pitied the rest of humankind, who could not become accustomed to the habit of not sleeping.

In December of 1970, I, too, stopped sleeping. I did not sleep for more than a month, and I did not feel any discomfort from lack of sleep. Strangely, this period of not sleeping began, not while I was going through the interrogations, but immediately after the investigation ended, after the day when I laughed hysterically.

At first I did not even realize that I was not sleeping at night. In prison at night, it is almost impossible to determine the time. You do not have a clock in the cell, and there are no markers to indicate how much time has passed.

The last time each day when we could determine the time more or less accurately was ten o'clock in the evening—bedtime. For several minutes before ten, the trap doors banged open and shut and at each cell the guard uttered the same phrase:

"Hand over your spectacles. Prepare for bed."

The guards wanted us to prepare for bed so that once we retired, we would sleep through the night. They did not want any of us to get up and wander around the cells. The supervisors watch the guards, even at night, but control then is relatively lax. If the *zeks* are sleeping soundly, then the guards can nap.

Why did they want our glasses? Out of concern for our health. They did not want any *zek* to accidentally slit his wrist with a lens from his spectacles.

The first night of my insomnia I went to bed as usual. After a while I drifted off. When I woke up, I heard the sound of a tram as it started, with an effort, to move along the Liteyny Bridge. As I lay there listening intently, I could hear other small sounds of movement in the street. It seemed to me to be about six o'clock in the morning. Very soon, I thought, they ought to be giving us the signal to get up.

I wrapped myself in the favorite world of the *zek*— dreams about the future, memories of the past. When I became aware again of my surroundings, it seemed as if a lot of time had passed. But still the guard did not give the signal to rise. My cell mate was snoring. And the sounds of movement along the Liteyny, instead of becoming livelier, had almost disappeared. The next time the guard came to check I asked him:

"Officer, what time is it? Why aren't we getting up?"

"It's one o'clock in the morning. Why aren't you sleeping?"

One o'clock. That means that the first time I woke up, the trams weren't just starting at the beginning of the day— they were still going at the end of the day. What I heard were not the first trolleys of the morning but the last trolleys circling the boulevards at midnight. That means that when I woke, the night shift hadn't even started work!

I tried to fall asleep—no luck. I began to count and was soon bored. I remembered hearing about a person who was fighting insomnia managed to count to a million and a half before he had to get up to go to work. Lying on a cot for eight hours without sleeping is harder than working for eight hours. Finally it was time to get up.

The next night the same thing happened. And the next night and the next. I was sleeping about forty five minutes each night. I didn't want to sleep during the day, either. Lying on the cot all night long without sleeping was unsettling. All kinds of thoughts—convoluted, endless, disturbing—crept into my head. I had to think of some remedy to cure this disaster.

My father had had insomnia for a while, I remembered. He had gone to the district library and selected books about the cultivation of corn and about the activities of the Soldier's Welfare League—boring literature. And that worked. He never managed to read more than a page before he started snoring.

I decided to try his solution. But when the librarian brought a list of available books, I noticed a little volume by Sholom Aleichem and forgot my good intentions. Each night I read those rich tales full of laughter and weeping and love. I experienced genuine enjoyment, particularly when I managed to imagine how some of the dialogues would sound in Yiddish. There was always plenty of light—the bulb hanging in the cell was never turned off. I just had to be alert, so that the guard didn't catch me reading when he peered through the hole. A *zek* is never alone—he is always being watched.

The nights no longer dragged on. Now they flitted by. I lived the sadly gay life of Sholom Aleichem's heroes and filled the gaps in my Jewish education—I had become a Zionist before I had become a Jew.

One day after the sentencing of the airplane group, eighteen Muscovites sent a telegram of protest to Nikolay Podgorny, the president of the USSR. Podgorny and his advisers were able to read that telegram in respectable Western newspapers even before their copies were delivered. The signature of our Moscow friend Villi Svechinsky was among those on the telegram.

The telegram was part of a larger occurrence. Waves of protest and solidarity for the defendants in the two trials rolled into the Kremlin from all sides. During the time of the Doctors' Plot, such protests would have been impossible.

The day that telegram was sent, Meir Gelfond, a former prisoner of Rechlag, addressed himself to all former prisoners of Hitler's and Stalin's camps, galvanizing them to join the struggle to get the sentences repealed. Still young in years, but already old in experience in the Zionist struggle, Meir was too proud to request anything of Podgorny, even if it was not for himself. Instead, he wrote under the auspices of Amnesty International: "the intention of these people to hijack a plane has been used as a pretext for reprisal. The real reason for the death sentences is to terrorize the tens of thousands of Jews who yearn to emigrate to Israel."

The activists in the Zionist movement in the Soviet Union were the first to realize what a unique opportunity Operation Wedding provided for focusing pressure on Soviet leadership. During those months the Israelis characterized the hijacking attempt as a provocation and refused to see it as a desperate effort to revive the issue of *aliyah*. They continued to be guided by the injunction, "Don't tease the bear!" It was our friends in the Soviet Union who correctly evaluated the situation. The first refrains of "Lighten the punishment!" and "Let my people go!" emanated from Moscow, Kiev and Riga—not from Tel Aviv or the West.

Muscovites wrote:

"We, the signatories of this appeal, are also striving passionately to reach our homeland in Israel. We declare that the spilt blood of our brothers will not stop us or frighten us. We are ready to give our lives for the right to live in our land."

From Jews in Riga came this appeal:

"No one anywhere in our history ever succeeded by violence, repression or threats in forcing Jews to renounce their dream of returning to Israel. And those methods will not succeed this time. Listen to the voice of reason! Repeal the unjust sentences! Permit the Jews who wish to emigrate to Israel to go to their homeland!" That was the appeal of the Riga Jews.

From representatives of the Russian human rights movement, the ideological grandchildren of the writer Korolenko, came these words:

"As long as people are forcibly detained in this country, the state cannot be protected against such attempts to escape. Everyone who wants to leave should be permitted to emigrate. Recognize the right of Jews to repatriation! Capital punishment and intimidation do not testify to the strength of the state."

A similar appeal by Academician Andrey Sakharov, friend of the humiliated, insulted and repressed, echoed loudly around the world.

From Sverdlovsk came this statement:

"Neither physical annihilation of those who wish to emigrate nor imprisonment for many years nor insults to human dignity can prevent a repetition of the Leningrad incident. The solution to the issue is complete observance of the guarantees of rights proclaimed in the Declaration of Human Rights."

From the Jews of Kiev came this affirmation:

"We declare that no repression can force us to renounce our struggle to emigrate to Israel. Normalization of the situation can be obtained in only one way—by guaranteeing the legitimate right of Soviet Jews to repatriation."

Ten of my acquaintances, the poet Iosif Kerler, his wife Anna and eight other Muscovites, appealed to the hearts of the deputies at the current session of the Supreme Soviet of the USSR:

"Citizen deputies! History clearly places before you a choice, and you have only two possibilities: to let us go in peace, or to start on the well-worn path of mass repressions. Because as long as we exist we shall—and each day more loudly—demand the freedom of emigration, and our voices will become unbearable to you."

From Kharkov, Iona Kolchinsky wrote to the defense minister:

"Since I am due to become a soldier in the Soviet army, it is not inconceivable that I shall be entrusted with the execution of the sentences of Dymshitz and Kuznetsov. I shall not shoot at my brothers! If the sentence is not repealed, I will not appear at the designated time at the conscription center and I will refuse to serve in the Soviet army."

Finally there was recognition in Israel and in the West of the need for action. The Knesset met in special session to adopt an appropriate resolution. Even Communist Deputy

Sneh spoke from the podium to the Knesset, expressing his condemnation of the Soviet government's position.

At about the same time, a group of Basque terrorists in Spain, fighters for an independent Basque country, were also sentenced to death. World opinion was aroused in support of them. The death sentences pronounced in Burgos and Leningrad were equated by some, and a struggle was waged to save the lives of both groups. Leonid Brezhnev and Nikolay Podgorny found themselves the objects of the same anger that was directed at their mortal enemy, Generalissimo Franco. Russian prestige, as well as trade deals and industrial cooperation between the USSR and the West, was threatened.

On December 31, 1970, the Soviet government decided to change the verdict. On the fifth floor of the Big House in Leningrad, doors opened and closed and people bustled around, even though it was Saturday night. The airplane group was summoned to the office of the director of the prison and asked to sign appeals. The law permits a prisoner to file an appeal within seven days of sentencing, and some of the group had not yet managed to write petitions.

But that did not matter. Appeals from all over the world for humanity toward the condemned had swayed the judicial college on criminal cases of the Supreme Court of the RSFSR. They commuted the death sentences of Dymshitz and Kuznetsov to fifteen years of imprisonment. Iosif Mendelevich's sentence was reduced from fifteen to thirteen years of imprisonment. And the sentences of Lev Khnokh and Tolya Altman were reduced to ten years.

World opinion was effective. On December 30, Franco had commuted the death sentences against the Basques. The Moscow sentences were changed on December 31, seven days after the end of the trial.

A few weeks later the military court of the Leningrad

military district heard the case against Vulf Zalmanson, an officer in the Soviet army who had deserted his military unit. We had all feared that Vulf, too, would get the death sentence. But the political climate had changed. Vulf received a sentence of ten years imprisonment.

That change also affected our "airplane-related" trial, which was to have begun on December 23 at nine in the morning. It did not start that morning. One of the lawyers, we were told, had not managed to read the case, and the administrative session of the judicial college of the Leningrad municipal court quickly gathered to postpone the case for two weeks.

Two weeks later, on January 6, 1971, we were again not summoned to the courtroom. This time we were told that Lev Yagman was coughing in his cell. The medical staff of the Big House was put on alert. Cough medicine was provided. The judicial college met again and decreed that the case was to be postponed until Lev was well. According to the authorities, Lev did not recover until May 1971.

Why was the case delayed? The next Party congress was approaching. Those who had to sit on the presidium of the congress were not in the mood for another anti-Soviet campaign.

While we were waiting for Lev Yagman's cough to disappear, the forty-two volumes of our case were sent to Moscow to be checked. The authorities had decided that they wanted us, at our trial, to look like straying lambs who had been deceived by bestial Zionism and saved by Soviet justice. Then our sentences could be lighter than those of the airplane group. This scenario required that all of us "deeply acknowledge our errors and sincerely repent." So in Moscow they examined the testimony that each of us had given.

Sitting there in the Big House from December 1970 to May 1971, isolated from each other and from the world outside the prison, we knew nothing of the government's trial strategy. Nor did we know that *aliyah* activists would soon be called to the OVIR visa offices in many cities and offered plane tickets to Vienna. We did not know that soon tens of thousands of Soviet Jews would be landing at Ben Gurion airport.

Perhaps if I had known all that, I would have slept. But then I would not have read Sholom Aleichem.

CHAPTER TWENTY-EIGHT

Awaiting Trial

Lev's lingering cough kept us in our abominable cells for four months. We weren't led to interrogations. We weren't summoned anywhere. The days were monotonous and gray, without variety, activity or companionship. But what I missed most during those months was sound.

The windows of our cells overlooked a courtyard that was surrounded on all four sides by high buildings. The courtyard was almost always empty, and as quiet as a cemetery. Only once in all those months of waiting was there a break in that silence. A car drove into the courtyard and the driver, when he got out, left the door open. Not only did he forget to close the door—he also forgot to turn off the car radio. My ears, yearning for sound, immediately scooped up the quiet melody. I opened the transom in the upper part of my window and the marvelous sounds of classical music flowed in. I stood by the window praying that the chauffeur would not return soon. I am sure that other transoms were opened during those minutes, that other prisoners were delighted by those few moments of beauty.

As the days passed, apathy began to engulf me. I did daily exercises and the obligatory kilometers pacing the cell, but I was spending almost all of each day and night in a dreamy stupor on the cot—I had to do something to prevent this from becoming a way of life. I was beginning to feel as if my brain were covered with cobwebs. The solution seemed to be some kind of mental activity. So I set about studying mathematics and languages.

From the prison library I got *Fascinating Mathematics*.

Each day I forced myself to solve problems—the answers were at the end of the book. And I dug into languages. Monday, Wednesday and Friday—English. Tuesday, Thursday and Saturday—Hebrew. Sunday—off.

Between the time I met Leah Lurie and the day of my arrest, I had studied the material in the first two volumes of the Hebrew book, *Elef Milim*. At the end of each volume was a list of root words for study: altogether a thousand words in the two volumes. Not only had I studied these lessons—I had taught them to others in the ulpan. Now I set out to recall the entire one thousand words—phrases, declensions of nouns and verb conjugations.

On Hebrew days, I opened the notebook on the little table before I started to walk the day's kilometers around the cell. As I walked I plumbed the depths of my memory for Hebrew words. Each time one floated up to consciousness, I went to the table and wrote the word in the notebook.

This purposeful activity of "restoring" the words from the Hebrew text pulled me out of the dreamy, vegetative state into which I had begun to slide. I got a second wind. Several weeks after I started, I wrote Hebrew word number 961 in the notebook. I just couldn't remember the other 39. But I was a rich man. With 961 words, a man could live comfortably, constructing rich combinations, little playlets, tales.

Several months later, Eva managed to get special permission to give me Shapiro's Hebrew-Russian dictionary. That volume has 28,000 words and a grammar section at the end. It accompanied me through all the islands of the Gulag Archipelago. During all the searches I went through, I worried most about the fate of that book. After long years together, we parted one beautiful day shortly before I left the Archipelago. It is a *zek* custom to leave such books in the zone because it is very difficult to receive them behind the barbed wire. My dictionary became the friend of Natan

Sharansky, who still had a long and tortuous road between the Gulag and Jerusalem.

During those months at the Big House in the Spring of 1971, I also had an English text, an old book from the 1930s with the big seal of the OGPU of the Leningrad region. It is better not to think about how that book with the seal of the predecessor of the KGB landed in the prison library, or about what happened to it former owner.

It is almost impossible to learn English without a human teacher. You need to know exactly how to pronounce the transcription marks. Otherwise it is possible to read almost every word in various ways. And so I was afraid to memorize words—it is better not to know a word at all than to learn it incorrectly. Relearning something is always harder than learning it the first time. What I needed was a cell-mate who knew how to read English.

The Leningrad winter passed. One day the trap was opened and the guard invited me to approach. By special permission, he handed me four photographs. I looked at them, and for several days fell out of the monotonous rhythm of the cell. The photographs were of Eva and Lileshka. I had difficulty recognizing them. Eva was as thin as a rail and hadn't even tried to smile. Probably all the other wives looked the same way. Jewish prisoners' wives—there's no way around it—are dragged through the same prison terms as their husbands. Only their daily routine was different. The pain and deprivation they suffered was the same.

But what stabbed me most deeply was the photograph of Lileshka. It bore no resemblance to the four-year-old girl I had put to bed on June 15, 1970, less than a year earlier. The sorrowful eyes of a long-suffering adult gazed at me. It was difficult to imagine that this little girl knew how to smile, sing songs, jump rope.

Regulations stipulated that prisoners at the Big House were to be taken to the showers once every ten days. So a shower was an eagerly anticipated event, and not just for the pleasure of getting clean. It provided a break in the gray monotony of our lives after the investigation. And it allowed us to hope, however futilely, that we might catch sight of one another. At the same time, a shower at the Big House was usually a traumatic experience.

The warden was obliged to see to it that all prisoners got washed, but in such a way that no prisoner, even accidentally, had any contact with any other prisoner. Each day the guard who was responsible for showers had at his disposal several hours and many dozens of unwashed men from many cells. The showers—all five of them—were at the very bottom of the prison, under the staircase. All the prisoners to be washed on a particular day had to go up and down the same staircase, and pass through the single dressing room, where they undressed and were given soap and a sponge, and where they later dressed. Each person was allotted half an hour for washing, including undressing and dressing. Half an hour should have been plenty of time, and each prisoner should have been able to return to his cell as clean and pure as a baby's kiss. But remember—no prisoner was to see any other prisoner. The logistics for preventing such meetings were complicated. So all day long the guards insisted on great haste, and each *zek* rushed nervously through the shower he had dreamed about for ten days.

The not-yet-arrested Soviet citizen has many rights. After all, it was not for nothing that people spilled their blood during the civil war. One of those indisputable rights was the privilege of washing in a bath house without any limitations on how long he stayed in the bath, how much water he used or the temperature of the water—he was free to regulate all these as he desired.

But the shower of the arrested Soviet man was a different matter. By the time the *zek* entered the shower stall, his half hour had long since started ticking by. But that didn't mean that the water was running. The faucet that controlled the water was in the corridor and was regulated by a guard. As soon as the guard turned the water on, you closed your eyes so you wouldn't get anything in them, and you soaped yourself up. Then you were ready to rinse off, but the water from the shower head was as cold as ice. You waited patiently, hoping it would get warmer. When it seemed to be getting warmer, you tried standing under it, then jumped back immediately because it was not. You could not regulate the water and you screamed and kicked your foot against the door.

"Officer, the water is cold!"

On the other side of the door there was silence. Then you would hear a stirring behind the door, only to discover that it was the guard who distributed soap. Regulating the flow and temperature of the water was either below his dignity or above his rights, so you had to wait for the return of the ruler of the tap.

At last he appeared and changed the position of the faucet handle. You felt the water becoming warmer rapidly. There, that was how it ought to be. Joyfully you jumped under the shower. And a second later you jumped back out—scalded. The water was boiling. You couldn't put your hand under it for even a second. The stall filled up with steam. Half-covered with suds, eyes tearing, you groped for the door and kicked it again.

"Officer, it's boiling! Make it colder!"

"You are never satisfied. Either it is too cold or too hot. Some people are too much . . ."

The officer grumbled with dissatisfaction. He seemed to be about to change the temperature of the water but then he called out:

"Stop washing. Your time is up—I'm turning the water off!"

But by then you were indifferent to everything. Circles were beginning to dance before your eyes. Your feet had turned to putty. Still half-covered with suds, squinting, suffocating in the whirls of steam, you began to lose consciousness and sink to the cement floor. The guard came in and carried you to the dressing room, where you lay until you came around.

That was shower day at the Big House. The finale was not always so dramatic. Once, for example, I managed to regain consciousness while still in the shower and crawled to the dressing room myself. But Viktor Boguslavsky's heart gave out, and he was unconscious when they carried him into the dressing room.

In the cell, too, you live at the whim of some administrator. He decides who your cell-mate will be, and it often seems that he finds pleasure in placing the most incompatible people in the same cell. Just when you have reached the depths of despair, when you wish you had a vial of sleeping pills so that you would never again have to wake up—that is when you are placed in a cell with a former sergeant-major from a sonderkommando, a man who has been convicted of murder and mayhem. Or you may find yourself with a pickpocket who has forgotten that you are not supposed to spit and blow your nose on the floor. The cell becomes a pigsty inhabited by two people who hate each other's guts.

Why is solitary confinement so feared? After all, it could be considered a dream come true—especially if you are self-contained, especially if you have something to think about; especially if you have books.

Imagine what it is like to have such solitude in prison. You can organize the room to please yourself. You can walk around the small space as much as you want, without having to relinquish the path to anyone. You can read for days and days without interruption. You are happy. One week passes, and then another. One day you notice, as you leaf through several pages of a book, that you haven't the slightest idea of what it is about. You read it again, and the same thing happens again—your eyes see the page, but your mind is wandering.

You realize that the solitude and the silence are beginning to affect you. You remember former cell-mates, and they don't seem so bad as they used to. You begin to dream of hearing a voice, any voice. You begin to dream about having a cell-mate. Not just any cell-mate, but a good one. One whose faults will complement your own faults. Better yet, two cell-mates or three, so that there will always be the possibility of variety.

In the weeks before the trial began, my cell-mate was Peter Ikonnikov, burglar and drug addict. When Peter reached the age of conscription, he had gone to serve in the Soviet navy. There he served inconspicuously but was caught at petty theft, received a sentence from a military tribunal and began a lifetime of incarceration in camps, years broken only by periods of freedom in which he earned new prison terms.

Peter talked quickly and continually. By the end of our first day together, I knew everything about him that I was supposed to know, and then some. In the beginning, when our relations were friendly, I did something that I later came to regret—I taught him the Israeli song *"Boker ba le-avoda."* After that I had no peace. If he wasn't chattering, he was singing, twisting the words. Or he was whistling the tune. I had no respite from it, in the cell or in the exercise yard. It became a form of torture.

The food at the Big House was not bad. It was supplemented by Eva's monthly packages and my allotment at the prison store. I realized that I could begin to save food for the time when I would be sent to a camp. Each month Eva sent me two kilos of good smoked sausage, the maximum permitted. Each day I cut slices of about 15 grams for myself and for Peter—and that left about one kilo of sausage each month that I stored away. Gradually I accumulated about eight kilos of sausage.

We had the right to acquire 250 grams of powdered sugar at the prison store each month. Of this I consumed nothing—it all went into the "savings fund," along with the sausages and the rusks I was also accumulating.

One day the guard handed out rags that we were to use to wash the cell floor. I saw, to my amazement, that around the perimeter of one of those rags was a design of faded, six-pointed stars. How could I preserve that rag from the guards? I asked for a needle and thread, saying that I had to mend my trousers. Then from half the cloth I made a little bag, and into it I poured the sugar that had accumulated. After that, during any search, the guards treated the little bag as a packaging for storing provisions. It went along with me on transports, comforting me with its little six-pointed stars.

At the prison store I bought cigarettes to use as currency in the camps. I kept the cigarettes, the rusks and the sugar in a bag under my cot. All the sausages but the one from which we were eating I kept wrapped in old newspaper on the window sill, the coldest place in the cell and the best place, I figured, to preserve them.

But the cold did not preserve my sausages. One day I decided to unwrap them to see how much I had accumulated. By my calculations, by then I had about eight kilos. I took the package down from the window sill. I found that it contained about 300 grams of sausage and lots and lots of air. I realized that Ikonnikov must have been eating about a kilo each night. He had done it secretly, under his blanket, so that I never heard a sound. He had consumed almost my entire cache of sausage.

From the time Peter Ikonnikov entered the cell, I had shared my food with him. The discovery of his theft was so unexpected that for several days I was silent. Finally I suggested to Peter that he leave the cell. He looked at me insolently and said:

"I'm fine here. You leave." And then, taunting me, he whistled his favorite Israeli song, *"Boker ba le-avoda."*

I could have asked to be received by the head of the prison so that I could explain the situation to him—and probably he would have had Ikonnikov taken away. But that was unacceptable to me. What we needed was a good fight in the cell—preferably a bloody fight. So I began to prepare for that.

Peter was a healthy lad, much taller than I am. And he had been fortified by seven kilos of smoked sausage. Justice was on my side, but that was not enough. I knew from experience that I had the usual Jewish intellectual complex—I couldn't punch a man in the face if he had not provoked me to the boiling point.

The antagonism between us electrified the atmosphere in the cell. Ikonnikov understood what was happening and began to prepare. Somehow he got hold of a piece of iron, which he sharpened in the cell when lax guards were on duty, and during walks in the exercise yard. I slept with my eyes half open. My nerves were taut, and I could not concentrate on preparations for the approaching trial.

Our Trial Begins

On the morning of May 11, 1971, a guard took me from my cell, through the prison, and out to a Black Maria. I could see that one of the compartments of the vehicle had already been locked—through the crack under the door feet were visible. I was locked into a separate compartment. Our destination, I knew, was the Leningrad Courthouse.

The Black Maria started, went just a short distance to the prison gates, and stopped. I heard the door open and the voices of the guards checking our documents. Then the door slammed shut, the prison gates clanked open, and the Black Maria rolled through the gates and onto the street.

Sitting inside the windowless van, I visualized the streets through which we passed during that excursion through the city I had once loved, the cradle of three revolutions, and of my personal one as well. After the gates closed I felt the van turn left (onto Voinov), then after about a hundred feet it stopped, and again turned left (onto Liteyny Boulevard).

It was after 8:00 am—the trial was to begin at 9:00 am I wondered how Liteyny looked. The buses overloaded with workers had already passed and the housewives had not yet come out to do their shopping. Most of the people on the street would be civil servants.

The van turned right—probably onto Pestel Street, I thought. Then left—probably Mokhovaya. Again right, again left. Then it slowed down and seemed to go up over a curb and across a sidewalk. We had arrived.

I heard the back doors of the van open and then the sound of a key being inserted into the lock of my compartment. The door opened and I got out and looked around. We were in the yard of the courthouse. An officer placed me between two robust young soldiers—one in front of me and one behind—who had the silver insignia of the internal forces on their epaulets. The officer was wearing a clean, well-pressed overcoat and a new cap; all three of them were carrying pistols in holsters. It was obvious from their expressions that they were on an important mission.

The four of us started off. Even going up stairs, the soldiers tried to keep in step. Instinctively I tried to fall in step also, even though I was miserably aware of being shorter than each of them by two heads. Thank heavens, I thought, that no one else can see me. But then we entered a corridor leading into a big hall. Bright lights were turned on and I heard the click and whir of movie cameras. I looked up and saw a whole brigade of cameramen along the length of the hall. The lights blinded me. I threw out my chest, raised my head, and tried to walk on tiptoe in order to ruin this miserable spectacle. But my efforts were in vain. When the film was shown to millions, I would look like a pygmy between those two giants. If I didn't stay in step, I would look like a pitiful little intellectual. Even walking in step and swinging my arms as they did, I looked ludicrous. Everything had been anticipated, everything planned.

We had reached the courtroom. In the middle was an elevated platform for the judges. The people's prosecutors sat next to the judges. Below the judges at one end were tables for the lawyers and, at the opposite end, an area set off by waist high partitions. Within that enclosure were four benches for the defendants.

The soldier in front of me opened a little gate in the partition and stepped aside, telling me to go in and sit on the front bench. He stood next to me, outside the enclosure.

I was told that I did not have the right to greet or address the other defendants—in Russian or any other language—when they were brought in.

I heard in the distance the sound of soldiers approaching the courtroom. The door opened, the spotlights blazed again. Now, I thought, I would learn whose feet I had seen under the door of the other occupied compartment of the Black Maria. A soldier brought Viktor Boguslavsky into the enclosure and seated him on the last bench, diagonally to the right of me. The soldier stood next to Victor, just outside the enclosure.

One at a time my friends made their way past the whirring cameras and the blinding glow of the spotlights. Finally the enclosure was full—nine of us were sitting on the four benches. Vladik Mogilever and I were on the first bench, Lev Yagman and Lev Korenblit on the second, Misha Korenblit, Solomon Dreizner and Lassal Kaminsky on the third, Viktor Shtilbans and Viktor Boguslavsky on the last one. David Chernoglaz, Tolya Goldfeld and Hillel Shur were missing. They were to be tried in Moldavia, with the Kishinev members of our Organization.

The so-called lawyers for the defense appeared. They were supposed to be defenders of the accused for accusers of Zionism. They walked up to each other, shook hands and began chatting.

The prosecutors—not so-called, but real—took their places. The face of Inessa Katukova had already assumed the expression of a relentless defender of socialism. Next to her was the six-foot-tall chief prosecutor Georgy Ponomarev, who was not very bright and would do Katukova's bidding throughout the trial.

And then I had my first surprise, as the guards began to admit the claque. Only then did I realize that this was to be an open trial. Some of the defendants, no doubt, had prepared speeches in their defense. Probably they had done so thinking that no one but those present at the trial in some official capacity would hear them in a closed court, and that their words would never reach the public. Now they might want to revise their speeches. On the eve of the trial, I had been preparing only for a fight with Ikonnikov. Whether the trial was open or closed, I would say whatever God put into my head.

The hall filled up. A small group of relatives was allowed to come in, to occupy the seats to the left of the aisle. I saw my mother and father. Eva came in, but was immediately forced to leave because she was on the list of witnesses, and a witness may not be present in the courtroom except when testifying. My sister was not permitted to enter at all. With other relatives who were not allowed entry to this "open trial," she sat in the corridor, awaiting an answer from the attorney general of the USSR, to whom she had sent a telegram requesting permission to attend. My only sister sat out in the corridor, while the hired claque hundreds settled in comfortably, awaiting the start of the spectacle. They had official status as representatives of the people. They were prepared to "seethe with indignation."

I scanned the rows of public observers, looking for someone from the Elektrik factory, where I had been working when I was arrested. And of course I found someone. The collective could not ignore the fact that one of their number had been accused of such serious crimes. Over near the aisle sat Comrade Bodrov, secretary of the Party organization of the factory. I wondered if he remembered the circumstances in which we first became acquainted. It was a situation a little out of the ordinary, at a kolkhoz where we had been helping with the potato harvest a year and a half earlier.

In Russia, five to six times as many people work in agriculture as in America. But even so, they are unable to succeed without the help of city dwellers. Each autumn, hordes of scientists and engineers go to the countryside to follow the potato-harvesting machines in the fields, and help gather the crop.

During one of those harvests, I landed in the same potato field as Bodrov. He was then secretary of the Party bureau of the planning section at the Elektrik factory. About half of the Elektrik brigade were male Jews; there were almost no women. Many of the non-Jewish men were alcoholics. They drank in the evening, and again in the morning, and during the day they lay in the bushes near the potato field, sleeping it off. Typically, there were many anti-Semites among them.

Bodrov was housed in the same barrack I was in. And so was "Aleksandr," one of the perpetual drunks. One evening Aleksandr was in a particularly bad mood. He fixed his dulled stare on my neighbor, Zhenya Fradkin, a modest Jewish laborer, and began to tell Zhenya what he thought of him in particular and of Jews in general.

Zhenya knew better than to tease a dangerous animal, and was silent. All the Jews were silent. All the non-Jews were also silent, including the secretary of the party bureau, Bodrov. An ordinary occurrence, the kind that makes some Jews thick-skinned and turns some Jews into Zionists.

I tossed around all night. Aleksandr's drunken diatribe against Jews—an overt and public expression of anti-Semitism—had to be answered. After reveille, I washed and dressed. Then, while the morning bustle was still going on, I ran around to all the barracks and warned everyone, especially the Jews, to eat breakfast quickly. A meeting was to be held in our section, I said, immediately after breakfast—an extraordinary occurrence had taken place and was to be discussed. Before the meeting started, I went to Bodrov and informed him that people had decided to meet in connection with the incident of the previous evening. Naturally, I told him, he was expected to say a few words.

A meeting in the morning before work was unusual,

and people were curious. Even some who never attended meetings came to that one. They crowded onto the cots and stood in the aisles. I addressed the assembled crowd and described what had happened the night before. And, I added, it had been suggested that the guilty individual should be severely punished for violating the Soviet constitution and the Criminal Code, which required punishment for inciting national hatred. Then Bodrov spoke, mumbling a few words about how "it hadn't turned out well."

He was followed immediately by several professional Komosomol speakers who automatically condemned the guilty party and warmly supported the suggestion of punishment. The sobered-up drunk stood up in front of the group and publicly repented. He submitted himself to sharp criticism, asked for Zhenya's forgiveness, and promised not to repeat his behavior of the previous evening. And then the meeting was over.

For days that meeting was the subject of conversations in the corridors. Both Jews and Russians were disturbed by that confrontation with anti-Semitism. To the Jews, it seemed that finally the struggle against anti-Semitism had begun. The anti-Semites could not understand what had happened.

In the USSR, a meeting—any meeting—takes place only on initiative from above. The agenda is known in advance. The leader of the meeting and the individual who is to "shoot the barbs" are designated in advance. But no one suspected that my "impostor" meeting was illegal. I had used such phrases as "it has been suggested that a meeting be convened" and "severe condemnation has been advocated" to obscure the lack of official sponsorship. Had Bodrov eventually understood what had happened?

Now, a year and a half later, we sat in the courtroom. Each of us had advanced on the path he had chosen. I was a defendant at a Zionist trial. He was secretary of the Party organization of the entire factory, and was in the courtroom as a representative of the people, prepared to welcome reprisals against me. At that barracks meeting Bodrov had had an opportunity to see why Jews become Zionists, to see how anti-Semitism creates them. I wondered if he remembered the incident now.

Bodrov sat near the aisle and looked over at the defendants in the enclosure. He would, in the days that followed, "severely condemn and unanimously approve."

The trial began. The judge, Nina Isakova, sat in her armchair and imperiously surveyed the arena of action, to see if everything needed for the performance was on hand. After the trial she would receive the title of meritorious jurist of the RSFSR, an award suitable for the director of this judicial production.

She saw nine "Zionist parasites" in place within the enclosure. Nine lawyers —of whom six were Jews—were in place in front of the enclosure. She knew that all of the attorneys, Jews and non-Jews alike, would perform their roles as expected. Looking into the hall, Judge Isakova saw the relatives of the defendants. They wouldn't applaud, she knew, but they wouldn't start a rebellion, either. Each one of them had a job. Each had children. The habits ingrained in them in Stalin's day had not faded. She looked over at the hired claque. They were ready. The trial could begin.

The defendants were identified, so that everyone was convinced that the right prisoners had been brought to the courtroom. The Soviet court was just—no longer was it possible, as it had been in Stalinist times, to try the wrong person.

Each of the defendants, in turn, was asked about his attitude toward the accusations. Each was asked whether he acknowledged that he was guilty. Each defendant was given an opportunity to testify about each of the matters covered in the interrogations. Each remembered the refrain of the investigator about "sincere confessions and heartfelt repentance." Each was supposed to believe that the more he confessed, the less severe his sentence would be.

The accused was not bound by his testimony during the preliminary investigation. And so it was possible for a man who had "confessed everything" during the preliminary investigation to change his testimony when he got to court—to renounce what he said in response to the interrogation and even, perhaps, to declare that he had given false testimony under coercion.

By law, a case is heard in court in order to confirm or refute the conclusions of the preliminary investigation. But what a defendant says in court can be ignored by the judge. She does not need to trust the court presentation of the parties. All of the words of the prosecutors, lawyers, witnesses and defendants can be heeded or ignored, as it suits the judge. She can decide to believe what was said during the preliminary investigation, or what is said in court—whichever suits the court's purposes.

During the months of the preliminary investigation, the nine of us had been completely isolated from each other. We were under intense psychological pressures, and we were by and large ignorant when it came to the Criminal Code. One result was that we gave different answers to the question about whether or not we acknowledged that we were guilty. Our answers ranged from complete acknowledgment to complete disavowal, with all possible shades and nuances in between.

The secretary of the court is responsible for recording testimony, including such nuances. In this court, that role was filled by Logvinova, a woman with whom I had studied at the law institute. There she had been known for her lack of principles. She retained that characteristic after graduation, recording the proceedings in a way that fulfilled the needs of the court, rather than accurately reflecting the testimony of the defendants.

It cannot be denied that the particular definitions of some words, the subtle nuances of some phrases, might escape the understanding of someone unfamiliar with the workings of a Soviet court. But common sense and an honest intent to record accurately what is being said will normally suffice. Not in Logvinova's case, however.

For example, if a defendant said that he acknowledged only the facts with which he was charged, then it should have been clear to everyone that he did not acknowledge the interpretation of those facts which made him guilty according to some article of the Criminal Code. But that was not clear to Logvinova. On the protocol of the court session she placed a check mark next to "confessed."

Similarly, if someone confessed to being partially guilty—that is, if he consented to the facts but not to the way they were qualified—Logvinova might write "partially." In legal language, the word partially in this context means that the accused agrees with the legal qualification but denies some of the facts.

Of the nine defendants, only Misha Korenblit and I were charged with treason for having participated in the preparation to hijack a plane. Misha confessed to being partially guilty according to this article—that is, he acknowledged that he had participated in the preparations for a time, but said that he then thought it over and declined to participate any further. That is, the facts in the charge were correct, but they had not been correctly qualified.

Misha's attorney, Buziner, a Jew, knew that Misha's refusal to participate further was evidence of his total voluntary rejection of the plan to carry out the crime—and that, in turn, meant that Misha should not be sentenced to any punishment. But Buziner never mentioned this to Misha.

I am sure that Logvinova understood what Misha meant, but she was also aware that neither he nor his attorney pointed out that Misha's rejection of the crime meant that he should not receive any punishment. She wrote on Misha's protocol: "Confessed his guilt." Perhaps she added: "Partially." But that was not an accurate record of what Misha was saying.

The judge began to read the indictment. This document had been drawn up by Colonel Menshakov, the senior investigator in the investigation division of the Leningrad KGB, district administration, attached to the Council of Ministers of the USSR. The indictment had been confirmed by the head of the division, Colonel Barkov, and the head of the KGB district administration, Lieutenant General Nosyrev.

In this case, No. 15, the sentence would resemble the indictment as two chairs from the same set of furniture resemble each other—only an experienced carpenter can tell them apart. I do not understand why, during sentencing, judges almost mechanically copy the indictments drawn up by the KGB organs. After all, that is incontrovertible evidence that the sentence is predetermined. Even a plagiarist will at least bother to change the order of the words he is stealing. Can it simply be that the judges are lazy?

Anyone in the audience who was able to follow the reading of the indictment might have observed that it had all the social realist elements of the style of Soviet writers— hostile activity by Zionist parasites and a sorrowful epilogue. The claque sat listening, brows furrowed, trying to understand what we were accused of having done. The story they heard is the following:

In November 1966 by virtue of Zionist convictions, Butman, Mogilever and Dreizner entered into a criminal pact with their like-minded friends Chernoglaz and Shpilberg (who have now been arrested in other cases). These five men created, in Leningrad, an underground anti-Soviet Zionist organization. They worked out its structure, program and statutes, and determined the tasks of the organization. Those tasks were to propagandize Zionist ideology, slander the international and national policy of the Soviet regime and incite feelings for emigration among people of Jewish nationality and so encourage them to emigrate to Israel.

The claque, most likely, did not understand what we had done, but they understood that it was something terrible on a large scale. The key word in the indictment was the common swear word "Zionism." In the USSR, Zionism had not been declared illegal, as it had been in tsarist Russia. And it was not mentioned in the Criminal Code. The simple Soviet citizen does not know what Zionism really is. But constant negative references to Zionism in the press had created the impression that it was both terrible and forbidden. So the claque frowned and shivered.

After Isakova had read for about an hour, she began to sound hoarse. She gave the indictment to her secretary, who read the rest of the text.

The introduction of the indictment contained an analysis of the domestic and international situation that formed the context in which our Organization was created. When that analysis was read, I heard for the first time one of the themes of the indictment: "The danger of the activity of Zionism is deepened by the presence of nationalist Zionist feelings among the politically immature segment of the population of socialist states." This jaw-breaking jumble amounted to an admission that something was rotten in the Union of the Soviet Socialist Republics. Half a century after the victorious October, Zionism was still alive and was the ideal—not of few individuals, but of "a segment of the population."

The claim of our "political immaturity" was, as even the claque understood, ridiculous. All nine of us were productive members of society. None of us led parasitic lives—we all worked. None of us had ever been tried before for any crime. And we all had done graduate work—among us were a lawyer, a graduate student in mathematics, three engineers, a physicist with a doctorate, an architect and two doctors.

Finally the secretary came to the end of the indictment and was silent. Isakova declared a recess. I was scheduled to speak next.

CHAPTER THIRTY

Statements of the Defendants

Judge Isakova resumed her place when the short recess was over. My time had come. This was my chance to respond to the charges—to give the court a clear picture of my activities, my thoughts, my feelings. Because of that damned sausage-stealing Ikonnikov, I was totally unprepared.

The hall was silent. Hundreds of eyes were on me: the judges, and lawyers, the claque, relatives and defendants all waited. Because I was the first of the nine defendants to speak, I felt a grave responsibility. I did not know how to begin.

I faced two major charges. The first was complicity in treason, in the form of organizational activity in preparation for the hijacking of a plane and a group escape from the USSR (Article 64a of the Criminal Code of the RSFSR). The second was anti-Soviet agitation and propaganda (Article 70 of the Criminal Code of the RSFSR).

The indictment included two other charges. One fell under Article 72 of the Criminal Code, which is an automatic appendage to the article about anti-Soviet propaganda and agitation and applies when two or more people jointly take part in such activities. The possible punishment under Article 72 is the same as the punishment for complicity in treason—probably a death sentence.

The other charge in my indictment was concealment of a crime (Article 189, Part 1 of the Criminal Code). That charge related to the concealment, by the Leningrad group, of the parts of the copying apparatus that had been sent to us by Organization members in Kishinev—parts that were to be used to build our own copying machine for Project Launch. The prescribed punishments under Article 189 are nothing, compared to the punishments for treason. I did not object to the charge under Article 189 and pleaded guilty to concealing the stolen machine parts.

The first two charges—treason and anti-Soviet propaganda and agitation—were the most onerous and complex. I did not plead guilty to treason because I remembered, from the course I had taken on criminal-procedural law, the legal implications of voluntary rejection of a crime: a voluntary refusal completely relieves one of responsibility for the execution by others of the planned acts. My actions after we received the negative reply from Israel contained all the elements of voluntary rejection of a crime. Moreover, according to the law, it was not significant whether my rejection was the result of my own initiative or someone else's influence. And so I did not confess to guilt on this charge.

But there is an exception to the exclusion of responsibility even with voluntary rejection: when there is a component of some other crime committed in the actions preparatory to the crime that is voluntarily rejected, the accused can be punished for that other crime. That "other crime," in my case, was anti-Soviet agitation and propaganda under Article 70 of the Criminal Code. The descriptive part of this article states that anti-Soviet agitation and propaganda can be conducted with the goals either of subverting or weakening the Soviet regime or of committing particularly dangerous state crimes—in my case, hijacking a plane.

It was clear to me that, for my role in organizing Operation Wedding, I would receive some punishment. And it seemed to me that the best I could hope for was that that punishment would come from within the framework of Article 70 of the Criminal Code. It seemed likely that the most favorable sentence I could hope for would be for anti-Soviet propaganda and agitation. For this, the maximum punishment would be seven years of imprisonment.

When I re-analyze the legal aspects of our trial today, it is clear to me that— even with my organizational role in the first version of Operation Wedding—the charge against me of anti-Soviet propaganda and agitation was inappropriate, just as it was for the other defendants, although for different reasons. My actions in organizing Operation Wedding could have qualified as propaganda and agitation directed at committing a particularly dangerous crime—treason—only if the airplane group had caused damage to the independence of the state, to its territorial inviolability or to the military might of the USSR. But the independence of the state was not damaged, nor was its territorial inviolability or its military power. So the charge against me of anti-Soviet propaganda was as trumped-up as the charge of treason against the airplane group.

Once I started talking, I was carried along by the momentum of what I was saying. For several hours I talked about my life. Two groups of ideas stood out: first, my rejection of capitalism as a social system that has no future and my belief that socialism is an especially just system; and second, my deep feeling of belonging to the Jewish people who have been dispersed around the world, compassion for the tragic fate of Jews in all generations and particularly in my own, rejection of anti-Semitism in any form, and emigration to Israel as a solution to the problem.

My life had been a series of clashes with anti-Semitism. Those experiences slowly but surely changed me from an indoctrinated member of the Komosomol into an ardent Zionist. My life had been a constant struggle to maintain my national dignity under conditions that made me defenseless. Having to call that meeting at the kolkholz during the potato harvest because the Party representative elected not to act was but one such example of the struggle.

I talked about the relevance of anti-Semitism in other countries, and about Meir Kahane and the Jewish Defense League in the United States. I said that although I rejected their methods, I accepted their goals—because anti-Semitism is increasing all over the planet and we are forced to defend ourselves against it.

Concluding my speech, I left open the question of whether anti-Semitism is state policy in the USSR or a manifestation of the prejudice of lone individuals, including government officials. The answer had long ago become clear to me, and had brought me to the Organization. The answer was also clear, in differing degrees, to those on both the left and the right sides of the courtroom aisle.

I wanted it to be clear to everyone in the room that it was anti-Semitism that had, quite directly, been responsible for the actions of which I stood accused.

Why did I talk so much about anti-Semitism? There was a time when I hated anti-Semites and anti-Semitism. By the time I was put to trial, my rational attitude toward anti-Semitism had changed. All that was left was hatred of anti-Semites. I realized that without anti-Semitism, the nine defendants in the enclosure would have been assimilated. Under the conditions in which we had lived, Jewish culture and religion had been completely destroyed; the Jews of the USSR would long since have been absorbed into the so-called "new international Soviet people" were it not for pervasive anti-Semitism. The suffering that each of us had experienced as a result of anti-Semitism had been an essential part of our evolution into Zionists. I finished my speech with these words:

> In the indictment it is stated that I confessed to being guilty of membership in an anti-Soviet, illegal

Zionist organization. But if one examines carefully the meaning of these words, it is evident that the "anti-Sovietism" of our Organization consisted only in indirect damage caused by our activity. Never was it our goal to weaken or subvert the Soviet regime. Yes, our Organization was illegal. But only in the sense that we were not able to be registered and did not register our Organization with the appropriate financial organs. Yes, our Organization was Zionist—but Zionist according to our understanding of Zionism, which is that Jews have the right to have their own independent state in their ancient homeland and the right to freely emigrate from all countries of the world and settle in Israel. This Zionism and the Zionism that is written about in Soviet papers have nothing in common.

My speech took almost six hours. I had thought only Fidel Castro had the strength to talk that long. By the time I finished I was hoarse. I sat down, completely exhausted.

One by one, in the days to come, each of the others had a turn to speak. During the rest of that first day I heard almost nothing. I put my head down on the top of the low enclosure and rested until I began to recover. The soldiers left the enclosure for a few seconds, long enough for Vladik Mogilever to whisper to me:

"Grisha Vertlib and Kreina Shur received visas. They are already in Israel."

Had *aliyah* really begun? I wanted to believe it, but I was afraid. Both Grisha and Kreina had been given categorical refusals when they first applied for visas. They were not old people or invalids—they were both in their thirties. So their release seemed like the first harbinger of spring. But was it? Was the government getting rid of two bad apples, two people they had already decided not to imprison, because the reaction of the West to our imprisonment had been so unexpectedly powerful? Or was it the long-awaited start of *aliyah*? Was it a only a thaw, or was it really spring?

Soon it would be Lev Yagman's turn to speak. He was sitting directly behind me, on the second bench. It was important to me that Lev mention my report to the last meeting of the members of the Committee, the report about my final conversation with Mark Dymshitz, after we had received the negative answer from Israel. But there was no way I could turn around. The soldier who was watching me was glued to his post, and he seemed to sense that I was planning something.

Fortunately, we were permitted to take notes during the trial, so I had pencil and paper in my lap. Pretending to make a note of something that had been said, I wrote a few key words in large letters. Then I picked up the paper, as if to better read what I had written, and held it high enough so that Lev could see it. Lev is an intelligent man. He would be able to figure it out.

I enjoyed listening to Lev's speech. I imagine that it was less pleasant for the judges. Although Lev is a maritime engineer, it was clear that he understood the legal aspects of the trial. Lev denied that he was guilty as charged under Article 70. He pointed out the provisions of the article that demanded that the individual participating in anti-Soviet propaganda and agitation have a direct intention to subvert or weaken the Soviet regime. In the absence of direct intent, Article 190, Part 1, of the Criminal Code is to be applied. Article 190, Part 1, is not part of the section that deals with particularly dangerous state crimes, and it carries a maximum sentence of three years. Lev insisted that in his indictment, Article 70 was to be replaced with Article 190, Part 1. His position was absolutely correct, the only correct position for those who were not charged with treason.

Lev also talked about his life. He spoke of the childhood of a small intellectual lad in glasses, who took boxing classes to learn to defend himself. As I listened to him, it seemed inevitable to me that the man who had been that boy should have become a member of our Organization.

Lassal Kaminsky spoke after Lev. Like Lev, he became a member of the Committee only thirty-nine days before his arrest. Lassal was to head what we referred to as Project Aliyah—to develop and implement measures for applying pressure on the Soviet government, with the goal of achieving mass *aliyah*.

Lassal spoke in the same spirit as Lev Yagman, but his speech had a sarcastic edge. He did confess to partial guilt in response to the charges of anti-Soviet propaganda and agitation, but apparently only because he was ignorant of the law. Nevertheless, it was clear that Lassal's partial confession meant, "I acknowledge the facts, but I reject the way they are interpreted." Lassal's sarcastic barbs were subtle, and it is possible that they were not completely understood by the deputy prosecutor, Georgy Ponomarev. But Judge Inna Isakova and Chief Prosecutor Inessa Katukova understood perfectly what defendant Kaminsky was saying.

Neither Lev nor Lassal took advantage of the fact that they had become members of the Committee only a short time before their arrest. They were not going to play that game. No "sincere confession" or "heartfelt repentance" for them—all of which counted against them when the judges, relying on their own socialist legal conscience, began meting out our sentences.

CHAPTER THIRTY-ONE

Witnesses

The defendants finished speaking. One by one the witnesses took the stand. Glebov, head of the planning-experimental section of the Elektrik factory, which had been awarded the order of the Red Banner, was first to testify. He talked for a long time, monotonously, telling the court that he had not wanted to hire the engineer Butman, but that the devil confused him. When Glebov left, an unspoken question hung in the courtroom. Why had he not wanted to hire Butman? After all, he had not known, then, anything about Butman's political views. So, clearly, he had not wanted to hire Butman because Butman was "an invalid of the fifth question"—a Jew. In protecting himself, Glebov inadvertently revealed the anti-Semitism in Soviet hiring practices.

Then Volodya Sharov, the second witness from the Elektrik factory, spoke. During Project Launch, Volodya, at my request, cut several plastic pieces of various shapes, to be used for the copying machine that was fabricated by Solomon Dreizner's group. He had no idea why I wanted those pieces, and I had not told him. We had picked potatoes together. I took advantage of this and, with the judge's permission, cross-examined Volodya.

"Volodya, do you remember when we were together in the fall of 1969 at the kolkhoz in the Lodeinopolsky district?"

"I do."

"Do you remember how, once in the morning, before work, I called a meeting?"

"I do."

"Do you remember what was talked about at that meeting?"

Volodya Sharov is a good fellow, and he remembered that meeting well. The talk at that meeting was different from the usual, boring speechifying at other meetings he had to attend. Volodya stood in the witness box thinking, then he blushed and was silent for a long time. Finally, he lowered his eyes, and he answered me in a subdued voice.

"I don't remember."

I, Hillel Butman, was forced to sit in prison, but he, Volodya Sharov, had to work. Every man for himself. Probably in his place I would have done the same thing.

"Call the witness Parela Tsinkovskaya!"

The door to the courtroom opened and a light rustle passed along the rows. A pretty, long-legged young woman with dark hair falling over her shoulders walked down the aisle, her high heels clicking. She wore Western style clothes—a short skirt and a bright, tightly fitting sweater. Her name and her proud carriage bespoke her Polish origin.

At the time of the trial Parela Tsinkovskaya was a saleswoman in a department store in Riga. Before that she was a stewardess for a domestic airline. The judge asked her to identify, among the accused, the citizen who entered the pilot's cabin during the flight from Leningrad to Riga on February 19, 1970.

The witness looked us over slowly, carefully. No, she could not identify any of us as that citizen. She left the courtroom and the door closed behind her. She probably paid a high price for her integrity.

Then the pilot of the plane entered the court. Even as he walked down the aisle toward the witness stand, he looked us over carefully. When the judge asked the pilot to identify the citizen who entered his cabin during that flight, he answered promptly.

"That comrade, there," he said amicably, pointing to me and smiling. A simple Russian fellow. Perhaps he remembered the bottle of wine I handed to him—a gift that, one could assume, he opened right after the flight. This was a simple man; he had not yet learned to play a role. Both his smile and his reference to me as "comrade" indicated that he realized how ludicrous it was for the prosecution to say that we wanted to kill the pilots.

Two years earlier, in 1969, when we had first made copies of *Exodus*, Lassal Kaminsky had given one of those copies to a Russian colleague, Aleksandr Verkhovsky. Lassal had hoped that reading *Exodus* would help his friend understand why Lassal wanted to emigrate. But now, because he had given Exodus to Aleksandr, Lassal was charged with subversion: an effort to convince Aleksandr—a Russian, not a Jew—to emigrate to Israel. Aleksandr was called before the court to testify on this subject.

Lassal's attorney, Rozhdestvensky, decided to use sarcasm to show that his client had *not* disseminated literature to encourage emigration.

"Tell me," he said to Aleksandr Verkhovsky, "why did you and your family decide to settle in Israel?"

Verkhovsky shuddered nervously and looked around the room. He was no fool. He knew that there were many KGB agents present in the courtroom. He knew that his fate—and also the fate of several generations of his descendants—would be determined by his response.

"I . . . to Israel? After all, I'm Russian," Verkhovsky began. But his voice cracked from agitation, his throat constricted, and he could not continue.

"I ask you, again, when did you, a Russian man, Aleksandr Verkhovsky, decide to leave your motherland and resettle in the Jewish state?" The voice of Lassal's attorney was stern.

The witness pulled himself together and—stuttering from agitation—explained that he had never entertained such an idea, even in his thoughts. Russia suited him completely, he said. It was simply that he was interested in historical and geographical literature about different countries of the world.

Rozhdestvensky had made his point: Lassal was not trying to convince anyone to emigrate to Israel. He was simply encouraging his friend's interest in historical and geographical literature. Rozhdestvensky glanced victoriously at the judges. But he had forgotten that he was an actor with a role to play—not the playwright. The KGB did not forget. After our trial, Judge Isakova was made a meritorious jurist of the RSFSR; Rozhdestvensky, on the other hand, was stripped of his membership in the Leningrad bar association.

It is interesting to compare the testimony given by the witnesses during the preliminary investigation with what was later said at the trial. Most witnesses told the truth both times. A few, alone with the investigators in the Big House, had not been able to withstand the pressure. But those few, once they were in court facing the defendants and their relatives, quickly corrected their testimony.

Near the end of the fifth day of the trial, a tall, strong lad named Aleksandr Fridman gave his testimony in court. Fridman said that he had not noticed anti-Soviet views among any of the members of the Organization, nor had he seen any anti-Soviet literature. Those of us within the enclosure knew how Fridman had described the Organization under pressure, during the preliminary investigation. Even though, in court, Fridman retracted the testimony he had given to the

KGB investigators earlier, we did not appreciate his earlier effort to exonerate himself.

Before the trial began, we had been permitted to read the case files. We learned then that Fridman wrote a letter to the KGB organs in July 1970, stating his desire to tell everything he knew about the Organization's criminal anti-Soviet activity. He would make his revelations under condition that the KGB arrested all the activists of the Zionist Organization who were not already incarcerated, and in particular Hillel Shur. Before Hillel's arrest, suspicious of Fridman, he had lured him to the backyard of a Leningrad house and, in plain Russian, had told him what awaited him if he started to talk to the KGB. But Fridman was willing to pay any price to remain a witness, rather than become a suspect in the case. And so he talked and escaped prosecution. But then, in court, he recanted what he had said to the KGB during the preliminary investigation. Seeing us all watching him from our benches in the defendants' enclosure, he told the court the truth—that he had not heard us express anti-Soviet views, or seen anti-Soviet literature at our meetings.

The Jewish witnesses spoke—our friends and relatives, unarrested members of the Organization, participants of the orphaned ulpans. When asked by the judge about some members of the Organization, they contrived to start their answers with the phrase "Former citizen of the Soviet Union . . ." And in doing that, they revealed to the defendants that the members about whom they were testifying were already in Israel!

I had already learned from Vladik that Grisha Vertlib and Kreina Shur were in Israel. Now I learned about dozens of other "former Soviet citizens." These included members of the Organization—Natan Tsiryulnikov, Rudik Brud, Benzion Tovbin, Gideon Makhlis, Ilya Elinson. It seemed that the ice was breaking up, that the long-awaited *aliyah* had really started!

My gratitude went out to the witnesses who started their testimony with those welcome words. After that, it was easier to return to the cell. No matter what sentences we were given, we would know that we were not "sitting" in vain.

The fifth day of the trial was almost over. If a Martian who understood Russian had sat through those first five days of our trial, he would have had a clear picture. He would have realized that none of the defendants had known anything about the plan to hijack a plane at the Smolny airport on June 15, 1970. He would have understood that none of the defendants had planned to subvert or weaken the existing order in the USSR. He would have known that the defendants had struggled against the forced assimilation of Jews and for freedom to emigrate to Israel, but that that struggle did not violate any Soviet law. But these facts did not fit the script prepared by the Soviet court.

State Prosecutor Inessa Katukova rose from her seat with a stern expression on her face and looked around. Then she began to thunder at the assembled defendants, witnesses, relatives and the claque. Pity the poor Martian. He would not have been able to believe that this woman had heard the same words he had heard. Why, he would have wanted to ask, was it necessary to listen to the witnesses and defendants for five days, if you now repeat as the summation what was written in the indictment? After all, it was now clear to even a Martian that the defendants were innocent.

Katukova read the prison terms she was demanding— and the Martian would have had a heart attack.

Butman, Hillel—10 years;
Korenblit, Mikhail—8 years;
Kaminsky, Lassal—6 years;
Yagman, Lev—5 years;
Mogilever, Vladimir—4 years;
Dreizner, Solomon—3 years;
Korenblit, Lev—3 years;
Boguslavsky, Viktor—3 years;
Shtilbans, Viktor—1 year.

We are not Martians. We knew that our prison terms would resemble those that Katukova demanded, just as the final sentence resembled the indictment.

The prosecutor thundered on to the end of her speech. Then the lawyers made their speeches. And then we, the defendants, made our final statements. But all that did not matter. The last act of the play had already been written.

On the tenth day of the trial, the judges did not sit down as usual after the standard exhortation, "Rise, the court is in session." Isakova remained standing and, following her example, so did everyone in the hall. In a solemn voice she began:

"In the name of the Russian Federated Republic on May 20, 1971, the Judicial Collegium on Criminal Affairs, of the Leningrad Municipal Court . . ."

Silence reigned in the hall, while she read the formal sentences:

"Butman, Hilya Izraylevich—ten years without confiscation of property, in the absence of such." Just as demanded by the prosecutor.

"Korenblit, Mikhail Semenovich—seven years without confiscation of property in the absence of such." They had taken one year off of the recommended sentence.

"Kaminsky, Lassal Samoylovich, and Yagman, Lev Naumovich—five years each." This sentence was in punishment
for their integrity during the investigation and the trial.
True, they subtracted one year from Lassal's recommended
sentence—the injustice to him, compared to the sentences
of the other defendants, was too blatant.

"Mogilever, Vladimir Osherovich—four years.

Dreizner, Solomon Girshevich, Korenblit, Lev Lvovich,
and Boguslavsky, Viktor Noevich—three years.

Shtilbans, Viktor Iosifovich—one year."

All as demanded by the prosecutor.

Just as in the joke about Soviet justice, the KGB recommendations became sentences that were signed by the
judge and the peoples' assessors. They sat quietly through
the court proceedings and they signed the verdict—all according to the scenario.

And then it was the claque's turn: time for applause. The
curtain fell. After all, they had not been sitting in the courtroom all those days for nothing when they could have been
working productively at their jobs. But the play in the
courtroom was more important. Applaud, applaud—but
know that your applause will be drowned out by the roar of
the planes as they take off from Leningrad and Moscow for
Vienna, filled with passengers headed for Israel. Applaud—
but know that we have had the final word.

CHAPTER THIRTY-TWO

Kishinev Group Trial

A year had passed since my arrest, and a month since the trial. On the morning of June 21, 1971, I found myself not in a loathsome cell, but between heaven and earth in an IL-18 Aeroflot airliner.

I was sitting in a soft seat in the small cabin of the plane. On each side of me sat a civilian dressed in a well-tailored suit, dress shirt, and tie. From time to time one or the other would smile pleasantly and exchange a few polite words with me. One even offered me his book, *When the Cherry Tree Blossoms*, to read during the flight. When the stewardess brought dinner, I saw that we were all given the same meal—meat, rice and a fruit compote. I could not tell from the expression on the stewardess' face whether she knew which one of the three of us was the prisoner.

Solomon Dreizner, Vladik Mogilever, Mark Dymshitz and Lev Korenblit sat in other seats in the small cabin, also enjoying pleasant and reliable escorts and the same fine service. The polite escorts had asked us to sit silently and not to look around. Solomon could at least see the back of my neck, but I, sitting in the front of the cabin, could see only Colonel Barkov, the chief escort.

The five of us were being taken to Kishinev, to be witnesses at the trial there of David Chernoglaz, Tolya Goldfeld, Hillel Shur and the others in the Kishinev group of our Organization. The escorts had brought us into the smaller of the plane's two cabins well before boarding time. When the other passengers started to board, two women tried to enter and take seats there, seeing that the small cabin was half empty but half full of handsome, broad-shouldered men in grey suits. But the escorts politely made it clear that the women were not welcome, and both disappeared into the main passenger cabin. Simple Soviet people do not ask questions.

I sat in the soft airplane seat with a book in my hands. I was wearing a suit and I was not handcuffed. Through the window I saw the forests and rivers of western Belorussia below. The next day it would be exactly thirty years since the columns of German tanks had moved along the sparse highways from here to the east. I looked at the book, then through the window, then back to the book. I couldn't concentrate—too much was happening all at once to a man who had been isolated in prison for more than a year.

After the trial in Leningrad had ended, my legal status had changed from that of a defendant to that of a convict. As a convict I could spend only five rubles per month in the prison store, and was permitted to receive only one package a year. On the other hand, my new status gave me the right to send two letters a month, and, theoretically, the right to receive an unlimited number of letters (the KGB also had the right to withhold those same letters without limitations). I even had the right to a half-hour meeting with Eva before being sent away to camp.

Early in the morning of the day they took us to Kishinev, they gave us our personal things and took us to the Black Marias for the ride to the airport. I immediately dug out and read all of Eva's letters, which I had accumulated in my suitcase while I had the right to correspond. The letters contained many subtle hints and much subtext, and my brain tried feverishly to decipher it all. My eyes, accustomed to seeing only the monotonous walls of the prison cell and yard, now flooded my brain with all this new information.

I looked up from the letters and saw the pretty stewardess in a blue Aeroflot outfit, the snowy white clouds next to the wings of the plane, the pilot with bulging back pocket passing through the cabin. Obviously the authorities had taken precautions, so that the witnesses aboard could not hijack this plane.

At the Kishinev airport some reconstruction work was being done, so the plane landed on a spare runway. After all the passengers in the main cabin had gotten off the plane, Barkov got up and declared solemnly: "The special group of workers of the Leningrad Committee of State Security has fulfilled their task of transporting witnesses to Kishinev." And then he added, more prosaically, "Hilya Izraylevich, you go out first."

From the airplane, we were loaded into Black Marias and taken directly to the Supreme Court of the Moldavian SSR, on Pirogov Street. This was my first visit to Kishinev.

When we arrived at the court building, we were led into a corridor. I was placed in a holding cell with a small window that opened on the corridor, to wait there until summoned to the courtroom. Directly in front of the window, on the wall, was a huge map of the world. All the continents and islands were cut out of wood, painted in various colors and tacked on. I hadn't seen a map for a year. My greedy eyes moved immediately to the juncture of Asia and Africa. Israel was in place. Then I looked over at the red-painted sixth of the hemisphere, which ran to the Finnish Gulf. There it was, the city that was a window to Europe, cut open by Peter the Great—Leningrad. There I was born and grew up. But I shall die in Israel, I thought.

When the guard came to take me to the courtroom, I realized that I had a problem—my pants were falling down.

Even though our status had changed from defendant to convict, the authorities in Leningrad had not yet cut our hair or distributed *zek* clothing to us. I had to put on the blue suit in which I was arrested. I had neither belt nor rope to hold up the pants. During the year in prison I had lost weight: my physique had been reduced to the *zek* standard and now my pants were falling down. As I followed the soldier along a corridor, I kept pulling up my pants, and thinking—with horror—about what might happen in the courtroom. I hitched them up one last time before we went in.

The guard accompanied me to the witness box. The presiding judge was the small, fat Dmitry Bordhiuzha, a member of the Supreme Court of the Moldavian SSR. He began the questioning, first to identify individuals, then about the essence of the case. I quickly became convinced of Bordhiuzha's stupidity and incompetence. He was the pushy sort, dedicated to the "older brother" (the government in Moscow).

Next to Bordiuzha sat the people's assesors—Ivan Kozaku, a Moldavian, and Nikita Sushkov, a Russian—and the chief prosecutor, Poluektov, also Russian. Several years later, after the Kishinev defendants had all been released from the archipelago, Poluektov spent time there for taking bribes. But at the Kishinev trial he was the chief prosecutor.

From the witness stand I looked over at the defendants in the enclosure. There were nine men on the benches— the same number as there had been at our trial in Leningrad. Three of them were from Leningrad. Pale, with their heads shaved bare, all nine looked identical. With some difficulty I identified on the first bench the round face of David Chernoglaz and the glasses of Tolya Goldfeld. But where was Hillel Shur?

One of the defense lawyers rose and addressed me:

"At the preliminary investigation, you testified that you informed defendant Shur about the plan to hijack a Soviet passenger plane. Can you assert with confidence that such a conversation took place between you and Shur?"

Aha, I thought, that means that Hillel denied the very fact of our conversation. As if on a television screen in my head, I visualized the two of us in the Victory Park in Leningrad, and I heard again our heated conversation. Hillel had even offered me a pistol with a filed-off firing pin as a weapon that could be used, if necessary, to intimidate the crew. I had said nothing about the pistol during the preliminary investigation, because I was sure that no one except the two of us knew about it. But I had spoken about the conversation and stressed that Hillel had rejected the idea of hijacking a plane.

The lawyer waited for my answer. The judges waited for my answer. As I stood there in the witness box, thinking about how to answer, I felt a catastrophe coming—my miserable pants had again passed the widest part of my hips and were about to succumb completely to the force of gravity. I had to solve both my legal and the sartorial problems immediately.

Pretending that I was digging in my pocket for a handkerchief, I pulled up my pants and then puffed out my stomach, so that they wouldn't slide down again right away. It was difficult to breathe. It was even more difficult to answer the question. My constitutional inability to lie prevented me from saying that the conversation had not taken place, as the lawyer wanted me to. What could I say?

"At that time," I heard my own voice saying, "I was terribly tense. Many months passed between that conversation and the time of the preliminary investigation. I could have forgotten or been confused about many things. My plan for selecting passengers for the plane required that I speak with dozens of people. Because of the confusion of those days, it was difficult for me to remember with whom I managed to speak in a general way about the possibility of an illegal escape from the USSR, and with whom I only planned to speak. I know for sure that I planned to speak to Hillel Shur, and this was so engraved on my memory that I certainly could have taken the desire for reality. Also, Shur's uncle died at that time, and Hillel wasn't up to anything then" (Hillel's uncle really did die at that time).

That statement was as much of a half-truth as I could tell. The lawyer got up immediately, went over to the man on the left end of the second bench in the defendants' enclosure, and began to whisper to him. I would never have guessed that that pale, shaven, half-dead person was Hillel Shur.

The lawyer finished whispering and returned to his place. It was evident to me that the atmosphere in Kishinev was different from the atmosphere in the court in Leningrad. There, no lawyer would have permitted his client to direct his own defense. Hillel, I learned later, had already challenged the composition of the court, declared a hunger strike, and refused to say a word to the court. After Hillel's lawyer had been instructed by his client, he turned and asked me the next question. It did not relate to a fact but was, instead, a request for my appraisal of Shur's activity in the organization.

In the Black Maria between the airport and the court, Vladik Mogilever and I had, rather brazenly and in front of the guard, agreed in oblique terms about how we would answer such a question:

"Look at that lousy Hillel Shur," one of us had said to the other. "A dummy with cold feet. Why did he creep into the Organization? And after he got in, he didn't do a damn thing except count himself a member. But all the time he was away, building his dacha in Toksovo." We repeated this at the trial.

Evidently our characterization of Hillel, together with his strange behavior at the trial and investigation and his silence, worked. He received a sentence of two years. The other defendants at the Kishinev trial received the following sentences:

Chernoglaz, David—5 years;
Goldfeld, Tolya—4 years;
Halperin, Sasha—2 1/2 years;
Voloshin, Aron—2 years;
Levit, Semyon—2 years;
Trakhtenberg, Lazar—2 years;
Kizhner, Kharik—2 years;
Rabinovich, David—1 year.

The Kishinev prison is a complex of squat buildings around a large courtyard. According to local *zeks*, it was built in the eighteenth century under Empress Catherine the Great, when Moldavia was conquered by Russia.

After my testimony at the trial I was taken down to a subterranean floor and led through an ancient corridor. On the left were wide, thick wooden doors. Across the width of each door was a heavy metal bar that was held in place with an enormous lock. I noticed that the distance between the doors was several times greater than the distance between the cell doors at the Big House. That meant that the walls in Kishinev were thicker. Everything was old, massive. You felt as if you were in recently excavated, ancient stables or storerooms.

The guard fumbled for a long time with the lock on one of the doors. Finally he removed it, threw the iron bar to the floor with a crash, and opened the door. I stepped into my new quarters and saw that I was not alone. At a large wooden table, under a barred window cut close to the ceiling and covered with a shade, sat a muscular fellow, writing something. He was bare to the waist and on his back were tattooed large portraits of Marx, Engels, Lenin and Stalin, in profile, with a profile of Adolf Hitler between Engels and Lenin. This grouping clearly constituted malicious anti-Soviet propaganda, and during the Stalin years the bearer of this living mural would not have survived.

This anti-Soviet back belonged to Filip. When he wasn't in the Kishinev prison for petty crimes, he used to cross the Soviet-Rumanian border and live in Rumania with his Moldavian relatives, or go pillaging with his Rumanian friends. Sometimes, just for variety, he sat in Rumanian prisons for crossing the border illegally. Filip didn't despair. He wrote stories and hoped to get them published under a pseudonym.

We had barely introduced ourselves and begun to chat when someone called Filip from the courtyard. He instantly jumped up on the table, leaped up, and grabbed a newspaper that had been shoved from the courtyard through the bars and into the cell. I could hardly believe my eyes. If a guard can deliver a newspaper from the courtyard, I thought, that means that in the same way it is possible to send notes, money, drugs, in both directions.

The door of the food trap opened and a guard asked whether a *zek* named Drokov was in the cell. Filip answered that that person was not there and never had been, and the guard closed the trap. Then we heard the traps in other cells slamming open and shut as the guards continued to search for the *zek*. I knew that in the Big House in Leningrad, a guard would go to the punishment cell for conducting a search that way. By asking for the *zek* by name, the guard had lifted the curtain of secrecy and revealed the name of someone who was in the prison.

The guards took us out for a walk in the exercise yard. About half a dozen large, triangular sectors, separated by prison walls, radiated from a hub at which stood the watchtower, with two guards on duty. There was a great hubbub in the yards, with whistling, cries and yelling between men in adjacent sectors and men in their cells. From behind the barred windows of the upper floors, prisoners shouted advice to their mates in the yards and in the other cell blocks.

I decided to try to take advantage of the chaos and the lax conditions to see if I could communicate with anyone else from the Organization who might be within range. I started to whistle the Israeli song of the Palmach, at first with the caution of a novice, then louder and more insolently. And from a distant exercise yard I heard an answer. I whistled with all my strength, but the din was so loud that I could hardly hear myself. And then I saw one of the guards on the tower wave to me to approach.

"Whistle more quietly," he requested. "You make it hard for us to talk."

I realized then that so much noise was coming from the exercise yards that the guards in the tower could barely hear each other. When Filip and I were returned to our gloomy underground cell, I felt as if I had just visited a madhouse.

On the day when *zeks* were permitted to make their monthly purchases, Filip brought out a list of the products available in the prison store. I looked at the list and could hardly believe what I saw.

"Filip, there are cucumbers and tomatoes and other vegetables on this list. Are they in cans?"

"Why would they be in cans? It is all fresh, and it's cheap, too."

But those of us from Leningrad had a problem. Prison rules gave us the right to buy five rubles worth of the wonderful things on the list, but our personal monetary accounts remained at the Big House. The authorities might decide to transfer those accounts, but by that time we would be back in Leningrad, or further. The only way we could get funds was to ask relatives to send money by telegraph. But how could I contact relatives?

"Filip, can you send a letter to the outside for me?"

"Sit down and write it. Tomorrow it will go out."

I took out a sheet of paper and a pencil, sat at the table, and wondered to whom I should write. Mama was being watched. My sister was being watched. And if the KGB intercepted my letter, that would mean trouble for Filip, too. I decided that if I wrote to Aunt Sonya, the letter would get through. Aunt Sonya was the matriarch of our clan, and she loved me. I was sure that she would act intelligently, quickly and efficiently. She would tell Eva, and Eva would tell the other families.

There are large Jewish family clans in which one of the old people, kind and wise, is silently acknowledged as the patriarch. In my mother's family—the Chernitskys from Northern Belorussia—there was no patriarch. But there was a matriarch, my grandfather's sister. Her double Jewish name, Sarah-Eidlah, always reminded me of the Pale of Settlement and of the Jewish town of Polotsk, from which the maternal side of our clan came. Even before the war, the family had combined the two names—Sarah and Eidlah—into the more compact Sore-Eda. After the war my generation, the great-nieces and nephews, called this beloved woman "Aunt Sonya."

Aunt Sonya belonged to the generation of Jewish women of Russia, born at the turn of the century, who knew anxiety and fear and deprivation throughout their lives. During childhood those women knew pogroms. They married during the civil war. And then, drawn by post-revolutionary opportunities, they left the shtetls, with the familiar patriarchal way of life and Yiddish as the shared language, and settled in the industrial centers of Russia. There they lived in basements and overcrowded communal apartments, giving birth to their children in an alien environment, surrounded by an unfamiliar culture and language.

Later the authorities came in the night and took away

their husbands. Some of the men were gobbled up forever by the gulags. Others were put to work draining swamps and building roads. The husbands who succeeded in returning were no longer breadwinners, but invalids. And so the Jewish women became the breadwinners and providers for the sons they had borne during the twenties. These boys joined the pioneers' youth organizations in the 1930s, and then fought and perished in World War II.

Aunt Sonya had two sons who gave light and warmth to her drab life. The older, Mordechai, was in the poorly planned counter offensive near Leningrad in the winter of 1942. He slipped on the ice of the snowy Neva, among the waves of attackers, and never got up. Aunt Sonya received a death notice: "He died the death of the brave in the battle near Moskovskaya Dubrovka." He was nineteen years old.

In 1944 Aunt Sonya's younger son, David, fell under Finnish bullets in the forests of Karelya. Aunt Sonya, after starving in blockaded Leningrad, read the second death notice: "He died the death of the brave during the liberation of the Karelo-Finnish SSR." He was also nineteen years old.

The war ended. Aunt Sonya's husband died and she was left alone. She placed enlarged photographs of her husband and sons in the most prominent place in her room. Returning from the long lines at the stores, where she heard endless conversations about the cowardly Jews who "fought on the rear front in Tashkent," Aunt Sonya would kiss the portraits of her sons in their caps with the red stars and weep silently.

I became like a son to Aunt Sonya. She singled me out from the relatives who visited her room in a communal apartment near the Sytny market. We held the first indoor meeting of our Organization in November 1966 in that apartment.

Aunt Sonya was with us at the dacha in Siversky when I was arrested. By then she was ill and in bed. But she recovered from her illness and said, "I shall live until Hillel returns, and then I shall die."

She wrote to me in the camp about that, in rare letters written in her broken Russian mixed with an abundance of Yiddish. She was impatient for my return, and afraid that she would not live that long.

Aunt Sonya immediately accepted Eva as a daughter, and Eva responded warmly. When Eva left for Israel, pregnant, she gave her word—if she gave birth to a boy, she would name it in honor of one of Aunt Sonya's sons. The baby would be a girl, and Eva would call her Geula-Davida. A double name like Aunt Sonya's. Geula (redemption in Hebrew)—a request to the Almighty and Omnipotent for my release, and Davida—in memory of Aunt Sonya's younger son, David Treister.

The name of my sabra justified itself, and in April of 1979 the gates of the Big House opened before the end of my term. Half an hour later I burst into the small room near the Sytny market and squeezed the almost blind Aunt Sonya to my shabby *zek* jacket.

Aunt Sonya kept her promise—she waited for me. And with a punctuality denied to most people, she died, true to her prediction, very soon afterwards.

Toward the end of my first day in prison with Filip at Kishinev, the guards brought Lev Yagman into the cell. Lev and I had barely managed to greet each other when the guards returned with more cell-mates for us, two Moldavian criminals. We began the usual exchange of information with the two newcomers, and what they told Lev and me forced us to act immediately.

The Moldavians told us that before being brought to our cell they had been in a large cell with dozens of criminals.

A short Jewish fellow who was brought into the cell told them that his trial had just ended and that he was to be sent off at any time. He gave the criminals some of his civilian clothes that he would not need in camp. The Jew's generosity turned out to be a mistake—his cell-mates wanted more. When he lay down on a bunk, they untied his bag and took all the clothes left in it. The Jew could do nothing.

Lev and I cross-examined the Moldavians and decided that the Jew was probably Tolya Goldfeld. It was not enough that on that day he had been sentenced to four years in the camps—he was then thrown in with criminals who stole his last few possessions.

We wrote two petitions to the local supervisory prosecutor, demanding that he intercede immediately. We didn't have much hope that these petitions would reach him, but it seemed possible that just submitting them would help. Then we called the duty officer, Lieutenant Ivanov.

Ivanov was as arrogant as a bull. In response to our oral appeal, he explained that Jews are to blame for everything that goes wrong, that they didn't like to work or to fight, that they lived like parasites, at the expense of others, and that, to be honest, Hitler was not so wrong about the Jews.

By the time he stopped talking, my ability to contain myself had evaporated. I told him what I thought about him and his kind, and I didn't mince my words. My reasoning powers were obscured, even scrambled, and I was ready to strangle this insolent hybrid of fascism and communism. Lev tried to stop me before things went too far, but without success.

Ivanov would not yield. He was stupid, brazen, fearless. He demanded that I come with him. I refused. Ivanov summoned the guards on duty, seven healthy, large men who stood in the corridor near the door of the cell, ready to tie me up and beat me. I was frustrated by my own helplessness. It was clear that if I did not go with him, they would beat me and Lev in front of the Moldavians, throw us in a punishment cell, and write a report that I attacked a duty officer.

I said that I would go with him, on the condition that not one of them put a finger on me. They led me across the yard, up to the second floor of another building, and down a long corridor. Judging by the signs on the doors, it was an administration building. One of the doors was open, and as we passed I caught sight of a high-ranking officer sitting at a desk, writing. He was, I decided, probably the head of the prison or one of the deputies.

I walked another few steps, then broke away and ran into the office before Ivanov could react. Quickly, I told the officer that I was a witness in the trial of the nine, in his prison only temporarily, and soon to be returned to Leningrad. There, I said, I would report to the attorney general the pillaging in the Kishinev prison and the attempt to lynch me.

The officer understood that my threat was real. He didn't want any publicity about the Kishinev prison—Moscow preferred that all the irregularities at the trials, which were publicized in the West, remain within the framework of the law. So he kept Ivanov from dragging me from the office, heard me out, and then forced Ivanov to sign an explanation. I demanded that Ivanov apologize to me, and that he be punished. Those demands were not satisfied, but I was returned to my cell, rather politely. And that evening Ivanov came to the cell and told us that the criminals in Tolya's cell had been lined up and searched. Tolya's things had been recovered and returned to him, and he had been transferred to another cell. As evidence that he was telling me the truth, Ivanov showed me a note from Tolya: "Hilya, don't worry. Everything is all right."

Late at night, as Lev and I were getting ready to go to sleep, the guard on duty looked through the trap door and said:

"You two, don't lie down. Get ready with your things."

Guards led us through the prison to the transit cell. There, for the first time, Lev and I witnessed the preparations for an *etap*—a transit trip. Prisoners who were to be transferred from the Kishinev prison to other places of incarceration had been brought to this large room. Their possessions were piled on long tables and on the dirty floor. Guards and soldiers stood behind the tables, sorting through the *zeks'* things, looking for forbidden items such as knives, razors, money. Other guards searched the *zeks*. Some of the prisoners had been stripped down to their underwear. Some were naked. Some were forced to squat while a guard checked their rectums.

The commander of the convoy came into the transit cell, carrying a pile of folders with photographs on the outside. He came over to me and started the official process of identification.

"Surname?"

"Butman."

"First name? Patronymic?"

"Hilya Izraylevich."

"Year of birth? Place of birth?"

"1932, Leningrad."

"Article? Term?"

"Articles 64-a; 70, part 1; 72; and 189, part 1 of the Criminal Code of the RSFSR. Term—ten years."

The commander handed my file to a soldier, who took me to a Black Maria. The process was repeated with Lev.

"Next!"

"Yagman."

"First name? Patronymic?"

"Lev Naumovich."

"Year of birth? Place of birth?"

"1940, Leningrad."

"Article? Term?"

"Articles 70, part 1 and 72 of the Criminal Code of the RSFSR. Term—five years."

"Move on. Next!"

The loading of the Black Marias was completed and the compartments were locked. The cordon of soldiers with submachine guns and guard dogs was removed. The prison gates opened, and one after another the vans rolled out of the courtyard into the night.

We were let out of the Black Marias at the train station, and the guards lined us up near the tracks. The commander spoke to us abruptly:

"Attention! Don't lag behind or talk on the way. A step to the left, a step to the right will be interpreted as an attempt to escape. The soldiers will use arms without warning."

The gray column of *zeks* started off toward the railroad tracks. The train was on a high embankment, and the steps of the cars were high. Not every *zek* managed to get up onto the bottom step on the first try. Some of the soldiers helped with a light kick in the behind, some with a heavy kick. I saw that Lev was having trouble getting up onto the step. Would they kick him? They didn't—his elegant coat in the midst of the quilted jackets, his black beard and intellectual's glasses stopped the soldiers. They waited patiently and let him scramble up by himself.

The soldiers accompanying the *zeks* had various assignments. Some "helped" the *zeks* up the embankment. Some counted the prisoners and made notes. A third group stuffed the men into the compartments of the Stolypin prisoner cars. Each of the cars had nine compartments, six large ones with three tiers for a total of about twenty people, and three small compartments that held three people. One of the smaller compartments was used as a punishment section for ruffians. The doors of that section could be sealed almost hermetically. A rowdy quickly exhausted the supply of fresh air and calmed down.

Lev and I were put in a large compartment. Now I could lie down on the lower bunk and doze off, I thought. But no, it was not that simple. The soldier explained that we were only permitted to lie with our heads toward the aisle. And we were not permitted to lie down at all until the new shift of guards was on duty.

Finally, the change of the guards was finished, and I lay down. A few moments later the bar that locked the compartment was moved with a clang and a soldier entered carrying a flashlight. He moved the beam around the compartment, checking to see if the walls were still intact. He climbed up, standing on the lower bunk with his boots level with my nose, to check above, then got down and looked under the lower bunk. Everything was all right. Nothing was broken. The soldier left, and we heard the door of the next compartment clang open. And then, finally we were able to sleep.

CHAPTER THIRTY-THREE

In Transit

For several hours I had been sitting in a holding cell in the Odessa transit prison, the first stop on the return trip from Kishinev to Leningrad. The box-shaped compartment was about three-and-a-half by two-and-a-half feet. A small wooden bench, coated with spit, was bolted to the dirty concrete floor. The walls—like those of all other such cells and indoor exercise yards of Soviet prisons—were covered with "fur," a rough, stucco-like coating that prevents *zeks* from writing on the walls.

We had been brought to Odessa early in the morning. Now, according to my calculations, it was about three o'clock in the afternoon. I was waiting to be taken for sanitation processing. Apparently this transit group was too large to be washed together. From time to time I heard the banging of cell doors. I couldn't make out if they were still searching *zeks* and putting them in cells, or if they had finally begun to take the prisoners to the bathhouse.

Even though I had been sitting in the cell alone for the equivalent of a full working day, I was not bored. There wasn't even time to concentrate and think things over. From the corridor came cries, banging, the guards' commands. A criminal in the cell opposite to mine howled desperately for forty minutes, asking to be taken to the toilet. Every ten minutes or so, when the noise of his banging and howling was at its loudest, the guard shouted the standard reply:

"Do it in your pants!"

Poor *zek*. He could have done that long ago. But he was

not alone in that cell, and if he hadn't held out, he would have been in trouble. On transit trips, the ones who suffer the most are the those who are sick and those who lack endurance, those who cannot adapt to the disorder and the succession of unpredictable events.

Suddenly the lock to my cell clicked and the door opened. Standing in the corridor was an attractive, brown-haired lad wearing a clean shirt and carefully ironed gray suit, shining boots and a cap—and carrying a string bag in which there was a huge crusty loaf of white bread. I began to salivate immediately, and realized that I hadn't eaten anything yet that day.

I squeezed over to one end of the bench so that the young fellow could sit down next to me. He barraged me with questions about what prison is like and how you deal with it. By then an experienced *zek*, I gave him thorough answers. Finally I got a chance to ask him what he was doing in prison. He shared his loaf with me, and I sat chewing while I listened to his story.

Companionship made the time pass quickly, and I didn't even notice when the screams from across the way stopped. Finally the guards came and took the two of us to the sanitation section. A dirty barber used dirty clippers to remove the pubic and underarm hair of each prisoner. And then with the same implement he shaved the face and head. He did this with the lazy sluggishness of a eunuch, cutting a strip here and a strip there, rather than finishing one whole area and then another. Perhaps he was lazy, or maybe doing it that way gave him some perverse satisfaction.

After the barber, all the sanitation activities seemed to take place in an unpeopled realm. We were ordered to strip and put our clothes on a hanger, so that they could be disinfected in an oven. Just the two of us were in the room. A small window opened and hands reached out to take our clothes. Then hands gave us soap. Voices came out of the wall and told us what to do next. As we followed the instructions, doors opened in front of us, parting as we approached. We found ourselves in a huge room with two long stone benches on which were basins. Along the walls on both sides of that huge room were about forty shower heads. My companion and I each stood under a shower, and turned the knobs. No luck. There was no water. And then, just as we were about to give up, suddenly water splashed out. From all forty showers. It was a gigantic water spectacle, like the fountain at the Lower Palace in Peterhof near Leningrad. Alone in that huge room, in that extravagance of plumbing, we were aware of our puniness in the belly of the corrective system.

As abruptly as the deluge had begun, it ended. A powerful voice, amplified by the bathhouse acoustics, advised us to finish washing quickly and to go through the door at the end of the room. We did, and entered another vast, empty space. A window in one of the walls opened, hands shoved our clothing out, and the window slammed shut. We extended our trusting hands to grasp the clothing and recoiled instantly, blowing on our fingers. Our rags, and especially the buttons, were as hot as boiling water.

We got dressed, and then it was time to part. I was taken with my possessions to the top floor of the prison. A powerfully built matron took me down a corridor and opened one of the cells. The stench of the latrine inside overpowered me; a cloud of tobacco smoke hung in the air.

"Hello," someone said from the depths of the cell, and I made out four dim figures sitting around a wooden table, playing with handmade cards. A fifth man lay on a bunk in the second tier and looked down on me with curiosity. There was no space for me on any of the bunks, but a bench had been improvised near the door from a board with one end on a small pillar and the other balanced on one of the bunks. I put my bag down and sat on the board. The criminals continued to play. Only when they had finished the game did they pay attention to me, and to my bag.

When dinner was brought, one of the criminals stood by the trapdoor. As each bowl of brown liquid was pushed through, he took it and handed it on. I looked at the first bowl and almost threw up. The bowl was filthy—you could tell by looking at it what had been eaten from it yesterday, the day before yesterday, and a week ago. Perhaps a tuberculosis victim or a leper had eaten from it, I thought, and my throat constricted. But I forced myself to overcome my squeamishness and eat. I knew that henceforth this would be part of my daily life, and no one was offering me a different prison system.

The men drank the soup, and then hot water—our "tea" was brought into the cell and poured into the same bowls. The result was more of the same swill, but thinner.

The guards announced bedtime. The men ignored the order and continued to play cards. Finally I realized that I'd have to find a place to spend the night amidst the confusion; I went back to the board bench. It was as long as I am tall, but narrower. I did a balancing act on that board all night long.

The next evening I was again loaded into a Black Maria, into a narrow compartment in which I found Mark Dymshitz. Farewell, crazy Odessa prison. Farewell, senseless, disorganized transit trips in Moldavia and the Ukraine! We were put on a train that crawled from the Ukraine to central Russia, and order was restored.

On our way from Odessa to Leningrad we passed through two transit prisons—one in Kaluga, the other in Kalinin. In Stalinist times all the *zek* trains passed through Moscow. In those days, the famous Matrosskaya Tishina prison in Moscow was always filled with activity and hubbub. In the post-Stalinist era, to relieve the pressure on the prison authorities and the facilities in Moscow, the Stolypin cars were detoured through Kaluga.

The calm, almost sluggish atmosphere of the Kaluga transit prison was as different from the craziness of the Odessa prison as the provincial Russian city of Kaluga is from seething, multilingual Odessa. Without any fuss or nervous tension, I went through the reception procedure. I was given a mattress that was barely torn, a pillow with a pillow case, and an aluminum mug and spoon. Then I was taken to an empty room that smelled of fresh paint—a refreshing change from the latrine stench of the cell in Odessa. Everything had just been painted: the floor, walls, iron bed, and a large perforated metal sheet covering a recess in the wall behind the bed (probably the heating pipes passed through the recess, I thought). By prison standards the cell was very clean, and few things please me more than cleanliness. I tested the paint with my finger to see if it smeared, and then sat on the bed and contentedly stretched out my legs.

"Greetings, countryman! Where are you from?" someone said loudly, right near me, and I shuddered with surprise.

I got up and looked around the cell. I was all alone. I sat down again.

"Why don't you answer, countryman? Where are you from?" This time two voices asked the question. I jumped as if I'd been stung, wondering if I was going crazy. My Marxist-Leninist materialist training saved me—I began to look for a scientific basis for this mystical phenomenon.

I heard the voices again, loud and distinct, and finally I realized that the sounds came from the other side of the perforated sheet. I pressed my ear against one of the holes, and recoiled immediately—the question shot directly into my ear.

"From Odessa," I yelled through the opening. My voice thundered and echoed in the space behind the metal sheet.

"Speak more quietly," said the voices from the neighboring cell. "Otherwise the guards will come. What's your name?"

"Hillel."

"What?"

"Hillel."

"We didn't get it. Repeat it!"

"My name is Hil-lel, Hil-lel," I enunciated quietly but distinctly. "It's a Jewish name, the name of my grandfather."

"Got it, got it, countryman. What are you sitting for?"

"Because of the airplane. You probably heard about it." I didn't consider it necessary to enumerate all my sins. My airplane sin was the main one, the one that led to the charge of treason. And it was important to me that the story about the airplane hijacking was told with the correct interpretation when it made the rounds of the camps.

"Of course we heard. In Leningrad, last summer."

Now, I knew from experience, interest in a conversation was guaranteed. We talked for a long time. Toward the end of the conversation, one of my three neighbors said to me, half jokingly and half seriously,

"Listen, Hillel, would you take us with you to Israel?"

"What do you guys need Israel for? After all, you're Russian, aren't you?"

"We're Russian, local born."

"Then why would you want to go to Israel? Your homeland is Russia. If you went abroad, you would soon long for your Kaluga. You would want to go home."

"I guess you're right, countryman," one of them said hesitantly. But the other two drowned him out.

"Like hell we need this Russia. It can go to hell."

We hadn't exhausted all possible topics, but it was late and the conversation was winding down. Then from the other side of the wall came the usual prison request.

"Countryman, what about something to smoke? We're all out—we smoked our last cigarette. Have you got any?"

"I have cigarettes, but with my personal things. I don't have any in here."

"Listen, at four o'clock the guards make the rounds. The supervisor will come and ask whether you have any requests or complaints. Ask him to bring the cigarettes to your cell, and when he brings them, ask him to hand them over to our cell. He's a good guy. He'll do it."

I did as they asked, and by the end of the day the three of them had five packs of cigarettes. When the guard came to get me for the next transport, the three of them called through the opening: "Have a good trip, countryman! May you get back to your family as quickly as possible. Early release, and a good trip to your motherland!"

At the last minute one of them remembered the cigarettes and yelled out, "Thanks for the smokes!"

I turned in the prison garb, received my own clothes and got into them, and was herded towards the Black Maria. Farewell, Kaluga. You are a delight for a *zek*'s nerves.

The train skirted Moscow in a wide arc and headed toward our next stop, Kalinin. I had been put in a compartment with Mark Dymshits—and about twenty criminals. One of them turned out to be a cheerful Georgian Jew. Within an hour he had told us all his secrets and given us a lot of information about when, to whom and for what he had given bribes. He gave us his Georgian address and swore that as soon as his sons finished the university, they would go to Israel.

Finally we arrived in Leningrad and were taken, again in a Black Maria, to the criminal prison of Kresty. During processing there, my supply of refills for my ballpoint pen was confiscated. I was led to the basement, to the transit cell. When the guard opened the cell door, I saw that about ten men were sitting on the bunks opposite the door. They were surrounded by water, like an island in a lake. I waded over and they made a place for me on the bunks.

All night long the guards brought *zeks* to that transit cell, and by morning it was full. The men on the bunks were pressed together like seals on a rock; latecomers stood in the water. Toward morning the guards began to take people off to their trials. Finally I was summoned, taken upstairs and put in a car that took me to the Big House.

The trip to Kishinev had taken about three hours by plane. The trip back took three weeks.

CHAPTER THIRTY-FOUR

On to the Gulag

In the first days after I was returned to the Big House in Leningrad, I rested from the events of the previous month. My spirit needed a respite and time to analyze my new life as a *zek* which I had experienced in such large doses during my time away from Leningrad. My body needed the calm and quiet and order of the Big House, the clean sheets on the cot and the visible chunks of fish in the soup.

Weeks passed, then months. And again I longed for people and impressions. Only Eva's monthly letters and the scribblings she enclosed from Lileshka breathed fresh air into my mausoleum. When I wrote to Eva the few letters I was permitted, I always included a separate little note to my daughter.

When Eva's August letter arrived, I saw that the censor had crossed out more than usual. It took me a long time to wash the letter and dry it. When I had done that and could read what Eva had written, I understood that almost all of the fellows were already on their way to camps, and that some had already arrived at camps somewhere in Mordvinia.

By that time Viktor Shtilbans had been released, without having been sent to a camp, because his sentence was for one year. Of those who had been in the two trials in Leningrad, only three of us were still in the Big House: Mark Dymshitz, Misha Korenblit and I. We were being kept there so that we could be witnesses at Boris Azernikov's trial. Boris had been arrested after we were tried. His trial was to begin at the beginning of October.

Boris had been a member of the same wing of the Organization as Misha Korenblit and I. He had a strong rational-materialistic streak that alienated him from many of his friends. But Mark Dymshitz, who knew that Boris was a wrestling champion, had decided that he could be a valuable participant in Operation Wedding.

As I rode to Azernikov's trial in a Black Maria, I realized that I had to choose a tactic for my testimony. I decided to present Boris as an unprincipled materialist who had been drawn into the Organization by me, to bring him into contact with Zionist ideas. That tactic left Boris with some choices: he could declare that after several months in the Organization he had changed. Or he could present himself as a deceived lamb to whom Zionism was alien.

Boris was given a sentence of three years. After Misha, Mark and I had testified, there was no reason to keep us at the Big House. By law, we were supposed to be sent on within ten days. We were soon told that we were to leave for camp by October 15, 1971.

I was given a letter from Eva, the last one I would receive at the Big House. It contained good news. Sima Kaminskaya had received a visa and would leave the Soviet Union by plane on October 14 with her daughters. I wondered if Sima was happy and decided that probably she was not at peace, leaving while Lassal was still in prison. But the Leningrad KGB would probably sigh with relief. Sima's intellectual and moral superiority made her a dangerous enemy for them, and she was part of the disturbing "wives' circle" that created problems for the KGB.

Sima understood that some would condemn her for leaving her husband. She felt, I realized, that she could be of more help to Lassal and the others from the other side of the iron curtain. She was right. One of the wives had to be the first to leave.

When it was time for the three of us to leave the Big House and start the journey to the camp, we were summoned to an office and given our personal possessions and dry rations for the trip. There, for the first time in almost a year, I saw Misha Korenblit. He had an enormous, handmade green rucksack that seemed to be dragging him down. Mark Dymshitz was carrying a half-empty rucksack, walking with a light and confident step.

A year earlier Mark had been sitting on death row. Now he was sure that he wouldn't have to serve all of his seven-year sentence. He was confident that soon the Americans would exchange us for someone. Misha, the hardened pessimist, was also sure that he wouldn't serve his seven years—he was sure that we would all be shot. And I, the moderate optimist, was confident that we would be released before the ends of our terms, but not as soon as Mark predicted.

On anti-Soviet maps printed in the early 1970s, two capitals of the USSR are marked. A red star in the center of the European part of the USSR marks Moscow, capital of Soviet Russia. Highways and railroad lines extend from Moscow in all directions.

A second red star, located some few hundred miles east in the depths of the Mordvinian Autonomous Republic, marks Potma Station, the capital of anti-Soviet *zek* Russia. Potma, which lies between Saransk and Yavaz, is a place known only to young pioneers who do well in geography class and to the families of political prisoners. One branch of a broad-gauge railroad line passes from Moscow all the way to Potma Station. From Potma, narrow-gauge tracks go off to the north.

I do not know why this God-forsaken spot, once renowned for its oak groves, was selected by Interior Minister Schelokov for the Gulag Archipelago. During Beria's time the many "islands" of the Archipelago that housed political prisoners were scattered all over the Soviet Union. By the time we arrived at the camps, after the Leningrad trials, only one island remained for political prisoners—Dubravlag, a group of camps clustered around Yavaz. From Yavaz, you went by narrow-gauge railway or along country roads through forests to the political camps of Dubravlag. This was also the site of a camp for foreigners and a camp for political recidivists sentenced to an especially strict and harsh incarceration.

Camps sprouted in these places immediately after the revolution. The local Mordvins who were our guards were the third generation to serve in that role. The oak groves were long forgotten—now wood for building new barracks was brought from far away. Only the retired oldsters remembered the early transports with social revolutionaries—first right-wing social revolutionaries, then left-wing ones, with Mensheviks, Trotskyites, Kamenevites, Zinovievites, Bukharinites, Tukhachevsky men. The kulaks were driven to Dubravlag in hordes. Today not even their graves remain. When the prisoners of the seventies and eighties dug up the earth, they sometimes stumbled across the bones of prisoners of the twenties, thirties and forties.

Our train left Leningrad on the night of October 15. Ahead of us, we learned, were transit points in Yaroslav, Gorky, Ruzaevka (near Saransk, the capital of Mordvinia) and Potma. Mark, Misha and I were put in a compartment for three. The other compartments, we soon saw, were overcrowded, with men pressed up against the bars. When the guards began taking people to the toilet, we could see who else was in the same car. The women prisoners were in the compartment next to the toilet. From that vantage point they could ridicule each man, making sarcastic comments as he went in to take care of his needs. But when it was Mark's turn, his appearance evoked a different reaction— they whispered to each other, "Look, the pilot went by!" They let me pass after him without comment.

The train crawled slowly, heading south from Leningrad, stopping often. Behind the locomotive were two cars—a mail car and our Stolypin car. The functions of the two were similar. From the postal car, bags of mail for the region were unloaded and sacks of local mail were taken on. From the Stolypin car, *zeks* who were headed for local camps were unloaded, and other *zeks* boarded on their way to trials in district or regional centers.

When a large group of *zeks* was to be unloaded or loaded, the preparations began long before the train stopped. The head of the convoy, usually an ensign, appeared with the files of those who were leaving. He found out which compartments they were in, checked the photographs, and asked routine questions. His helper, usually a sergeant, recorded the data. The sergeant was responsible for what occurred inside the car when it was time to unload the *zeks*, the ensign for what happened outside. A soldier was also posted on the platform.

When the train stopped, each soldier or officer went to his post. The doors of the compartments clanged open and the sergeant called out the names of the *zeks* who were to get off the train. Any dawdler got a kick of encouragement. The *zeks* who stayed behind tried, under cover of the commotion, to snatch the bags of those who were leaving.

As the *zeks* filed past the sergeant, he counted them. As they stepped down onto the platform, a local militiaman counted them. In Stalin's day, the sergeant had to utter the ritual phrase, "I handed over such and such number of enemies of the Soviet Union," and his counterpart had to reply

"I received such and such a number of enemies of the Soviet Union." By the time we got to the gulag, that practice had been abandoned.

When the train started moving again, the soldiers on duty removed their overcoats and went to a special car to rest; some of them returned to pace the corridors. If you were lucky, the soldier in your corridor decided to open the frosted glass window, pushing it far down enough so that, from the second tier of bunks, you could see what you had not seen for months, sometimes years: grass, trees, cows grazing. The countryside seen in that brief glimpse, even in the cheerless northwestern weather with its constant drizzle, looked marvelously beautiful. The forests were broken only by swamps, occasional fields dotted with stacks of hay and small railway stations, each with a small wooden station house, a kitchen garden, a shed and an outhouse. There was deep mud everywhere.

The guard in the corridor changed. The new soldier banged the window shut and returned us to reality. I decided to try to establish contact with him—I wanted to send a note to Eva. My strategy was simple. I attracted him to the compartment with some interesting conversation, postcards, pictures. Then I offered him a cigarette. And then I asked him to send a letter. When a soldier agreed to do that, he would simply throw the letter out of the train window near a station, on the chance that a passerby might pick it up and drop it in a mailbox. A soldier who was caught mailing a *zek*'s letter faced punishment. In this way during the trip from Leningrad to Potma I sent three letters to Eva via convoy soldiers. She received only one of them.

Two weeks after we left Leningrad, we arrived at the Ruzaevka junction in Mordvinia, the republic of the *zeks*, and were taken to the transit prison. Ruzaevka was once famous: in the days of the first Russian Revolution of 1905, some of the first soviets of workers' deputies were formed here. But today Ruzaevka is known for its transit prison, not for its revolutionary traditions.

That night would have left no trace in my memory if we hadn't been visited by a member of the administration who sat in a locked cell with the three of us for two hours asking questions. His behavior was so different from the rude encounters of the previous two weeks that our visitor might have been from another planet—or at least a high-ranking foreign diplomat who had come from Moscow to arrange the details of our exchange. We allowed ourselves to indulge in these fantasies. When this unexpected visitor departed, Mark was overflowing with optimism—he was certain that we were about to be released.

But the next day we were on the train again, in a comfortable compartment for three, heading toward Potma.

After the long months of exhausting monotony in the Big House, I had been glad to leave Leningrad. But, as the saying goes, the grass is always greener on the other side. The trip from Leningrad had already taken two weeks. I wanted to be at the camp, to see my other friends and breathe fresh air. I even wanted to work. When the train reached Potma, I joyfully gathered my rags and got in line behind Misha Korenblit and Mark Dymshitz.

We marched, stumbling up to our ankles in the soupy mud. But what was going on? The three of us alone were being taken to a broad-gauge railroad track. That meant we were not going to a camp. The rest of the prisoners remained at the Potma transit point.

The train took us back to Ruzaevka. There, instead of taking us to the transit prison, the guards led us over a bridge above a railroad track and into the city, to the district police department, where a car was waiting for us. Had Mark been right? Were we going to be exchanged?

The car took us through the streets of a city. We were unloaded at a small building and taken to the second floor.

The building was clean, and the beds had been painted recently. But the windows were barred and the doors had peepholes and food traps.

Mark was externally calm, but shining inside. He declared his conviction that we were about to start on the road to Israel. I was not so sure. Mark and I made a bet: if we were released before January 1, 1974, I would buy us twenty bottles of cognac; if not, Mark would. He would have agreed to an earlier date, but I wanted to be a gentleman. Either way, I would come out fine—I'd win cognac, or I'd win freedom.

CHAPTER THIRTY-FIVE

Escalating Expectations

After a few days it became clear where we were, but not why. Our prison was in Saransk, the capital of the Mordvinian Republic. The first floor of the building housed the prison cells of the Ministry of Internal Affairs, the second floor those of the Committee of State Security.

The procedures on those two floors were as different as the working methods of the two departments. The second floor of the Saransk prison was clean, neat, quiet; the prisoners there were addressed with the formal "you" and treated politely. The first floor was ruled by a Darwinian process of natural selection: there it was strictly survival of the fittest. Although our second-floor quarters were relatively clean, Mark, Misha and I quickly became involved in a struggle to get enough to eat, since our meals came from the first floor.

Within a few days after our arrival, we had consumed all of our private stores and were completely dependent on the prison allowance. The Russian word for "allowance" has the same root as the Russian word for "enough"; but in Saransk the allowance was not enough. We had had neither psychological nor physiological preparation for the change from the relative plenty in the Leningrad prison to the starvation rations at Saransk . Soon we were starving. Our daily meal was a half-inch cube of "meat" floating in hot water. What strength we had began to leave us.

And then, late one night, the KGB captain came into our cell. He took off his fur hat, sat down wearily at the table, and looked at us kindly. Then he dug into the string bag he had brought with him and pulled out—we couldn't believe our eyes—a crusty round loaf of white bread, warm and fragrant, a package of butter, and a large piece of delectable sausage. (Even now, as I write these words many years later and with a full stomach, my mouth begins to water.)

Three times during our three months in Saransk, the "chief" fattened us up, and three times we felt hunger even more acutely the following day. Once, during a conversation I had with him in his office, this man offered me sweet-smelling apples from his own garden. That was too much.

"Listen," I said, "what is the reason for your great civility toward us? I don't understand why you do this. And now these apples. Do you want to recruit me?"

"Really, Hilya Izraylevich, what makes you think so?"

"We don't understand why we were turned back from Potma. Why weren't we sent to a camp? Why are you keeping us here?"

"What's the matter? Do you have it so bad here? You don't have to work. They will bring you books from the library—I'll give the order. And if you want to meet with Eva, we can try and arrange it."

"Of course I want to meet with Eva, but I am permitted a meeting only after my arrival at camp. And only then will I be able to receive the permitted annual parcel."

"Your rights in camp are ahead of you. Here we are the masters. Everything is in our hands. A lot depends on you and your friends."

"I don't understand what depends on us. I'm not a diplomat. Be clearer."

"You see, Hilya Izraylevich, you and your friends are a special group with special interests. You say that you are not anti-Soviet, that your only goal is to go to Israel. But the behavior of many of your friends who are already in the camps makes us doubt that. They are cooperating with the worst enemies of the Soviet regime, with nationalists of all kinds who hate not only us but also you Jews. What do you have in common with such people? After your release, no one will hinder you from emigrating. Moreover, the Soviet government is not interested in your serving your term to the very end. But it is difficult to say that early release is likely when there is such behavior in the camps. Think about that very carefully."

I didn't need to think about it. When I got back to the cell, I told Misha and Mark about the conversation I had just had with the KGB captain, and added that I personally agreed with him completely—and not because of the apples. We did not need to cooperate with other nationalists in the camps—our interests did not coincide with theirs. We had achieved our goal—*aliyah* had started. Now it was time for us to sit quietly and not rock the boat.

Misha Korenblit immediately supported me. Mark Dymshitz was more evasive.

"We'll see when we get there," he said, and went on with the task he had set for himself.

Each day Mark worked at copying the sentence in our trial onto the lining of his civilian coat. Mark was certain that we would soon be exchanged, and he wanted to carry the words from the trial out with him. Mark and I made another bet, this time for five more bottles—if we got out by the first of January 1974, when we got to Tel Aviv I would give Mark twenty-five bottles of Israeli cognac.

It began to look as if Mark might win our bet. A few days after our wager, a colonel from the political division of the KGB arrived from Moscow. He was wearing a carefully pressed gray suit, a light-colored shirt, a tie with a big knot and shining boots. He displayed flawless KGB politeness.

One by one the three of us were called in to talk with this man. We each talked a long time, and he recorded all of our complaints and claims in detail. I requested that my sister be granted an exit visa. She had already received a refusal in Leningrad. The colonel promised to look into the matter.

After the colonel's visit, we were in a state of vague but pleasant expectation. Mark was more confident than ever that he would not have to buy the cognac.

The captain had more surprises for us. One day I was called to his office for another talk. When the door opened in front of me, I stopped in my tracks. Was I dreaming? Near his desk was a small table, and on it was. . .a small sample of the kind of refreshments offered during a congress of Party leaders. Candies, cakes, chocolate, fruits. All in beautiful bowls. And an elegant little teapot.

I was starving. I did not need these special effects. With difficulty I tore my gaze away from the food and looked at the captain's smiling face.

"I won't bother you. Sit down. Eat, Hilya Izraylevich, don't be embarrassed. The water is boiling now."

And he slipped out of the room, closing the door firmly after himself. Only then did I notice that I was not alone.

In the room was a man about forty-five years old, with the sad eyes of a diaspora Jew, wearing a rumpled suit and a crooked tie. He introduced himself, stressing his typically Jewish name and patronymic. He told me that he worked as a senior instructor at a local university, that he had a good salary and a nice apartment, that he enjoyed the respect of his co-workers and did not feel any anti-Semitism. He said he couldn't understand how anyone could leave such a good life to go to Israel, with its pitiless capitalist exploitation, constant wars, intercommunal conflicts and discrimination against immigrants from Russia.

He delivered this speech in a monotone, almost without breathing spaces or punctuation marks, with the sound of a record that had been recorded at 33 rpm and then played at 45 rpm. When he had finished his recitation, the man remembered suddenly that he was supposed to play the role of host. He began to pour the boiling water into the mugs, adding an aromatic brew from the teapot.

"Fat, don't be embarrassed," he said, smiling guiltily.

"Did you finish high school in the Stalinist days?" I asked.

"Yes."

"University, too?"

"Yes."

"Did you do well in your studies?"

"I was close to the top of my class."

"Where did you work after graduation?"

"For several years I lived in a little backwoods Mordvinian village, in the lap of nature. I worked as a teacher. I was treated well."

"Have you been teaching at the university for a long time?"

"Since the beginning of the sixties."

This man was very glad that we were having a free-flowing, unrestrained conversation—the KGB would be pleased. Once I had gotten the answers to my questions, I switched from interrogation to narration.

"You keep asserting that you are treated well, that you don't feel anti-Semitism, that you would never go to Israel. But your personal history contradicts what you say. You were a city dweller, you had an apartment in Saransk, you finished the university with a brilliant record, you were a philosopher with promise, your degree work was devoted to the religions of the East. And what did they do with you? Did you begin your career by teaching philosophy or Marxism at an institution of higher learning? Did they at least trust you to be a teaching assistant? No. You, with a head full of philosophical questions, were sent to be a simple teacher in a backwoods Mordvinian village where, probably, no one else wanted to go. Probably it was a village where there was only an elementary school, and they offered you a pitiful salary. And your fellow students, who had not done as well as you, remained at the university as instructors. How do you explain that? You know the answer. The answer to that question is the same as the answer to the question of why I shall go to Israel, sooner or later."

Halfway through my monologue, the man put his fingers to his lips and, pleading with his eyes, pointed to the walls. "They are eavesdropping on us," he was telling me with his gesture. But I didn't want to spare him. He was a descendant of the Jews who remained in Egypt, near their fleshpots. In a few minutes I would have to return to the near-starvation of the cell, with eight and a half years of imprisonment in front of me. This man was a teacher of philosophy at Saransk University, the owner of a three-room apartment in the center of town, "with a fine view of the sea." Nevertheless, I felt fortunate in comparison to him.

The KGB captain came back—the time for the "pleasant" conversation had run out. Insolently, I had already filled my pockets with cakes for Misha and Mark. I put my hands behind my back and left with the guard.

It was clear to the KGB that my conversation with the philosopher had been counterproductive. But that did not stop them. Someone had devised this plan, and budgeted it (to cover the cost of the refreshments) and put it in motion, and there was no stopping it. Misha was summoned to a similar meeting with a professional colleague. The KGB evidently couldn't find a pilot to talk with Mark, so they came up with a Jewish engineer.

They arranged two final meetings in their efforts to persuade us to abandon our desire to emigrate to Israel. They arranged for Eva to visit me at the end of January. After she arrived, they left us alone for two hours in the investigator's office. They also allowed Eva to give me an illegal "five-kilo" package. And they permitted Polina Yud-Borovskaya— Misha's "bride" for Operation Wedding and now his wife—to visit him. Polina brought a suitcase full of canned goods—Misha's "five kilos" seemed even heavier than mine.

Eva and Polina also brought good news, telling us that a massive *aliyah* was underway. Planes were flying via Berlin and Budapest, trains were going via Brest. And all the tickets had been sold for months in advance. Many of our acquaintances, including former ulpan students, were already in Israel.

When we got back to our cell and poured out the contents of our two packages so that we could divide the food into three piles, the stuff covered the floor. Even if the three of us were to end up in different camp zones, there would be enough food for several good parties. I included in my portion an enormous torte that Eva had bought just five days earlier in the best cafe in Leningrad.

In the midst of this abundance, we permitted ourselves to eat until we were stuffed. Our mood brightened, and Misha began to sing in his pleasant tenor. His repertoire included my favorite songs. For several hours he and I walked around the cell singing. Mark was sentenced to listen.

We sang because we were full. And we sang because we rejoiced in Eva's and Polina's visit, and in the news they had brought, that *aliyah* truly had begun.

CHAPTER THIRTY-SIX

The Twenty-Sixth Bottle

Five days later we were sent on another transfer. This time we passed quickly through the transit point at Potma and reached the narrow-gauge rail line. We were at the entrance to Dubravlag, one of the islands of the Gulag Archipelago.

The cars on line were small-scale Stolypins. The three of us were put in a compartment with other *zeks*. One of them was being taken to a strict regime camp, the camp where Edik Kuznetsov, Yuri Fedorov and Alesha Murzhenko were. Ordinarily *zeks* destined for that camp are transported in isolation. But all the compartments were full—the guards had no choice but to put this man in with the rest of us.

It is possible that the *zek* lied to us, to take advantage of our sympathy and skim off some cream. And there was cream. I had five packs of cigarettes left. Four were the cheap Pamirs, and one was a pack of good cigarettes with a picture of a sailboat on the wrapper. Under the sailboat I wrote a short greeting to Edik, and then I gave the package to the *zek*. For his trouble in delivering the pack to Edik, I rewarded him in advance—I gave him the four packs of Pamirs. I realized that the chances that the cigarettes would reach Edik were almost nil.

Finally the train arrived at the last station of the narrow-gauge line, Barashevo. There is no camp at Barashevo, just a hospital for the camps in the area. The guards started to unload the *zeks* assigned there, but for some reason we were not among those taken off the train. Mark's great expectations were revived. The train whistle sounded and the train started to move in the direction from which it had come. We were being taken back! Perhaps that colonel in the immaculate suit who had traveled from Moscow to Saransk to visit us had not made the trip for nothing. Mark made another bet with me. This time our wager was almost symbolic—for just one more bottle of cognac, the twenty-sixth. The compartment was full of noise and laughter as Mark and I shook hands.

And then someone in the next compartment banged on the partition and called out:

"Hilya, is that you?"

"Yes—who is it?"

"Lev Yagman. Greetings!"

"Lev, greetings! How did you wind up here?"

"I'm going back to the camp from the hospital in Barashevo. Are you going to the zone?"

"Yes. Misha Korenblit and Mark Dymshitz are here with me. How did you know that I was here?"

"By your voice. Do you know what zone you're going to?"

"No."

"Well, in Yavaz they'll start unloading. Then we'll see."

Indeed, they unloaded us at Yavaz. I jumped from the train into the snow. Lev Yagman, thin even in a padded jacket and a hat with ear flaps over his bearded face was standing on the ground with other *zeks*. I stood next to him. The air was frigid, about 40 below zero centigrade. The men without mittens pushed their hands into their sleeves and danced in place. All around us was deep snow. The guards had on warm fur coats and padded hats with ear flaps. Even the dogs had their own fur. But the frigid air penetrated our bones.

In a few hours I would be at the camp, part of the group. Finally the order was given and we were loaded into the Black Marias.

The vans traveled along the wintry forest road, bumping

over hummocks, pot-holes and tree roots. Those who were not clutching the bench flew into the air and were smacked down again. We began to feel sick. Some turned pale and breathed heavily.

After an hour I felt as if I were barely alive, and the others felt no better. Finally the Black Maria stopped. The chiefs of the convoy appeared with folders. Whose? My name was called and I gladly got out of the van. Lev and I had arrived at Camp Number 19. The van left, carrying off Misha and Mark. Lev and I stood in the snow near the gate, waiting.

I still felt sick—not nauseous, but weak—and my feet and arms were numb. Then the guards arrived and began the reception process. Lev, as a returnee, was immediately admitted into the zone. I was taken to the guard house. There my hair was cut off and I was given the uniform of a *zek* to put on. Someone brought me a tray with pea soup and gruel. I began to eat at a corner of the table.

The rest of the table was covered with the contents of my rucksack and suitcase. When all that had been sorted through, I was permitted to keep the regulation amount of underwear (for summer and winter), a hat with ear flaps, scarf, socks and handkerchiefs. Also toilet articles, towels, some other small things and some of the food that Eva brought. All of my books and notes were taken to be checked over. I was not permitted to have the rest with me—it would be kept in the warehouse outside the camp, to be returned when I was released. Only then was I permitted to enter the zone.

I was welcomed and embraced by my friends, who had learned about my arrival from Lev. The Zionists in the zone were one unit—I felt that immediately. That evening, in one of the sections where three of our men lived, we held a Zionist bash. Officially we were forbidden from going from one section to another. But in camp as in prison you learn to distinguish between the rules that cannot be broken and those that can.

The men gathered stools from other sections. Someone meticulously cut Eva's torte into equal portions. Then one person turned his back to the table and another, pointing to a portion, asked him "For whom?" This *zek* method of dividing any treasure is the most just and prevents any suspicion of favoritism.

The Zionist group of Camp 19 consisted of nine men. My arrival brought that number to ten—a *minyan*, a quorum. Of those who sat on the defendants' bench with me in the airplane-related trial, Lev Yagman and Viktor Boguslavsky were there. From the Leningrad airplane trial, Tolya Altman and Boris Penson were also in Camp 19. Tolya Goldfeld, Sasha Halperin and Kharik Kizhner from the Kishinev trial and Misha Shepshelovich from the Riga trial were also there. The ninth Zionist was Yura Vudka, a former student from Riazan University who was serving time for participating in one of the Marxist youth groups that rejected the Soviet form of Marxism. Yura, like many other Jewish dissidents, joined the Zionists who arrived at the camp in 1971 and became an ideological member of the Zionist commune at Camp 19.

We ended without having had any interference. During the entire evening not one guard came into the section, and no one reported a violation of the rules. The torte I had brought disappeared, except for the pieces that were saved for those who worked the evening shift in the industrial zone. We decided not to tempt fate, and before it got too late we cleaned up the table, put the stools back where they belonged and went outside.

I reported to my friends about the three months Misha, Mark and I had spent in the Saransk prison, and about my conclusions—that we had made our statement and done what we could, that *aliyah* had begun, and that now the thing for us to do was to sit quietly and not do anything that would impede early release. The group voiced violent disagreement with this view. They told me about the hunger strike they had carried out on December 24, the anniversary of the sentencing at the first Leningrad trial. Suddenly I understood why our troika (Butman-Korenblit-Dymshitz) had been turned back for "reeducation" at Saransk. The men told me, too, about the appeal that had been sent from Camp 19 to the public at large, all around the world, and especially to all Jews. Many years later I finally was able to read that appeal:

"Today, December 24, 1971, on the anniversary of the harsh sentences at the first Leningrad trial of Jews who want to emigrate to Israel, we, the victims of this and succeeding trials, declare a three-day hunger strike. We declare that we were never guided by malice or hatred in our relations with the Soviet state. We did not intend to subvert it. We considered and still consider Israel to be our homeland, and only fervent desire to live there has led us into conflict with Soviet organs.

1. In declaring the hunger strike we demand the free emigration of Jews from the Soviet Union to Israel.
2. We are seeking to have our papers for Israeli citizenship drawn up, and we reject our Soviet citizenship. In this connection we are today sending a letter to the Presidium of the Supreme Soviet of the USSR and to the Dutch embassy.
3. We demand a review of all of our cases and the immediate release of Silva Zalmanson.
4. Since we henceforth consider ourselves citizens of Israel, we don't want to live with people who stained themselves with Jewish blood during World

War II. We demand to be moved immediately to the sector for foreign citizens until our case has been reviewed.

5. In connection with the harsh way that we are treated by the administration, we demand the presence of some representatives of the International Red Cross.

We appeal to world society and to Jews all over the world: Support us!

Altman, Boguslavsky, Halperin, Goldfeld, Kizhner, Vudka, Penson, Shepshelovich, Yagman"

All the Jewish prisoners joined those who signed the appeal, except Lev Korenblit and Vulf Zalmanson (they joined the others when the hunger strike began) and the three of us, who were, at the time, in the Saransk prison.

The prisoners who took part in the hunger strike of December 24 were: Solomon Dreizner, David Chernoglaz, Vladik Mogilever, Izrail Zalmanson, Shimon Levit, Aron Shpilberg, Lassal Kaminsky, Aron Voloshin, Iosif Meshener, Aryeh Khnokh, Iosif Mendelevich, Hillel Shur, Lazar Trakhtenberg, Anatoly Altman, Viktor Boguslavsky, Aleksandr Halperin, Anatoly Goldfeld, Eduard Kuznetsov, Yuri Fedorov and Alik Murzhenko.

That letter demonstrates that by December 1971, our fellows who were experiencing the conditions of the camp had decided to struggle, rather than to coexist peacefully with the administration. The letter also shows how well the Zionists in various camps were able to communicate and to coordinate their actions.

When I was faced with the realities of the camp, the illusions of the Saransk hothouse quickly evaporated. I realized that justice is indivisible, and that the price for a peaceful life in the camp was moral degradation. I consciously accepted the attitude of struggle. But I was one of the moderates and whenever possible I tried to prevent unnecessary confrontation with the administration.

A few minutes before bedtime I made it back to my assigned place, a second-tier bunk in the one-story wooden barrack of the fourth unit. About fifty men were already lying in their beds. Some were still talking. Others had already begun to snore after a hard day's work. In the bunk under mine slept a solid little fellow, a collaborator who had served in the Nazi occupation police force.

It wouldn't be easy to get a different neighbor—most of the men in the section were like him. The rest were Ukrainian nationalists, Baltic nationalists and criminals. There were almost no dissidents, and no other Zionists.

I had barely managed to reach the bunk when the orderly turned off the light. What a blessing that seemed to me—for the first time in a year and a half I was in total darkness, without the bright intrusion of the overhead lamps of the prisons. I took off my prison garb, hung it over the back of the bed, and crept under the blanket. The guard came in for the first check-up of the night, to make certain that everyone was in his place.

I fell asleep thinking, "Tomorrow I must write a letter to Eva."

I fell asleep with the three sisters of mercy by my bed—faith, hope and love.

EPILOGUE

The long detour on our trip to Jerusalem began on June 15, 1970, with the arrest of the Jews who committed no other crime than to desire to quit the Soviet Union. Ironically, that was the birthday of KGB chief Yuri Andropov—our arrests must have been a fine birthday gift. Our ordeal ended at Ben Gurion Airport in Israel on April 29, 1979, almost nine years later. Thanks to the benevolence of fate and the employees of El Al, that day coincided with an anniversary in my family—Eva and I had become husband and wife on April 29, 1962. We had been separated for nine of the seventeen years of our marriage.

As the blue and white El Al plane made its final approach to Israel's only international airport, the passengers changed their watches to local time, about 5:00 pm. The captain announced that five of us, the newly released "traitors to the Soviet Motherland," would be given the privilege of stepping out of the plane first.

We stood facing the exit doors while the plane rolled down the runway, on the land that we had dreamed of for so long. As the only family man, I was first in line. Behind me were Tolya Altman, Vulf Zalmanson, Aryeh Khnokh and Boris Penson. Mark Dymshitz and Eduard Kuznetsov would fly in the following day. Iosif Medelevich, Aleksey Murzhenko and Yura Fyodorov were still in prison. The others had been released earlier and were already in Israel.

A few minutes more, I thought, and the door would open—I would step onto Israeli soil, and I would see my family. Eva and Lilya were older, but I would know them.

And our small family had another member now, one I had never seen.

The earth orbits the sun once every twelve months. Once in every twelve months, a maximum security prisoner in a Soviet prison is allowed a personal visit from his wife. Provided that no "critical remarks" have been made about his appearance or his behavior, at work or in the living zone. Provided that no KGB agent has whispered into the ear of the camp boss (in my case, Senior Lieutenant Khramushkin), "No visitation rights for that man—use any pretext."

My second personal visit was on March 19, 1973. That morning Eva got out of the train at Vsesvyatskaya (All Saints), the small Ural station not far from the camp. By then she was an experienced prioner's wife, and she was in a hurry to make sure that Khramushkin did not deprive us of our meeting. We were to spend one day and one night together in the visiting room of the prison camp.

Our meeting took place. Four months later, when Eva left the country where it had been our fate to be born, she carried within her one more member of our family, invisible to the guards at the airport. On December 12, 1973, soon after the Yom Kippur War, Eva gave birth in Israel to our second daughter.

The plane moved in an arc as it approached the terminal building. A few more moments and the door would open.

In 1979, Eva was working at the Naan Kibbutz, in the factory where irrigation systems are manufactured. She had been living on that kibbutz for about five years, waiting for my release. She expected to have to wait for at least another year.

April 19, 1979, was an ordinary day at the kibbutz. When Eva reached home, the children were waiting for her—Lilya, then thirteen, a child already grown when she was born, and Geula, then five, our gift from fate. That day a telegram was waiting for her: "Released today. Soon we will be together forever until the grave. Your own Hillel."

Until she read those words, Eva had thought that I was in a small prison on the outskirts of the town of Chistopol, where I had been serving my time along with Iosif Mendelevich. Natan Sharansky was in the cell next to mine. She knew that a prisoner at such a place could not send a telegram. She read the telegram again and then rushed to the telephone to call the Israeli Ministry of Foreign Affairs to confirm that I really had been released.

When the door of the plane opened and I stepped out onto the stairs, I smelled orange blossoms.

"If you don't believe it, pretend it's a fairy tale"—that's what they say in the Gulag camps. And it really was like a fairy tale.

The plane was about three hundred yards from the terminal building. The space between the building and the plane was filled with people. Over their heads fluttered hundreds of tiny blue and white flags.

I started down the steps and then saw Lilya running toward me. We crashed into each other halfway up the steps. Everything that happened after that left only vague impressions on my memory, like fragments from a film seen long ago.

I stood on the airfield beside Eva and Lilya, with Geula perched in my arms. Menachem Begin, then Prime Minister of Israel, stood a few feet away, hardly able to hold back his tears.

Geula, sitting in my arms, looked disappointed, deceived. This man who had picked her up and was holding her looked nothing like the father she knew only from his photograph, the smiling, youthful papa with a shock of black hair. She had known that photograph for as long as she had been aware of herself. But the man who was holding her had an alien, pale, unsmiling face. He had sunken cheeks and the little hair he had was grey. She didn't want to kiss a father who looked like that.

Another fragment. It was just a few minutes after I arrived. The five of us were sitting at a table in a room in the airport with the Prime Minister and a representative from the Jewish Agency. I had already received the identity papers of a new immigrant and a Bible. I couldn't hear what the Prime Minister was saying. I was looking through the doorway down the hall where I could see other members of my family, friends, people I knew, people I hadn't seen for many years. My mother I would never see again—she had died in Israel two years earlier.

Then I was taken by car to the kibbutz. At the wheel was Izrail Shternfeld, the kibbutznik who looked after my family during their years in Naan before my release. A minibus drove alongside the car, and from it came the sounds of my favorite Israeli songs—the kibbutzniks probably had learned from Eva which songs I like.

At the entrance to Naan, the kibbutzniks were lined up along the roadside with a big "Welcome" banner flapping above their heads. When we reached the center of the kibbutz, I got out of the car and was squeezed through a crowd to a freshly dug hole in the ground. There a young pyramid cypress sapling that reached just to my waist was waiting. That was the first tree, but not the last, that I would plant in Israel. (Today that cypress, not far from the entrace to the dining hall, is three times my height. Each time I visit, the kibbutzniks smile and say, "We see you every day—actually, three times a day!")

Then I climbed up onto an improvised rostrum and for the second time that day made a speech in Hebrew. From then on I would speak the language—which the Soviets consider "reactionary"—every day. Lilya already spoke Hebrew like an Israeli, and Geula knew no other language.

That night I was kept awake by the singing of the birds. In the gulag archipelago, the birds are quiet even during the day.

I worked for almost six months in the fields of the kibbutz. Those months were the channel from the low water of my monotonous existence in the prisons and camps to the high water of my bustling life in Israel. Like many people who have spent long years behind bars and barbed wire, I experienced periods of depression—that is how my nervous system reacted to the rapid and radical restructuring of my life. The people and the life of the kubbutz helped me maintain my stability during that abrupt transition.

It was due not to my luck or virtue but to the intelligent, prescient planning of Izrail Shternfeld that I worked in Menakhem Rusak's field brigade. As I looked at that quiet, reserved man, I found it hard to believe that during the War of Independence he had been second in command of the Palmakh's legendary Harel Brigade. But after I got to know Menakhem, I could understand easily how his son, an officer in the Israeli army, had died of dehydration in the Sinai desert while all the soldiers serving under him had survived.

Menakhem Rusak and his fellow workers were reserve soldiers, on leave eleven months of the year. They liked working the land and tried to do it well. As I walked around the fields with Menakhem, I could see his brow furrowing involuntarily as he examined the grafts on the fruit trees. "This was done by someone with two left hands," he would sometimes say, pulling out his knife and correcting the problem.

Manekhem work team didn't exactly "look after" me, but they treated me well. I think I fitted in, although I can think of at least one occasion when they gave me special treatment. I accidentally put the tractor into first gear instead of reverse. Menakhem and some of the other men were sitting nearby, in a jeep. Before I managed to slam my foot down on the brake, the tractor nearly crushed the jeep. The men jumped out and ran over to me. "Well done, Hillel," Menakhem said. "To hell with the jeep. The main thing is, you saved us from getting crushed. Thanks." I wondered what their reaction would have been if someone else had done that.

Before the end of 1979, I learned about special one-year courses that were to be given in Tel-Aviv for lawyers who had recently immigrated. So I moved to Tel-Aviv while the family moved to Jerusalem. Among the things I took with me was the almost completed manuscript of the first part of my book, which I dedicated to the Naan kibbutz. A year later I finished the courses, passed the exams, and started working in the department of the Israeli State Controller. I am still working there today.

Eva is one of the mass of immigrants who arrived in Israel from the Soviet Union as a result of Operation Wedding. After she moved to the capital, Eva went to work at a defense factory. But soon she realized that the hours there were too long for a woman with two children. She changed jobs and went to work as an engineer/inspector in the Labor Ministry, where she still works. Almost every evening after dinner, she takes out her files and does whatever work she hasn't had time for during the day.

When I put Lilya to bed for her nap on June 15, 1970, she wasn't even four years old. When she woke up, I was gone. I was gone for the next nine years. When I reached Israel, the Lilya I had known was no longer. In her place I found a thirteen-year-old girl, a typical sabra. She was uninhibited and independent and recognized no power or authority. Compulsion did not work on her, only persuasion.

And I was no longer the playmate papa she remembers. Nine years in prisons and camps had not taught me to be persuasive or tolerant. I was accustomed to applying force. Our characters were similar, and soon my blade came up against her stone. A crisis developed in our relationship, as our family continued to pay the "old bill" presented to us by the KGB on June 15, 1970.

Now that is all in the past. After high school Lilya served two years in the Israeli air force. And then, like many other Israeli soldiers after demobilization, she got a backpack and traveled in Southeast Asia. She journeyed around almost every state in India, spent some time in Thailand and climbed the Himalayas in Nepal. When she came back to Israel, she enrolled as a student of biology at the Hebrew University, and she is studying there now.

Although Geula had been disappointed by the man at the airport who didn't look like the picture of her father, we have had few problems since that day. She had not known any father before then. She got used to the one who had been in prison and learned to accept his pluses and minuses. Gradually we became friends.

Eva sent Guela to the only secular school in Jerusalem where the pupils are given a thorough education in the Jewish religion and traditions, a school operated under the auspices of a conservative synagogue in the United States. Eva, Lilya and I are not religious. We wanted Geula to be able to compare the two lifestyles—religious and not religious—and decide which suited her better. Now she is in the eleventh grade. In two years she will enter the army, which could be called into action at any moment. She will do that because there are still too many people in the Arab world who think that Israel is the result of a technical error, an oversight by Arab leaders, a mistake that can still be rectified.

We live in Ramot, a beautiful area of Jerusalem not far from the place where the prophet Samuel is said to have been buried. Three other immigrant families—from the United States, France and Zimbabwe—live in our building, which houses only one family of sabras.

As I walk along the streets of old Jerusalem, where an entire town from the times of Herod the Great has recently been uncovered by archaeologists, I think about my ancestors who walked along those same streets two thousands years ago. Did they survive in the burning city when Jerusalem was set aflame by the legions of Titus Vespasian? Were they taken to Rome in galleys? What happened to their children? To their children's children? What path did they follow before they reached Polotsk, my mother's birthplace and Pustoshka, the little town where my father was born, in northern Belorussia? I will never know. The family tree I put together before my arrest includes only the last five generations. But what I do know fills me with happiness and pride. Now, after about eighty generations, I have returned to Jerusalem.

Jerusalem
March, 1990

Appendices

Principal Characters

NOTE: Names are listed in alphabetical order. Names in parentheses are either Russian diminutives or Hebrew names currently used by the individuals. The spelling of the names is based on a commonly used system of transliteration of the Cyrillic alphabet and occasionally may differ from that chosen by the individual. The information in this listing is that available to the author in 1989.

Alexandrovich, Ruth arrested and tried with the Riga group. Sentenced to 1 year. Emigrated to Israel after serving full term. Lives in Jerusalem.

Altman, Anatoly (Tolya) was a member of the Leningrad Zionist Organization. Participated in the attempted hijacking, arrested and tried with the "airplane" group. Sentenced to 10 years. Deported to Israel after serving 9 years. Lives in Haifa.

Aronson, Rami Norwegian doctor, visiting Leningrad in April, 1970. Agreed to transmit message to Israel from the Leningrad Zionist Organization regarding the first version of Operating Wedding.

Azernikov (Agami), Boris was a member of the Leningrad Zionist Organization. Arrested after the second Leningrad trial for arrogant behavior at the trial, sentenced to 3 1/2 years. Emigrated to Israel after serving full term. Lives in Tel Aviv.

Blank, Alexandr (Sasha, Asher) was an unaffiliated Jewish activist in Leningrad, his apartment served as a Jewish gathering place. Emigrated to Israel. Lives in Jerusalem.

Bodnya, Mendel participated in the attempted hijacking, arrested and tried with the "airplane" group. Sentenced to 4 years. Emigrated to Israel after serving full term. Lives in South Africa.

Boguslavsky, Viktor was a member of the Leningrad Zionist Organization. Arrested and tried with the second Leningrad group. Sentenced to 3 years. Emigrated to Israel after serving full term. Lives in Moshav Barkan, Israel.

Brud, Rudolf (Rudik) one of the founders of the Leningrad Zionist Organization. Emigrated to Israel. Lives in Kiron, Israel.

Butman, Hillel (Hilya, Grigory, Grisha) one of the founders of the Leningrad Zionist Organization. Arrested and tried with the second Leningrad group. Sentenced to 10 years. Deported to Israel after serving 9 years. Eva (Ella), his wife, emigrated to Israel with daughter Lilya. Daughter Geula born in Israel. Butmans live in Jerusalem.

Chernoglaz, David one of the founders of the Leningrad Zionist Organization. Arrested and tried with the Kishinev group. Sentenced to 5 years. Emigrated to Israel after serving full term. Lives in Moshav Arugot, Israel.

Dreizner, Solomon one of the founders of the Lenin-grad Zionist Organization. Arrested and tried with the second Leningrad group. Sentenced to 3 years. Emigrated to Israel after serving full term. Lives in Givat Zeev, Israel.

Dymshits, Mark originator of the plan to hijack a plane and leader of the attempted hijacking. Arrested and tried with the "airplane" group. Death sentence commuted to 15 years. Deported to Israel after serving 9 years. Lives in Bat Yam, Israel.

Elinson, Avram former member of the Union of Soviet Writers (pen name Belov). Taught Hebrew in a Leningrad ulpan. Emigrated to Israel. Lives in Jerusalem.

Epshteyn, Rosa was a member of the Leningrad Zionist Organization. First met Butman during the annual Simchat Torah gathering of Jews in the Leningrad Synagogue. Later introduced Butman to Leah Lurie. Emigrated to Israel. Lives in Kiriyat Yam, Israel.

Feodorov, Yury was a dissident, one of the two non-Jews who participated in the attempted hijacking. Arrested and tried with the "airplane" group. Sentenced to 15 years. Emigrated to the USA after serving full term. Lives in the USA.

Furman, Boris was a member of the Leningrad Zionist Organization. One of the ulpans functioned in his apartment. Emigrated to Israel. Lives in Rishon Lezion, Israel.

Goldfeld, Anatoly (Tolya) joined the Leningrad Zionist Organization while a student in the Leningrad Polytechnic Institute. Arrested and tried with the Kishinev group. Sentenced to 4 years. Emigrated to Israel after serving full term. Lives in Beer Sheva, Israel.

Halperin, Alexandr (Sasha) joined the Leningrad Zionist Organization while a student in the Leningrad Polytechnic Institute. Participated in organizing clandestine summer camp for Jewish youth. Arrested and tried with the Kishinev group. Sentenced to 2 1/2 years. Emigrated to Israel after serving full term. Lives in Beer Sheva, Israel.

Jacobson, Anna aunt of Mikhail Korenblit, born in the USA, was a member of the U.S. Communist Party. Was deported to the USSR with her husband in 1933. Her husband was killed in a "gun accident" in the late 1930's. Allowed meetings of the Leningrad Zionist Organization in her apartment. Died in Leningrad.

Kaminsky, Lassal was a member of the Leningrad Zionist Organization. Arrested and tried with the second Leningrad group. Sentenced to 6 years. Emigrated to Israel after serving full term. Sima, his wife, emigrated to Israel in 1971. Kaminskys live in Jerusalem.

Khnokh, Lev (Arye) participated in the attempted hijacking. Arrested and tried with the "airplane" group. Sentenced to 10 years. Deported to Israel after serving 9 years. Lives in Moshav Barkan, Israel.

Khnokh, Meri sister of Iosif Mendelevich, was married to Lev and participated in the attempted hijacking. Arrested with the "airplane" group. Released prior to trial because of her youth and her pregnancy. Emigrated to Israel, subsequently divorced Lev. Lives in Tel Aviv.

Khorol, Iosif was a member of the Riga Zionist Organization. Emigrated to Israel in 1969, carried with him the letter (without signatures) described in Chapter 7. Lives in Moshav Elkana, Israel.

Kizhner, Kharik joined the Leningrad Zionist Organization while a student in the Leningrad Polytechnic Institute. Arrested and tried with the Kishinev group. Sentenced to 2 years. Emigrated to Israel after serving full term. Lives in Haifa.

Knopov, Valdimir (Zeev) was a member of Leningrad Zionist Organization. Emigrated to Israel. Lives in West Germany.

Korenblit, Lev was a member of the Leningrad Zionist Organization. Arrested and tried with the second Leningrad group. Sentenced to 3 years. Emigrated to Israel after serving full term. Lives in Beer Sheva, Israel.

Korenblit, Mikhail (Misha) (not related to Lev Korenblit) was a member of Leningrad Zionist Organization. One of the first supporters of Operation Wedding. Arrested and tried with the second Leningrad group. Sentenced to 7 years. Emigrated to Israel after serving full term. Lives in Jerusalem.

Kuzkovsky, Iosif painter, was a member of the Union of Soviet Artists, resided in Riga. Emigrated to Israel in 1969, where he died shortly afterward. His paintings are exhibited in a private museum in Ramat Gan.

Kuznetsov, Eduard (Edik) in 1962 arrested for dissident activities, served 7 years in prison. Afterwards moved to Riga and married Silva Zalmanson. Participated in the attempted hijacking. Arrested and tried with the "airplane" group. Death penalty commuted to 15 years in prison. Deported to Israel after serving 9 years. Subsequently divorced Silva. Lives in Paris.

Levit, Shimon was a member of the Leningrad Zionist Organization. Emigrated to

Israel. Lives in Rehovot, Israel.

Loitershtein, Boris was a member of the Leningrad Zionist Organization. Assisted with the assembly of copying machine received from Kishinev. Emigrated to Israel. Lives in Tel Aviv.

Lurie, Leah was born before World War II, crippled at birth, survived Leningrad siege. Arrested in 1949, released after Stalin's death, became an ardent Zionist, and opened her home to Jews who wanted to learn Hebrew. Awakened Zionist feelings in Butman and Dreizner, among many others. Died in Leningrad in 1960.

Mafzer, Boris was a member of the Leningrad Zionist Organization. Arrested and tried with the Riga group. Sentenced to 2 years. Emigrated to Israel after serving full term. Lives in Jerusalem.

Mendelevich, Iosif was one of the principal advocates of the attempted hijacking. From childhood a religious Jew, early became a member of the Riga Zionist youth group, later became member of the AUCC repre-

senting Riga. Participated in the attempted hijacking. Arrested and tried with the "airplane" group. Sentenced to 12 years. Deported to Israel after serving 9 years. Lives in Jerusalem.

Mirkin, Ludmila sister of Hillel Butman. Emigrated to Israel. Lives in Haifa.

Mogilever, Vladimir (Vladik) one of the founders of the Leningrad Zionist Organization. Arrested and tried with the second Leningrad group. Sentenced to 4 years. Emigrated to Israel after serving full term. Lives in Haifa.

Murzhenko, Aleksey was a dissident, one of the two non-Jews who participated in the attempted hijacking. Arrested and tried with the "airplane" group. Sentenced to 14 years. Released after serving full term, rearrested, emigrated to the USA after serving additional time. Lives in the USA.

Penson, Boris was a member of the Leningrad Zionist Organization. Emigrated to Israel. Lives in Netanya, Israel.

Rabinovich, David was a member of the Kishinev Zionist Organization. Involved in the theft of the copy machine. Arrested and tried with the Kishinev group. Sentenced to 1 year. Emigrated to Israel after serving full term. Lives in Acco, Israel.

Rabinovich, Shimon was a member of the Leningrad Zionist Organization. Emigrated to Israel. Lives in Tal El, Israel.

Sharansky, Natan was an active dissident. Arrested and tried on charge of espionage. Sentenced to 13 years. Deported to Israel after serving 9 years. Currently serving as President of the Soviet Jewry Zionist Forum in Israel. Lives in Jerusalem.

Shekhtman, Pinhas assisted Butman and others with transporting illegal books from Riga to Leningrad. Emigrated to Israel. Lives in the USA.

Shepshelovich, Mikhail was a member of the Riga Zionist Organization. Arrested and tried with the Riga group. Sentenced to 2 years. Emigrated to Israel after serving full term. Lives in Moshav El Khana, Israel.

Shpilberg, Aron was one of the founders of the Leningrad Zionist Organization. Arrested and tried with the Riga group. Sentenced to 3 years. Emigrated to Israel after serving full term. Lives in Lod, Israel.

Shtilbans, Viktor was a member of the Leningrad Zionist Organization. Arrested and tried with the second Leningrad group. Sentenced to 1 year. Released after serving full term. Remained in Leningrad.

Shur, Hillel was a member of the Leningrad Zionist Organization. Arrested and tried with the Kishinev group. Sentenced to 2 years. Emigrated to Israel after serving full term. Lives in Nes Ziona, Israel.

Shur, Kreina was the only woman member of the Leningrad Zionist Organization. Refused to testify during interrogation. Emigrated to Israel. Lives in Jerusalem.

Starobinets, Boris was member of the Leningrad Zionist Organization. Assisted with the assembly of the copy machine received from Kishinev. Emigrated to Israel. Lives in Tel Aviv.

Tovbin, Benzion (Ben) was one of the founders of the Leningrad Zionist Organization. Emigrated to Israel. Lives in Vienna.

Trakhtenberg, Lazar was a member of the Kishinev Zionist Organization. Arrested and tried with the Kishinev group. Sentenced to 2 years. Emigrated to Israel after serving full term. Lives in the USA.

Treister, Sonya Hillel Butman's aunt. Died in Leningrad shortly after Butman's release from prison.

Tsiryulnikov, Natan was a member of the Leningrad Zionist Organization. Emigrated to Israel. Died in Haifa.

Vertlib, Grigory (Grisha) was one of the founders of the Leningrad Zionist Organization. Emigrated to Israel. Lives in Vienna.

Voloshin, Aron was a member of the Leningrad Zionist organization. Arrested and tried with the Kishinev group. Sentenced to 2 years. Emigrated to Israel after serving full term. Lives in the USA.

Yagman (Agmon), Lev was a member of the Leningrad Zionist Organization. Arrested and tried with the second Leningrad group. Sentenced to 5 years. Emigrated to Israel after serving full term. Lives in Haifa.

Yankelevich, Iosif was a member of the Riga Zionist Organization. Emigrated to Israel in 1969. Lives in Tel Aviv.

Yud-Borovskaya, Polina unaffiliated Zionist, was designated to play the role of the "bride" in the first version of Operation Wedding. Emigrated to Israel. Lives in Haifa.

Zalmanson, Izrail participated in the attempted hijacking. Arrested and tried with the "airplane" group. Sentenced to 8 years. Emigrated to Israel after serving full term. Lives in the USA.

Zalmanson, Silva sister of Izrail, participated in the attempted hijacking (at the time the wife of Edik Kuznetsov). Arrested and tried with the "airplane" group. Sentenced to 10 years. Released after serving 4 years. Emigrated to Israel after release. Lives in Rishon Lezion.

Zalmanson, Vulf (Zeev) participated in the attempted hijacking. Arrested with the "airplane" group, but tried by a military courtmartial. Sentenced to 10 years. Deported to Israel after serving 9 years. Lives in Bet Arye, Israel.

Chronology of Events

N O T E: Precise date given when available. Otherwise only month or season and year indicated.

1941   June 22   Hitler invaded Russia.

1948   May 14   State of Israel established.

December 10   Universal Declaration of Human Rights adopted by the U.N. General Assembly.

1953   January 13   Nine Jewish doctors arrested in Moscow, accused of plotting to kill Soviet leaders. The case became known as "The Doctors Plot."

March 5   Josef Stalin died in Moscow.

Amnesty granted to the Jewish doctors shortly after Stalin's death.

1956   February 14   The Twentieth Communist Party Congress held in Moscow.

Stalin's crimes secretly denounced by Khruschev at the Party Congress.

Denunciation revealed by Western press several months later.

October 29   Israeli Defense forces, responding to border attacks and blockade of Straits of Tiran by Egypt, within days forced Egyptian Army to withdraw from Sinai and Gaza. This operation, known as the Sinai-Campaign, played an important role in awakening Jewish spirit in the Soviet Union.

November 4   Soviet tanks crushed Hungarian revolt.

1966   July 6   Israeli singer Geula Gil gave concert in Leningrad.

November 5   A Zionist group was organized at a meeting in Pushkin Park, suburb of Leningrad. Present at the meeting were: Butman, Dreizner, Brud, Shpilberg, Chernoglaz and Mogilever.

December 16   Human Rights Covenants on economic, social and cultural rights and on civil and political rights, extending 1948 Declaration, adopted by the U.N. General Assembly.

1967 September   First ulpan started in Repino, suburb of Leningrad.

1969 Spring,   Several Jewish families allowed to
      Summer   emigrate to Israel, among them Blank, Khorol, Kuzkovsky and Yankelevich. Many others denied permission to emigrate.

      August   All-Union Coordinating Committee of Zionist groups formed in Moscow.

      Fall   Operation Wedding conceived during conversation between Butman and Dymshitz.

1970 Winter,   Several versions of Operation Wedding
      Spring   considered; hijacking scheduled for May 2.

      April   Operation Wedding delayed (finally cancelled on May 25).

      June 15   Hijacking attempted by Dymshitz, Kuznetsov, Mendelevitch, Zalmanson (Silva, Izrail and Vulf), Altman, Khnokh (Lev and Meri), Feodorov, Murzhenko, Penson and Bodnya. This group was arrested before boarding the plane and later tried as the "airplane group." Another group, including Butman, was arrested the same day in connection with Zionist activities and planning of Operation Wedding. Later tried—known as the "second Leningrad trial" group.

      September 27 Mikhail Korenblit arrested, later tried with the group in the second Leningrad trial.

      December 15   Trial of the airplane group began.

      December 24   Airplane group sentenced.

      December 30   As a result of worldwide protests by Jewish and non-Jewish groups, the Supreme

		Court of the RSFSR (Russian Soviet Federated Socialist Republic) reduced the sentences of the airplane group.
1971	May 11	The second Leningrad trial began.
	May 20	The second Leningrad trial group sentenced.
		Azernikov arrested for arrogant behavior at the second Leningrad trial.
	June/July	Butman, Dreizner, Mogilever, Dymshitz and Lev Korenblit flown to testify at the trial of the Kishinev group. Returned to Leningrad prison by train.
	October	Butman, Dymshitz, and Mikhail Korenblit testify at Azernikov trial in Leningrad.
		Sima Kaminsky, with her daughters, leaves Soviet Union for Israel.
		Butman, Dymshitz and Mikhail Korenblit leave Leningrad for the Gulag. (Others were transported to the Gulag earlier).

1972 Fall   Senator Henry M. Jackson introduced an amendment to the East-West trade bill in the U.S. Senate which proposed that the most favored nation treatment of the Soviet Union be contingent upon an end to restrictions to emigration from the USSR. This became the basis for the Jackson-Vanik Amendment passed by Congress in 1973.

1979	April 29	Group including Butman, Altman, Zalmanson, Khnokh, Penson, Dymshitz and Kuznetsov released from prison and flown to Israel. Mendelevich, Murzhenko, and Feodorov remained in prison. Others, released earlier after serving full sentences, were already in Israel.